FATE UNKNOWN
Reflections of a Combat Tour

FATE UNKNOWN
Reflections of a Combat Tour

Labuela
Published by: Labuela Enterprises, LLC

BY: FIRST SERGEANT
GALEN G. MITCHELL
USA (Ret.)

FATE UNKNOWN
– Reflections of a Combat Tour
Copyright © Galen G. Mitchell, 2014

All rights reserved. No part of this book may be reproduced or transmitted in any form or by any means, electronic or mechanical, including photocopying, recording, or any information storage and retrieval system without written permission from the copyright owner, except for the inclusion of brief quotations in a review.

Published by: Labuela Enterprises, LLC.

Category: Autobiography, Vietnam, Military, History, Combat

ISBN: 978-1496082206

Written by: First Sergeant Galen G. Mitchell (USA Ret.) | FATEUNKNOWN@comcast.net

Edited by: Kathryn Hughes | Labuela Enterprises

Cover Design & Text Layout/Formatting by: Eli Blyden | CrunchTimeGraphics.com

Printed in the United States of America

Contents

Dedication	IX
Acknowledgments	X
Chapter 1 Professional Private First Class	1
Chapter 2 History of The Abu Mascot	19
Chapter 3 USNS General Leroy Eltinge	23
That Rusting Crate	35
Chapter 4 An Khe (Ann-Kay or On-Kay)	45
Chapter 5 Hasty Ambush	53
Chapter 6 Collateral Damage	63
Chapter 7 Rocky	67
Chapter 8 Hard Times	79
Chapter 9 Mama-San	91
Chapter 10 Meet The FNG	125
Chapter 11 Phan Rang: Our New Base Camp	141
Chapter 12 Promotion	149

Chapter 13
Tuy Hoa (Too-Ee Waa) 155

Chapter 14
Nasty Rumor 161

Chapter 15
Lieutenant New's Old Indian Trick 165

Chapter 16
Ham and Lima Beans 171

Chapter 17
MIAs 175

Chapter 18
Doc Jackson 179

Chapter 19
Water Re-Supply 183

Chapter 20
Meanwhile Back In The Jungle 185

Chapter 21
Staff Sergeant Ira H. "Perk" Perkins, Jr. 189

Chapter 22
Perkins Brew 195

Chapter 23
Reality Check 199

Chapter 24
Red Rain 201

Chapter 25
Rotation 211

Chapter 26
My Phu (My-Foo) 213

Chapter 27
Objective Bit 215

Chapter 28
Surprise Targets 227

Chapter 29
Rendering Assistance 233

Chapter 30
Assault 237

Chapter 31
Friendly Fire 245

Chapter 32
Pucker Factor 247

Chapter 33
Tactical Withdrawal 253

Chapter 34
The Grim Reaper 255
    Exhausted 261
    Who Goes There? 264
    What About Me? 271
    Abu Company (13) 278
    Bravo Company (7) 280
    Charlie Company (1) 281

Chapter 35
Recovering Our KIA 283
    "Harry The Horse" 289
    "Sweet Daddy Grace" 294

Chapter 36
Walk Through 297

Chapter 37
And So It Went! 303

VII

Chapter 38
In My Opinion 325

Chapter 39
PFC Clarence E. "Griff" McKinnis 331

Chapter 40
Premonition 335

Chapter 41
McNamara's 100,000 351

Chapter 42
Gut Checks 355

Chapter 43
Gathering Eagles 391

Chapter 44
In Retrospect 393
Glossary 397

Annex A
Movement Order 403

Dedication

This book is dedicated to my comrades in arms and especially to those who "Gave all."

It is also dedicated to the many support soldiers, without whom the infantryman would not succeed, and who don't get the recognition or credit deserved. It takes a high ratio of military specialties to support the combat soldier. These specialties include: nurses, medics, engineers, indirect fire specialists, chopper pilots, Air Force pilots, cooks, clerks, and far too many others to name. They know who they are, those unsung heroes that keep the military machine well-oiled and functional. Although they may not receive the kudos deserving of their role, we infantrymen recognize their great contribution.

It is said, "Behind every great or successful man stands a great woman." Through my personal experiences and knowledge of the real-life characters in this book, and my contact with each of their wives at our reunions, I believe this to be true. I can attest to the fact that the greatest influence on their lives has been their wives, who have always stood behind their men. This book is also dedicated to them.

To all those Screaming Eagles that have served, or presently are serving with the 101st that have made the Division known throughout the world and feared by our enemies—this book is dedicated to you.

Special thanks to Billy "Abu One Zero" Robbins for all his encouragement to embark on this mission.

And last, but not least, this book is especially dedicated to my wife of over 47 years, Irene. She has always been there in the most troubling of times, and in my life Irene has been the greatest influence of all.

* * *

Acknowledgments

Special military consultants: LTC Billy R. Robbins (USA Ret.), Major Eugene R. New (USA Ret.), CSM Robert A. Press, (USA Ret.)
Special civilian consultants: Kathryn Hughes, Tampa, FL and Laura McCormack of The Villages, FL

Chapter 1

Professional Private First Class

As a normal, free-spirited child playing war using sticks for rifles, or Cowboys and Indians with cap guns...death had no meaning. We played dead like the characters seen on television, without ever knowing its true meaning. Even into my teen years death was something that only happened to older people like grandparents. The war however, changed everything. I realized that once exposed to the cruelties of war, there is no returning to the innocence of youth.

My name is Galen Gene Mitchell. I was born on August 8, 1944 in Chester, Pennsylvania, to Laurene "Rene" Keilmann and Joseph Allen Mitchell. My mother named me after a doctor she knew named Galen Young. It's an unusual name to say the least, but women have always seemed to like it. The name actually dates all the way back to the Romans; there was a man named Galen of Greek bloodlines who became the personal physician for Julius Caesar. Additionally, he was the doctor for the gladiators, whom he used as subjects to perfect his study of anatomy. This Roman Doctor Galen also invented state of the art surgical tools. The name Galen has been linked to several other emperors and prominent members of the Roman society.

My mother was an LPN (licensed practical nurse) by profession, but later became a full-time housewife and devoted mother of six children. She always made sure there was food on the table for all us kids when we were growing up. There's no doubt my mother liked my name, but she never had any thoughts of me becoming a doctor. In fact, about the closest I ever came to it was by acquiring some first aid training in the Army and then applying some of those skills, like bandaging up wounds and giving out morphine shots, to my wounded men in Vietnam.

My father was a welder by trade. He worked mainly for Westinghouse, but the company always seemed to be out on strike, one time for a year and a half. During that period Mom became both the bread winner and the bread maker. Mom was a local product of nearby Parkside, Pennsylvania, and was from a middle-class family. Dad was from a poor family of Greensboro, Maryland. His entire family had migrated to Chester, Pennsylvania in search of jobs because the area was the most industrialized in the country.

We were a poor family who saved money everywhere we could. For instance, my dad gave us haircuts, and I even put cardboard from cereal box tops in my shoes because of holes in the soles in order to go to school. Mom and Dad grew up during the Great Depression and were frugal about everything. If you came out of the kitchen and left the light on Dad was all over you like a cheap suit.

When I was about eight years old we moved to a small town named Upland; it was located right next to Chester where I had grown up. Once, when Pop was on strike for over a year, our shoes were so badly worn we couldn't walk to the Upland school which we attended. I remember the principal knocking on our door to see why we weren't in school. Well after my father explained why, the principal commenced to quote the law to my Dad. That was a big mistake, as Dad quickly went after him, with the principal making a quick retreat. My Dad said, "If you want them in school, you buy them shoes." The cops showed up a short time later, however nothing happened except for a few days later we had shoes. I believe they were from the school, but I really don't know for sure. We were a close family. Mom was a great cook so we ate well. You just didn't ever want to be late for dinner because the food would be gone. I was always the first at the table and the last one to leave.

I joined the Boy Scouts, enjoying camping out, cooking breakfast, making beans and weenies for supper and sleeping under the stars, which for a city kid was an unbelievable experience. I never had a clue that

I would be doing that for a living with a career in the Army. There were many lessons learned that carried over from scouting to the military which helped to shape my successful military career...the most important of which was discipline. Pop also was a strict disciplinarian and a firm believer in corporal punishment, as were many from that era, unlike today's kinder and gentler approach. We ended up none the worse for wear from it. That lasted until I was about thirteen years old, when I had the cojones to stand up to him. He never put a hand on me after that.

At the age of thirteen I also began to hang out with the older guys that I met playing football. They had a bad influence on me. I began smoking, chasing girls with those raging wild oats my body was making, learning to play penny poker, and drinking beer. One time while four or five of us were in a car drinking, the cops stopped us. I ended up having to go to juvenile court, receiving a fine plus a warning.

My English teacher, Miss Mabel Jackson, was also the detention teacher. I was always in there for one reason or another, primarily for not doing the homework she had assigned me. The last to be let go at 5:30 pm each night, I walked home in the dark many a night. Hell, I thought I was going to night school. There was no love loss here as our relationship culminated into one of hate. Once having said she would break me,

PROFESSIONAL PRIVATE FIRST CLASS

naturally with my stubbornness I flunked English, which was mandatory to pass, despite passing all other subjects with some A's and B's. At this point I was ruined, and had the same result the following year. After all, I wasn't about to get up in front of the class and recite poetry like some candy ass or do book reports for homework. There was too much going on in the streets for that kind of stuff.

When I turned fifteen, I lied about my age in order to work in a factory on third shift. It felt really good to be earning my own money and paying for my own clothes and room and board. This lasted about three months. One Friday night, while out drinking and double dating with my friend Bob Richmond, we all drove to my work place. Upon arrival, I told them to wait in the car for ten minutes; I went in and quit, returning to party hard. At the time, it was a tough choice, but school was getting ready to start anyway. At sixteen years old, I quit school and continued to aimlessly go nowhere until I turned seventeen. On 21 August 1961, after having my parents sign some papers and getting a couple teachers to write letters for me, I went into the Army. And no, Miss Jackson was not one of them. Had I not joined the Army, I probably would have ended up in jail, only going in through the back door as an inmate instead of working in one for a second career and going in and out through the main entrance.

We arrived for Basic Training at Fort Jackson, South Carolina, about 0300 hours, after flight delays and a bus ride. I spent the first hour learning to make my bunk bed with hospital corners, and finally about 0400 hours they let us rack out. At 0500 hours, in they came, screaming and hollering at us to get up and make our beds. My immediate thought was, "Oh no, what the heck did I get myself into." I ended up with an upper respiratory infection and spent three days in the hospital while my newly met friends from Philly moved on to basic in nice wooden barracks. I ended up in tent city with crushed coal roads. We wore combat boots to and from the shower because if you didn't, by the time you got back to the tent, your ankles were black from the crushed coal. They made us roll the sides of the tents up every day for ventilation for the August heat, and the wind was constantly blowing the dust and dirt around inside. I ate more dirt than a worm while I was there.

Author with M-1 rifle during Basic Training in Tent City at Ft. Jackson, S.C. in October 1961.

After several weeks, I was granted a pass for the main post area. I was enjoying a beer at the canteen on Tank Hill when someone pointed skyward and said, "Hey look!" We observed men and their parachutes dropping out of Air Force planes. As the parachutes opened, the men drifted downward and disappeared behind buildings and trees. A few hours later several paratroopers came into the canteen dressed in outstanding class-A khaki uniforms and spit-shined jump boots. They were quickly swamped by trainees asking questions. The paratroopers looked better than any cadre we had in basic training! I was hooked, and soon volunteered for airborne.

After basic training, I stayed at Fort Jackson for AIT (advanced infantry training). This was much easier than basic with a lot less harassment, plus we were in wooden barracks. Then it was on to Fort Benning, Georgia for jump school—so much for the laid back training of AIT. We had a week before jump school started, so actually it was four weeks of intense training. Anytime we stepped out of a building we had to either double time or run to wherever we were going. If you were caught walking, the penalty was push-ups. Running, sit ups and pushups were the key points of emphasis throughout the course. During our lunch time, we all ran at least a mile to the mess hall, did sit-ups, and then quickly ate our food with screaming cadre hovering over us like a screaming buzzard before we ran back to the training area. That was all taking place in the Georgia heat, with quite a few men falling out to throw up and then quickly rejoining the formation. Whenever we were given a ten-minute smoke break at the school, we had to run about a quarter mile to our break area. At the end of the break, our platoon (a unit of approximately 43 men) formed up and a sergeant would tell us where our next class was—naturally it was always back where we came from or a quarter mile away. At the end of jump school one of the requirements was to complete a five mile run or flunk out. Later, a three to five mile run following other physical training was common practice in the airborne units.

During jump school training, none of us had any rank; each of us was given a number which was painted on our steel helmet. Consequently, a trainee never knew if they were standing next to a captain or a private. There was an inspection every morning, and if a trainee accumulated too many demerits they were flunked out of the school. I was going along great with no demerits the first couple weeks. I decided one night to shave my head, as most of us did to beat the heat and prevent gigs, and during inspection on the following morning, I got a demerit for needing a haircut. One gig short of flunking puts a lot of pressure on an individual. I finally figured out that putting pressure on us was the whole purpose. There was a blackboard outside of the cadre building and the cadre would exit and place student numbers on the board every time a man broke a rule or got a demerit.

If anyone was a screw up, they were harassed by every cadre every place they went, and most ended up quitting the jump school program. One day after lunch I found my number on the blackboard, apparently for some dumb thing I had done in the morning. I was sure glad it was on there for only half a day. With approximately four hundred soldiers in the class, the numbers on the blackboard changed frequently, unless they were a real dud. All I can say is that Miss Jackson's blackboard and detention was petty in comparison to this forced fed learning curve and harassment.

After completing jump school, Basic Airborne Class # 22, on 23 February 1962, I was assigned to B Company, 506th Airborne Battle Group of the 101st Airborne Division at Fort Campbell, Kentucky. The unit paralleled jump school in many ways, with a wakeup call every day at zero dark thirty (0500 hours), with the first hour devoted to making our bunks in a way that would bounce a coin, dressing into our physical training uniform (PT), and taking care of personal hygiene needs. Formation began sharply at 0600 hours with inspection and accountability, followed by PT, which culminated with a three to five mile run. These units were firm believers in the lean and mean philosophy. We were in such great shape at the time that troopers could get in at 0500 hours, still drunk from a night of heavy drinking in town, and complete the five

PROFESSIONAL PRIVATE FIRST CLASS

mile runs without a hitch. They were damn sure sober when the run was over. Between 0700 hours and 0830 hours, there were showers, barrack maintenance, and breakfast; with every squad (a unit of 10 or 11 men) and platoon having specific areas of cleanup. Teams would rotate to chow and barracks cleanup. During the 0830 hours formation, uniforms were inspected for clean starched fatigues and spit-shined jump boots. The remainder of the day varied daily and included classes on all kinds of military subjects, weapon's maintenance, etc.

The one thing I quickly learned was attention to detail and organization. Everything had to be in a specific place and lined up with the tile blocks of the floor, to include footlockers, beds, and footgear, so if you stood at the opening of a platoon bay, everything would be in perfect alignment. This was standard operating procedure (SOP) on a daily basis, not just for inspections, while just becoming a routine way of life. Troopers had to come up to standards or face the wrath from peers. A trooper would face court at night or get knocked on his butt if he walked down the center aisle of the platoon bay, which received a coat of paste wax every day. After all the sergeants were gone for the day, court was held by the old timers and all the cherry jumpers (only 5 jumps and just out of jump school) had to appear. The court and jury would give out sanctions such as giving a dirt bag a shower with hard bristled brushes and making someone participate in "blanket parties." I've seen sergeants move men out of the barracks and into a pup tent for being a real goat-smelling dirt bag. Teamwork and unity was stressed, and if the paratrooper couldn't measure up quickly, he was run off either by his peers or the sergeants. Those who couldn't cut it would have their jump status terminated and be reassigned to a leg unit (non-airborne unit). It was not unusual in those days for troopers who had not gotten any inspection gigs to be out on a pass on a Saturday afternoon, and see men in the street breaking rocks with a sledgehammer because they had received discipline from the Company (an Army unit of about 225 men at that time) Commander in the form of an Article 15.

I was a natural, except for a few hiccups along the way. An example of one such hiccup was going to the field for the first time on a night movement and breaking contact, as branches were smacking me in the face, when all of a sudden the man in front of me disappeared. Before that field trip was over, I was number one on their most wanted shit list for a while and was getting my ass smoked. Thankfully there were several cherries besides me that had been recently assigned to the platoon. I rapidly assimilated into the unit, while earning the respect of peers and supervisors. This helped me to

PROFESSIONAL PRIVATE FIRST CLASS

hone military skills that would give me a foundation to greatly enhance my future military career.

Jump pay for the enlisted troopers was $55 a month and for the officers, it was $110. A large part of our pay was spent on laundry for breaking starch every day on our uniforms. The fatigues were so heavily starched they could stand up on their own and appeared to be frozen stiff. We had to run our hands through the sleeves and pant legs before they could be put on– thus the expression of "breaking starch." There was also the additional expense of mandatory weekly haircuts for Saturday inspections, which cost 50¢. A typical laundry bill was $20 to $25 a month, and cigarettes ran $1.80 a carton or 18¢ a pack. Wow, imagine that! Of course it was all relative in that as a Private First Class (PFC) my pay was $99.37 per month. My jump pay was huge and more than half of my base pay per month.

    I also became a professional Private First Class for my first enlistment, which came about because of my stubbornness. The company's policy was that to be promoted after being selected by squad and platoon sergeants, a trooper had to appear before a promotion board consisting of the platoon and first sergeants who asked questions of the trooper pertaining to job skills. If a soldier finished in the top three, the policy was he didn't have to reappear and was promoted as the allocations became available to the company. I finished second, and the following month I was told I had to reappear. Based on the policy, I refused. I had to report to the Company Commander, who asked me why I had refused; after informing him of my reason, the Company Commander dismissed me. The following day First Sergeant Grady Trainer, whom we called Gravy Train, called me to the orderly room and said, "I heard what you told the Company Commander and if you had told me that I would have knocked you on your ass!" My thoughts were, "If you had asked me I would have told you the same thing." Then he said, "As long as you're in my company you'll never get promoted, now get your ass out of here!" Well, my peers were promoted, but no one ever harassed me because I knew more than any other Private First Class and many who were promoted. I remained a professional Private First Class in the Bravo Bulls of the 506th.

I took the General Education Development (GED) tests as the unit schedule allowed, and passed each one to receive my equivalent of a high school education of twelve years. Others had to go to classes for months in order to pass these tests, so I guess I wasn't all that dumb after all. After completing jump school I realized that I could accomplish anything I set my mind to.

My enlistment was up in August 1964 after three years in the Army. I returned home to Pennsylvania

PROFESSIONAL PRIVATE FIRST CLASS

where my best friend Bob Richmond talked me into going to work for General Motors, in Newark, Delaware; it was one of the highest paying jobs around the area at the time. It didn't take long to become disillusioned with the repetitive and boring assembly line job, where I had to perform the same task roughly every two minutes. One day I was working with a man who had worked there over forty years and was about to retire, when it occurred to me that I couldn't see myself continuing this sort of work and wanted something more out of life. Additionally, I was missing my old flame, Carol, from Hopkinsville, Kentucky, with who at one time I mistakenly thought I was in love with. So, after eighty seven days, I reenlisted in the Army and returned to Fort Campbell, Kentucky. Had it been ninety days or more, I would have lost my stripe or rank.

On my return, I was assigned to A Company, 1st Battalion (an Army unit of 4 to 5 companies), and 501st Airborne Infantry and immediately was jilted by Carol, who had hooked up with an Air Force guy—a leg (non-airborne) of all people—while breaking my faithful heart. Faced with three more years of service, I decided to make the best of it–get promoted to make as much money as possible and then get out. As I was sitting on my footlocker spit shining my boots one day after training, First Sergeant DuPont approached and asked me my name. After replying Mitchell he said,

"You know you have more time and grade as a PFC than anyone in the Battalion–over three years. We'll have to get you promoted to Spec/4."(Specialist Forth Class) I'm thinking, "Sure," but then a week or so later I received orders promoting me to Specialist Fourth Class, no board or anything. I was definitely surprised. My base pay rose to $194.70 per month. It wasn't long before Platoon Sergeant Rivera had me running a Fire Team, doing the job of a sergeant; it was interesting and allowed me to gain additional experience. After several months, First Sergeant DuPont summoned me to the orderly room to inform me he had been tasked to find the best men in the company to fill some slots in a unit that was going to combat in the Southeast Asian country of Vietnam. I volunteered, and on May 20, 1965 was assigned to A Company, 1st Battalion, 327th Airborne Infantry of the 1st Brigade.

"War is delightful to those who have had no experience of it."
~Desiderius Erasmus, Dutch author, philosopher, & scholar. (1466-1536)

We had about six weeks before moving out to Vietnam. Everyone took a 14-day leave of absence to go home, and the rest of the time they devoted to weapons qualification, familiarization of all the weapons in the unit, squad and platoon formations, plus arm and hand signals. On my leave of absence, I visited a friend named Irene. I had known her for some time and it was strictly a platonic relationship. We hung out at a place named "Bernie's," which was a local hoagie shop that had a juke box and pool table that many of us teenagers had often gathered at. I learned that Irene and her 21-month-old daughter were living with her father, who was helping her to get a divorce from an abusive marriage. Irene's husband had taken to beating her and once even broke her nose. She promised to write me and keep me up to date about home, our mutual friends and the happenings about town.

FATE UNKNOWN

Chapter 2

History of The Abu Mascot

Soldiers assigned to A Company 1/327th Infantry learn that the company is called Abu (pronounced Ay-Boo). But just how exactly did the name come about? The Abu's actually evolved from another unit, the Ibu, AKA (also known as) I Company of the 187th Regiment Combat Team (RCT). As the story goes, in 1952 the companies of the 187th decided rather than use standard military phonetics (i.e. Able, Baker, Charlie etc.) to identify themselves, they would give themselves animal names: L Company became Lion, M Company became Mighty Moose, and K Company became King Kong. But poor I Company found that the only animal that began with an "I" was a wading bird called an Ibis. This was a wimpy looking tropical wading bird with a downward curved beak; it obviously would not do justice as the mascot of an airborne unit. It was the I Company Commander, Captain Shannon and his XO, Lieutenant Patrenus, who came up with the mythical Ibu (in fact, Ibu is the acronym for Is Best Unit). Then all they had to do was decide what this mythical creature would look like.

Remarkably, they accomplished this task in a very short time; they just took various parts of the mascots from other units and then put them all together. The Ibu ended up with a gorilla's body, a lion's head, a moose's horns, and an alligator's tail to help stabilize the Ibu and make him amphibious. Lastly, the Ibu was given Corcoran jump boots and human hands. The original Ibu (I Boo) did not wear a parachute, nor clutch a pistol in its right hand and a knife in its left hand; these features were added over time as the mascot evolved.

After the Korea War, the 187th RCT was deactivated. Then in 1956, when the 101st Airborne Division was reactivated and I Company 187th RCT was activated, it was incorporated into the 1/327th Infantry. Instead of bowing out gracefully, Ibu, the beloved mythical mascot and fierce figure of yesteryear, simply changed its name to Abu, to fit its new company designation—A Company, 1/327th Infantry. The Abu proliferated quickly, finding its way on to the units' company signs, orderly room and platoon bay walls, as well as tattoos on the left calves of proud paratroopers. Additionally, the image of a ten-foot Abu sprung up in front of the mess hall of building 6930 facing the company street. He leaped into the hearts of all who served in the mighty Abu Company, 1/327th. ABU! Above the Rest!

Although still an Abu, the current mascot of Abu, 1/327th, has changed with the times. They are no longer

HISTORY OF THE ABU MASCOT

airborne, arriving into battle by helicopters; they are now airmobile, arriving instead by helicopters. The parachute is gone but the tradition of the Abu mascot lives on. Today's Abu Company continues the heritage and standards previously set by those who preceded them. The history of the Abu mascot was provided to me courtesy of John C. Haughain, a former Abu paratrooper who served in Vietnam with the 4th Infantry Division during the Tet offensive. Abu John was originally from England. Thanks for your service. You are truly "Above the Rest!"

PFC John C. Haughain
Abu Company member and Vietnam Veteran.
Courtesy of John C. Haughain.

Our beloved Abu mascot that began in 1952 and is still in existence today with Abu Company, 1/327th. Courtesy of LTC. Billy "One Zero" Robbins (USA Ret.)

Chapter 3

USNS General Leroy Eltinge

We departed Fort Campbell and Campbell Army Air-Field by civilian commercial aircraft, on the evening of 6 July 1965. I was somewhat surprised the Air Force wasn't doing the transport, but after all, what did a peon like me really know. The flight to San Francisco went smoothly, and it reminded me of being in a bar in Hop-Town (Hopkinsville, Kentucky) on a Friday or Saturday night.

Our duffle bags were stowed and we boarded the plane carrying only our standard issued service-rifle, the M-16. Upon entering the aircraft, we were greeted by several truly beautiful Stewardesses. I mean they were knock-out gorgeous beauties. In those days there was no such thing as equal opportunity; being a natural beauty was a prerequisite of the job.

Once the flight leveled off, most of the troopers never did; they were in love at first sight. The local bars normally had one or two waitresses who generally were married and had a boyfriend on the side, sometimes even the bartender. Most of the time there were a few dozen drunken troopers, each of them thinking they were the best looking of the bunch, and each of them thinking they would be the only one that would win her heart and take her home for the night. This flight wasn't much different and troopers didn't necessarily need booze to be struck by the love bug. But for the most part, leaders kept things under control until the lights went out and they finally dozed off. While others slept, some played cards, some shot dice, and after the lights were dimmed, the booze came out. Troopers were trading their wings for the stewardess' wings, phone numbers, etc. A couple of them were just as wild as the paratroopers on board. No, this wasn't Spirit Airlines, but the plane was definitely full of free spirits. This also was the first time I had ever heard of the Mile High Club. The girls were very nice about the whole situation, and although they were probably used to getting some attention, I seriously doubt they had ever experienced a prior flight with over a hundred young virile men as passengers at one time. Some let their hair down as much as the men and it was a fun flight. Perhaps the stewardesses realized many of the men would never return. This flight was special in more ways than one, as their next one might be an angel flight.

By the end of the flight, a real special bond had developed between us all. As we approached the exit, the stewardesses were lined up and adorned with pinned on 101st patches, name tapes, cloth jump wings, and even some metal jump wings. One of the stewardesses was even wearing one of the trooper's dog tags. The troopers proudly wore the lipstick imprints on their cheeks from being kissed by a stewardess. As they left the aircraft, just about every trooper received a kiss or a hug, along with lots of good luck wishes. A few of the well-wishers had real tears running down their cheeks.

Next we took buses to Oakland Army terminal, where we were greeted by an Army Band, Red Cross Donut Dollies who were dispensing coffee and doughnuts, and a ship sitting dockside, bearing the name USNS General LeRoy Eltinge on its bow. It was nice of the Red Cross to volunteer their time to see us off and provide some small but special treats; it was a totally unexpected surprise and appreciated gesture. This was my first contact with a Donut Dolly; I had never heard that expression before. We mingled around, drinking some coffee while waiting the word to board.

The USNS General LeRoy Eltinge was first launched in September of 1944 and already was over 20 years old. It was solid grey in color and was not in the best of shape. In fact, I cannot recall anything inside or outside on this relic that wasn't grey. The rumor was it had recently been taken out of mothballs for this mission. Without a doubt, it had seen better days when it was used primarily as a cargo and troop carrier vessel. It measured 522 feet, 10 inches long, and had a beam of

71 feet, 6 inches. After we loaded onto the boat, the deck quickly became crowded. An unidentified trooper from Arizona remarked, "Gee, I wonder what battle General Eltinge lost to have it named after him?" A voice from the crowded deck informed him, "He was Custer's S-2." The S-2 of all Army units, from battalion on up, is the intelligence section. It has been suggested by some historians that George Custer, a respected U.S. Army officer and cavalryman, suffered a disastrous defeat in The Battle of Little Bighorn against a coalition of Native American Indian tribes, partially due to inadequate intelligence-gathering (reconnaissance) and his failure to heed the warnings of his Crow scouts. In the Army, every infantry soldier learns the acronym SAULTE, which stands for size, activity, unit, location, time, and equipment.

> Author note: See Annex A for Movement Order and list of original Boat Troopers.

We departed in early evening and passed under the Golden Gate Bridge into the bay. The wind was blowing and I was struck by how cool it was, especially since this was July on the west coast. I quickly went to put on my field jacket, and returned to see a last glimpse of the United States. Our unit was housed five or six floors/decks down, where we slept on canvas cots stacked four high and about 18 inches apart. Every morning, except for the cleanup detail, all others had to go up top to the main deck. It didn't take long to realize how over-crowded the Eltinge was, I suppose to keep the unit intact. There were thousands of troopers and I could hardly move as some men played cards, shot dice or slept while others smoked and joked.

The overcrowded USNS General LeRoy Eltinge enroute to Cam Ranh Bay. Courtesy of LTC Billy R. Robbins (USA Ret)

The chow line ran all over the boat, up and down stairs, through doorways or whatever the navy calls them. About half way there I was totally lost and by talking with the men around me, found we were all in the same boat. Every door, stairs and hallway all looked the same and everything was painted Navy Deck Grey. The chow line was continuous because as soon as breakfast was over, they started serving lunch, and then supper. Upon arrival, we entered this big room and went through the chow line. The room was made entirely of steel; there was poor circulation and it was hot as hell. Not only were the cooks sweating profusely, but so were the walls. Once through the chow line, we ate standing since the tables were about the width of the tray and chest high. The boat was rocking; those that were finished eating looked like they were ice skating on the wet slippery floor, with one man falling on his fourth point of contact (buttocks) as they were leaving. Trays were sliding off the make shift tables that were held up by two-by-fours. A trooper on the other side of the room turned around and barfed all over the floor. This caused some of the troopers to start laughing, but caused another to barf. Even on jumps there is always one or two that get sick and other troopers are quick to seize the moment to mess with them. One man hollered out, "Barf in the tray so we can save the big pieces." Oh this place sure didn't smell like a mother's kitchen at all. Yeah, this man's Merchant Marines were a real class act and I suppose they perceived it to be a four or five star dining facility. Some men resorted to skipping meals, but real men would have none of that, so they just dealt with it and drove on to the airborne objective as trained to do so many times. Our hard times and hardships were only the beginning of what would lay ahead for us.

One day I reported to the kitchen for my Kitchen Police (KP) duty. A cook handed me a small knife, took me to this huge room (hole) and said, "Get peeling!" I couldn't believe the sight before me—this huge room, the size of a whole house, was filled with potatoes from floor to ceiling, and there were a couple dozen troopers already at work. At least back at Fort Campbell there were actual potato peelers. I'm not even sure a potato farmer has seen that many spuds in one place before. We sat on big steel cooking pots, and as we peeled them we threw the potatoes into another pot filled with water. I was glad to see the day end, and the only damn thing I learned was that thousands of men can devour a lot of damn spuds in one day.

After a couple days we received word that the showers were now open, so I stripped down to my boxers, grabbed a towel and a bar of soap, and took off to beat the crowd. On arrival, all the shower heads were already taken. As I waited for my turn, the troopers in the showers were lathering up when suddenly they began cursing and bitching because the soap would not rinse off. The soap just became a white paste all over them from the salt water, as if they were smeared with toothpaste. Some had it all in their hair, a couple all over their arms, and one of them even all over his private parts. I thought, "Oh shit, I'm not getting in there." There were a few serious troopers waiting and making comments like, "Why won't it rinse off?" and as someone entered the room, "What's going on?" I felt elated now by not being the first to arrive and I began to see the humor of the situation at hand. I jokingly told a black trooper from my squad by the named of Private First Class David T. Rogers, who was tall, thin, lanky and always was a happy-go-lucky soldier, "Hey Rogers, you look good man." He still found a smile even though the rest were some unhappy campers. I beat feet out of there. We weren't sure if this was some kind of joke by the Merchant Marines or an honest mistake. They turned on the water every other day for showers and the next time issued us soap that worked in salt water. As they say, just another day in this man's Army.

John T. Humphries took us to the bow of the boat one morning for physical training, but due to the rough seas, that idea was quickly abandoned to prevent any injuries. The up and down motion of the boat was throwing us around the deck like rag dolls, requiring some quick PLFs (Parachute landing falls). Our platoon sergeant, whom everyone just called John T., was a slightly rotund Korea war veteran. His appearance was deceptive, however, as he made the daily runs and kept up with the best troopers. I recall one time shortly after arrival we were training on hand and arm signals, when he caught a man not paying attention and jumped in his shit like he was a drop zone. The trooper told the platoon sergeant that he already had this training in his previous unit. Whoa trooper...wrong answer! John T. said he didn't give a damn what he learned in his previous unit and he was going to learn 3rd platoon's arm and hand signals. There was absolutely no question who the MMFIC (main mother fuc-er in charge) was of this unit.

I was 20 years old at the time and viewed Platoon Sergeant Humphries as being really old. In making contact with him some 40 years later, I asked how old he was back then. I was shocked when he told me he was thirty five. There's a lot more than beauty held in the eye of the beholder. He passed away before I could hook up with him for a visit. At the time, I wrote the following:

PSG John T. Humphries, Qui Nhon, October 1965.

John T. Humphries recently soared from the mandatory muster we all must answer to. "Jumping" John T. was an Ibu and original Abu going back to 1952. He had Abu tattooed on his left calf and was our Platoon Sergeant when we deployed to Vietnam on the USNS Eltinge in July of 1965.

We were fortunate to have a leader with combat experience from the 187th Regimental Combat Team in Korea. As John T. honed our skills we became a fighting force to be reckoned with by our enemies.

"Jumping" John T. Humphries went from the wings of eagles to the wings of angels on 26 April 2007. May this great eagle finally have found peace on a perch in heaven...that elusive peace that evades a soldier while here on earth.

~Written 23 July 2007, By Sgt. Galen G. Mitchell

After the PT fiasco on deck, someone pointing forward of the boat and its bow hollered, "Look...flying fish!" Several of us made our way to him and were astonished to see fish flying through the air out in front of the boat, way ahead of where the boat was breaking water. I observed it for quite some time, not because of something never seen before, but because of the tranquility and quality of the time. The experience was enhanced by the wind blowing clean fresh salt air into my face. I would return there several times during this cruise and on one occasion even saw dolphins running with the boat in a somewhat playful gesture.

As we moved along it became warmer and downright hot as the trip grew longer. The bowels of the boat where we slept became too hot with stinking stale air and everyone started sleeping on deck to escape it. How we never lost a man overboard in the night was a surprise to me, since they slept on the edge of the deck without even a safety rope or rail. This relic of a boat broke down enroute and we just aimlessly floated around, bobbing up and down for about a day and a half until the engine crew had it running again. We limped in or slowly made our way to Subic Bay in the Philippines for repairs.

Once there we were allowed to go ashore for a four hour period and began exploring the Naval Base. Everyone pretty much ended up in the one or two bars located on the base, because a bunch of paratroopers could find a bar faster than an alcoholic bloodhound. We were putting down some local beers by the name of San Miguel's, but the only problem was they had twice as much, if not more, the alcohol content than did American beer. After being pent up for some time, troopers do store up a lot of aggression, and if no one is around to take it out on, they start fighting between units for entertainment. Fights broke out and the bars started getting torn up, so they sent the Navy Shore Patrol to control us. That didn't go over too well; it ended in a standoff until our MP's (military police) arrived and the base commander ordered us to return to the boat. I suppose he gave our brass a piece of his mind. We were confined to the boat for about two days until the repairs were made, and then our luxury cruise continued. Chaplain Bowers stated to us, "Twelve years ago I rode this same ship to Europe." Now how's that for a rugged cross to bear? First Sergeant Robert A. Press told us he had made several trips across on troop carriers and this was the worst ship he had ever been on.

This luxury excursion is summed up best in the following poem, which is all factual, including the trooper in the Brig.

That Rusting Crate
~A poem by Peter S. Griffin

Orders were cut, the men well trained,
The 1st Brigade of 101st Airborne fame....
3700 Paratroopers, all hand-picked,
To Viet Nam, they'd soon be shipped....

In early July of 1965,
At Oakland terminal, we did arrive....
Thoughts of combat, we had surmised,
But not the hulk that met our eyes....

"Donut Dollies", cheerfully, gave us their wares,
As if to lessen, our growing fears....
Donuts and coffee, not enough to relieve,
Life on land, we'd soon grieve....

FATE UNKNOWN

Moored to the dock, The "USNS GENERAL LEROY ELTINGE",
On THAT RUSTINNG CRATE our lives would hinge....!
A mothballed troopship, of years gone by,
Crossing on it, would we survive....?

Was it seaworthy?, would it stay afloat....?
Drowned in saltwater, our bodies would bloat....
All envisioned a watery grave,
Against a shark, could you be brave....?

Only 510 feet from bow to stern,
Of personal space, all would yearn....
Fighting the crowd, to get to the rail,
Bumping each other, like cows corralled....

Moored in place, for two long nights,
Staring at the city's lights....
San Francisco, a great place to be,
But California, we had not come to see....

Finally, we were underway,
Passing Alcatraz, along the way....
Then, under the Golden Gate, we passed,
Wondering, how long, this voyage, to last....?

USNS GENERAL LEROY ELTINGE

Entering, the pacific, oh so blue,
Thousands of jellyfish, of many hues....
Flying fish led the way,
From this prison, none would stray....

Chow lines ringed the ship, all the long day,
Standing at tables, we ate that way....
As soldiers regurgitated, in their trays,
The swaying of the ship slid it your way....

Saltwater showers, soap, no lather,
On the decks, friends, struggled, to gather....
On THAT RUSTING CRATE, there were no latrines....!
"Oh My God", I heard someone scream....!

Sweltering holes, in the bowels of the ship,
Personal space just did not exist....
Stacked four high, on canvass cots,
Swaying of sea, stomachs in knots....

The man above you empties his guts,
Drenched in vomit, just your luck....
Wiping yourself, with your last towel,
Thanking God, it be not, his bowels....

FATE UNKNOWN

Every day, they broke up fights,
Hoping no one, pulled a knife....
Quarters too cramped, nerves too frayed,
To keep the peace, our Chaplains prayed....!

Boredom became everyone's enemy,
Gambling, not considered obscenity....
Not much to do, see or read,
A fight or two, to make them bleed....!

One day, all fought for the rails,
Excitement!, the carcass of a whale....
In its center, a huge, bloody crater,
Feeding Albatrosses was "Mother Nature"....

Across the ocean, we plodded along,
Of Terra Firma, we did long....
Ten long days and nights, at sea,
No gravy, in this damned navy....

There was no laundry, on the boat,
We tied our fatigues, to a rope....
Across the water, they would skip,
Saltwater stained, as they dripped....

No room at the bow, but....we attempted PT,
Like the Macarena, barely, could touch our knees....
By the numbers, one, two, three, four,
"Tell the people, what she wore"....

USNS GENERAL LEROY ELTINGE

Only peanut brittle, sold at the ships store,
Boxes of "Pecos Pete", we did hoard....
"Crunch, crunch, crunch", became an annoying sound,
One more bite, we'd go twelve rounds.....!

On clear nights, a movie, some saw,
Only a small unit, could answer that call....
Too many men, for all to see,
A sudden downpour, our first fatality.....!

A trooper asleep, on a lower deck,
The stairwell crowded, getting wet....
Unknowingly, a soldier leapt,
Landing full force, crushing his chest.....!

No space, so into the brig, his body went,
No air-conditioning to purge deaths scent..
Suddenly all was quiet, not a sound,
The engines failed, our hearts did pound....

For a solid day, we were adrift,
Prayed for something, anything, to give us a lift....
Finally, the crew, got us underway,
Another prayer, to keep us going our way....

Into Subic Bay, for repairs and rest,
They docked the ship, three abreast....
Ashore for just two hours, but it was swell,
Enough to down, some "San Miguel's"....

FATE UNKNOWN

Our casualty disembarked with prayers,
As mechanics completed, much needed repairs....
Never had I seen a place so green,
As we said "goodbye," to the Philippines....

Only two days from Cam Ranh Bay,
New anxieties came our way....
Can you kill? are you prepared to die....?
"Ours is but to do and die, not ours to reason,
WHY?".....?

One day out, miraculously, the struggling stopped,
For each other, suddenly, we cared a lot....
On that ship, a band of brothers, we became,
Calling each other, by first names....

Suddenly, a fighter plane, flew by,
Tilting its wings, a welcoming "Hi"....
An immediate bond, to other military branches,
The NVA would fight, all our lances....?

Excitedly!, someone shouted, "LAND",
Of mountainous jungles, palms and sand....
As evening fell, "The Eltinge" docked,
Reality! Viet Nam, now our lot....

USNS GENERAL LEROY ELTINGE

THAT RUSTING CRATE, now a refuge,
one last night,
Concussion grenades, boomed, to morning light....
Into a hostile land, we disembarked to meet our fate,
A sentimental, "GOODBYE",
to THAT RUSTING CRATE.....!

Grif wrote: The above poem was inspired by my lifelong friend, Jim Soprano, who proudly served with Headquarters Company 1/327 Infantry. Jim and I went over to Vietnam on the Eltinge. We also flew home on the same plane after our tour was over. When I was suffering from a relapse of Malaria during the trip, he took care of me all the way to my house in upstate New York! He was an "Above the Rest!" paratrooper, and he is still the same caliber of a person and friend. Thanks for everything, Jim.

Sincerely,
Grif

* * *

Peter S. Griffin was a member of A Company, 2nd/502nd Airborne Infantry Battalion (Widow Makers). They upheld their Battalion motto and a long tradition dating back to WWII by leaving many VC and NVA widows as they fought in Vietnam.

Word spread quickly of land sighting and the deck of the USNS Eltinge became crowded.

As elements of the 101st Airborne Division Screaming Eagles gathered, everyone wanted to get a glimpse of Vietnam, our final destination. My first impression of Cam Ranh Bay was of a beautiful green emerald set in blue water that was very serene and hospitable. It was a very picturesque sight with the bluest water I had ever seen. There wasn't even one sign of conflict or war. We arrived on 29 July 1965 and with only one pier there we had to wait until the following day to un-ass this luxury liner. During the wait, precautions were taken as concussion grenades exploded around the ship throughout the night. After being cooped up for several weeks, we couldn't wait to spread our wings.

Because of the rolling wave action, which after a few attempts put a halt to our physical training on the boat, we quickly lost our physical conditioning in that short period of time. The environment literally just kicked our asses and the weather elements were cruel. It took the better part of a month to become acclimated, while we got our water consumption down to normal.

The days brought temperatures of over 100 degrees and if wet when darkness came, especially in mountainous terrain, the drop in temperature brought chills with uncontrollable shaking. At night if one man fired, the whole Company would open fire. The men were wound tightly and nervous and were fast to react to any unnatural sound. It takes discipline not to fire and give away your position at night. It's even more important and critical for crew served weapons, like machine guns. An enemy will probe a defensive perimeter just to locate them and to find the weakest area to attack. Of course once a position is given away, well, here come the grenades. We became acclimated and adapted to the combat situation faster than we did to the weather.

FATE UNKNOWN

Chapter 4

An Khe (Ann-Kay or On-Kay)

In August of 1965, the 1st Brigade, 101st Airborne Division commanded by Colonel James S. Timothy, moved to secure the area of An Khe for the incoming 1st Cavalry Division. Our missions were to clear and secure the following: Highway 19, which ran from the coastal city of Qui Nhon; An Khe Pass; and the area above the pass, where the 1st Cav. would establish their base camp, conduct operations for the control of the Central Highlands, and block key infiltration routes from Cambodia.

The road slowly wound up through the mountains as the elevation increased from the rice paddies and floor of the valley below. Highway 19 meanders through the steep, winding and rocky Mang Yang Pass (U. S. troops just called it An Khe Pass) for about ten miles, and forms a defile, or what's known in the military as a D-File, and a perfect one at that. D-Files can be man-made such as by mines, booby traps or naturally by nature. Some of the best occur naturally and it's a matter of a leader taking advantage of the terrain to deploy his force. The right-side of the road of An Khe Pass or curve of the D-File for the most part went straight up so fast that it couldn't be climbed by man without some kind of special equipment. The left side of the road or left side of the D-File dropped straight off and down more than 900 feet. The road is also flanked by dense elephant grass and jungle foliage on either side. The famed Mobile Group 100 of France was annihilated at this exact location on 24 June 1954, about eleven years before our arrival. Their rusting hulls could be seen at the bottom of the drop off, south of the road or left side of the D-File. This road at the time was made of raised dirt and now was a paved, barely a two lane-wide improved road. This Battle occurred shortly after the French were defeated at Dien Bien Phu; the French Army sought to consolidate their troops for the anticipated withdrawal. GM 100 was ordered to retreat to Pleiku some 40 miles by enemy-held roads and merge with other French units.

Group Motor (GM) 100 originally contained a total of approximately 2502 men, plus 400 men from the 10th Colonial Artillery, whose weapons were towed. Approximately 300 French civilians were allowed to convoy with GM 100, even though this was against high command's orders! Their signal staff was short twenty radio operators. The Viet Minh's (VM) 803rd Regiment was composed of 1,500 men, actually just a battalion, though 400 support troops also reinforced the 803rd. They had many machine guns (light and heavy), 57 mm recoilless rifles, and mortars (an indi-

AN KHE (Ann-Kay or On-Kay)

rect fire weapon that fires an explosive projectile–also light and heavy). Both sides were fully aware that the Pass was ideal terrain for an ambush, but the French assumed high-tech communication and fast moving trucks on the road would give them the element of surprise. They abandoned earlier plans for recon and security in favor of maximum speed. The 803rd knew that to get to Pleiku, ten miles of the GM 100 route was through the Pass itself and the 803rd deduced that GM 100 would travel through it.

The French leader, Colonel Barrou, split his force into four battalions and they departed about a half hour apart. At 1300 hours, two VM formations were reported seen at about one mile and four miles north of Highway 19 and they proceeded without concern of other possible VM formations in their path. At about 1415 hours, Colonel Barrou was informed of a stone barricade on Highway 19 and, if found to be covered by interlocking fires, removing it would be a difficult and extremely dangerous task. It was covered, and at 1420 hours the battle had begun. The troops spotted had been decoys–a favorite tactic used on U. S. Units throughout the Viet Nam war by the VC (Viet Cong) and NVA. Once spotted, Americans would give chase with abandonment and run right into an ambush.

At 1420 hours, they came under fire by the VM, who picked the perfect ambush site. Then the VM disabled the first and last vehicle blocking any vehicle escape route; the French were trapped and unable to move in any direction. The stone barricade was covered by interlocking fires, making it impossible to move. Simultaneously as the 1st Company came under fire, all the vehicles surrounding Colonel Barrou, the Group Commander, also came under massive and accurate recoilless rifle and mortar fire. Then at 1425 hours, a 57mm recoilless rifle struck and destroyed their radio truck, killing everyone inside. At this point they had no command and control. From the right side of the D-File and high ground that the French couldn't climb or assault, the VM lobbed grenades down on them. They shot 57mm recoilless rifles along with 50 caliber machine gun into their vehicles. By 1450 hours the VM swarmed what was left of GM 100's Headquarters, rounding up and executing every French soldier they could find…no prisoners…no survivors…and no exceptions. The kill zone of this ambush location couldn't have been a pretty sight, and while a major victory for the VM, it was devastating for the French, who once more had violated security for speed.

At 1620 hours, French B-26 Marauders (planes) arrived to provide close-air support. The two sides were so close together and "friendly" strafing runs so indis-

AN KHE (Ann-Kay or On-Kay)

criminate, more French troops were killed by air strikes than by VM fire. At the same exact time, French artillery ran out of ammunition. By 1715 hours, GM 100 was ordered to abandon its vehicles and link up with GM 42 on foot. They left behind the wounded and medical supplies, but their ordeal was far from over. The Viet Minh Commissar immediately confiscated the medical supplies and forbade the medics (at gun point) from treating the wounded. The medics could only watch as their wounded died.

The remaining leaders yet again decided to split up into platoon size units (about 40 men), as they fled to the supposed safety of GM 42. For days, GM 100's survivors endured thick jungle, VM ambushes and assaults by mountain tribesmen. Finally, at 1130 hours on 25 June, the remnants of GM 100 were rescued by GM 42. However, even after GM 100 survivors had been rescued, the VM continued to ambush their units for the next seven days before they finally reached Pleiku on 29 June 1954.

GM 100 lost 85 percent of its vehicles, 100 percent of its artillery, 68 percent of its signal equipment, and 50 percent of its weapons. Over 1000 of GM 100 men were killed—40 percent of the unit—and most were killed within a few hours. Of the 400 men from the 10th Colonial Artillery, 259 were lost. The U.S. Army has re-created the GM 100's concepts with their use of Stryker vehicles, and formation of Stryker Brigades Combat Teams units. Hmm...Go figure! Author's note: The above account of the French unit GM 100 was taken from internet research and historical facts, *The Real Stryker* (Chapters 1-3). Additionally, this battle is very briefly depicted at the beginning of the movie, *We Were Soldiers Once*.

One day in early September 1965, I was perched on the right side of that D-File in a two- man defensive position to protect Highway 19 and the Pass. When I was first assigned there my foxhole partner surveyed the situation and said, "If we're attacked, there's no place to go!" Behind us dropped straight down about 70 feet or so and I said, "I don't think we'll be retreating." My foxhole buddy just gave me a blank stare; our backs were up against a wall, so to speak, however I was sure our unit would fight like cornered rats.

After digging in, there was time to survey the area and take it all in as I sat on my steel pot smoking a cigarette. I could see some remains of GM 100 vehicles, rusting ever so slowly, down in the draw off the road, and was surprised that in this environment they even still existed. I wondered what the heck they were thinking. Then again, hindsight is always perfect, isn't it? Having heard by now of the battle I had a better feeling and insight into that day on 24 June 1954. It's one thing to read about history and imagine the events,

AN KHE (Ann-Kay or On-Kay)

while quite another to be able to be at the actual location to get a real visual. It just transports you back in time. I perused the valley below and we were so high up that I could see clouds below. The scene was an array of colors from the puffy white clouds, blue sky and green from vegetation, and it was then I realized just how beautiful a country Vietnam truly was.

The mountains were much cooler than down in the valley although we were operating in both while moving around from time to time with different missions. I preferred the cooler mountains, but at night the temperature would really drop and when I was wet from sweat it actually was downright cold. We didn't have a lot of extra clothing and I remember being wrapped up in a poncho literally shaking as the wind was blowing hard one night. The wind hindered our sense of hearing and my foxhole buddy kept hearing something all night long. Too cold to sleep it was a long night and we were glad to see daylight. I learned to take off my t-shirt during the day keeping it dry and to put it on at night, as it made a huge difference in warmth.

The enemy's knowledge of the terrain created an advantage, giving them the element of surprise as to when or where to strike. We were continually adapting to our environment, the enemy and the situation at hand. As men left we obtained their canteens, rifle magazines, boots and anything else we could scrounge from them to keep going. The Army's concept of a basic load just wasn't hacking it! Come on, one canteen in this environment??? We started carrying our c-rations in our socks and tied them to our web gear and if it rained, "Presto!" We had clean socks. By now our regular boots were beginning to fall apart from water and the environment, men resorted to holding them together with commo wire (communication wire). Our leaders saw the 3.5 rocket launchers were useless in the jungle and, plus the enemy had no tanks. They were turned in and we were issued lightweight M-72 LAW's (light anti-tank weapon) which were good against bunkers. The men that carried the 3.5's in weapons squad were made additional ammo bearers for the M-60s (machine guns). The plastic bags that radio batteries came in were a premium and were re-used to keep things dry such as my wallet that was also carried in the helmet liner of my steel pot to additionally keep it dry. The communication in the chain of command was working to address operational problems except for that slow boat for resupply. Hmm…must have been the Eltinge and was probably broke down at sea.

Chapter 5

Hasty Ambush

Author as M-79 Grenadier Gunner, October 1965.

Author loads an 8 oz. HE (high explosive) round into his M-79 Gun, October 1965 near Qui Nhon.

On 10 September 1965 we were being briefed on a platoon size combat patrol to the north of the Pass into the mountains. We were delayed a bit because a newspaper reporter that was going out with us had his orders abruptly changed. Orders came over the radio to escort him back to the Company CP (command post). Our mission was to search and destroy an area to the north and return by a different route. We were informed that no other friendlies or civilians were in the area, only the enemy. On some operations, such as in the valley, we would encounter civilians in villages and some working out in the rice fields. Additionally, the Battalion Chaplain was going out with us on this one. I was impressed because I'm sure he volunteered and didn't have to go out. Chaplain Curtis Bowers was from Lancaster, Pennsylvania, not too far from where I was born and raised. He was well built and strong looking, not wimpy as one would expect a chaplain to be—all of which would be needed to travel the trails we were blazing. We were giving new meaning to the term pathfinders.

When the escorts returned, someone asked the sergeant, "What's up with the reporter?" The sergeant replied, "Effective this day the Brigade Commander has barred any reporters from going with any 101st units." He further went on to explain that apparently a reporter did a story on a unit that was going out on night patrols armed with only hatchets and cutting off enemy heads. We looked at each other in total disbelief; none of us believed it. Some of those looks turned to smiles and head shaking in the negative at the stupidity of such a thing. First of all, where would they come up with a bunch of hatchets, and who in their right mind would go out without their rifle. Sounds like either something the reporter made up for the publicity, or his heat-oppressed brain from the environment or the stress of combat had gotten to him. Troopers are bad to the bone but not totally insane…well maybe just a bit. The reporter was gone and in fact I never saw another news reporter with the 101st Airborne except for an interview with General Westmoreland in the Phan Rang base camp at Christmas time, three months later. I thought it was a good idea; we had enough to worry about without having to worry about their candy asses tagging along and getting in the way.

 We encountered elephant grass on this mountain top at our turn around point. This stuff was downright nasty, six to eight feet tall with razor sharp edges that would cut the hell out of the men if their shirt sleeves weren't down. Even a minor cut in this humidity and dirty conditions quickly became infected, and these weren't paper cuts. This stuff was so dense it reduced the air flow and while the sun was beating down on our heads from above it, we were soaked with sweat. This probably was very similar to walking through a cornfield that was many times thicker without the rows that provide nice paths for walking. I was lucky that I was in the middle of the formation and most of it was cut or matted down by the lead element. Obvious to me also was that no man had passed by here in many a moon with all this grass so upright, or ever at all for that matter.

We reached our objective, made the turn and were on the last leg of this nature walk back to the rest of our company about a mile away; when we finally entered back into the jungle where it was much cooler and humid, but the triple canopy jungle blocked the sun. This area was very thick and the point man had to use a machete to cut through it. Every fire team (4 to 5 men) was issued one; we also carried some shotguns for the jungle. We were constantly tailoring the platoon and all units for situations we encountered. The progress was slow and the point man with the machete had to be changed over every ten to fifteen minutes. We were in a single file with the men bunched up like it was a night patrol and they weren't maintaining their interval. The file formation didn't resemble a bunch of ducks in line but was more like a snake as the point moved around obstacles in its path. Constant stop and go was the situation, moving perhaps four or five feet at a time as the point man progressed. While standing there waiting to move, I observed several bugs and creatures on the leaves and vegetation of the jungle. They were things I have never encountered in the United States. My thoughts wondered as to their possible harm to man or if they were even known to man. Has man ever even been here before?

Our nature walk continued at a crawl and the day was now getting into late afternoon. Suddenly Vietnamese voices could be heard on our left flank! Arm and hand signals were given to halt, the direction, quiet, and to get down. We alternated every other man facing left and right and took up the prone position. I went to sight the M-79 (a grenade launcher) that I carried and realized it was totally useless because the round has to travel several feet and/or spins to arm the round, and the jungle was so thick that it was impossible. I realized then that I had to get out of carrying it any further, even if I had been handpicked to do so. This was later denied. I took out my .45 caliber pistol and felt somewhat naked and defenseless without at least an M-16 rifle.

The voices stopped as if they also heard us; then I could hear them coming closer, directly to our front. Lieutenant John D. Howard was to the front with the lead squad while Platoon Sergeant Humphries and Staff Sergeant Billy R. Robbins were with the trailing squad, along with an M-60 machine gun. My squad, the 3rd, was located approximately in the center. We heard a voice again that definitely was a male voice speaking in Vietnamese. I immediately received chills while my total body heightened to alertness, so much so that if a mosquito pissed on a cotton ball, I would have fired. Right after that, Lieutenant Howard gave the command, "Fire!" A huge volume of fire erupted simultaneously with the M-60 machine guns sounding like a platoon firing an FPL (final protective line) to stop an all-out assault on its position. I fired four to five rounds from my pistol but observed no assault, so I changed the magazine and waited for a visible target. There was a sharp decrease in the volume as men changed magazines, but sporadic fire continued. Then all of a sudden the volume increased dramatically to reach its original pitch. By that time I realized no fire was coming in our direction. Lieutenant Howard began hollering, "Cease fire, cease fire!" Gradually the firing subsided and came to a halt. Each man had fired about two magazines (about 40 rounds each) and it was a good thing they had gained some experience by now and didn't throw any grenades, because in that thick jungle they would have just bounced back into us.

The jungle now was full of smoke and smelled of gunpowder. It was unusually quiet as every man listened intently, nearly to the point one could hear even sweat dripping. The smoke was drifting up through the trees as we listened. Word passed down the line to get ready to move out, so everyone policed up their empty magazines. A few minutes later Lieutenant Howard gave the order: "Move out!" We picked up and moved forward, trying to get through the jungle. We hadn't gone much more than ten meters or so when I was able to observe the kill zone. There lying on the jungle floor were about a dozen Montagnards (Mountain-yards). Montagnard is a French word meaning mountain people or dweller. They are primarily nomadic but practice some farming and forage of the jungle. They hunt with crossbows, dress in little more than just loin cloths, and no shoes. They inhabit the central highlands of Vietnam. They don't look like Vietnamese, but rather more resemble Indonesians and Cambodians who have a darker skin tone compared to the Vietnamese. Plus the Vietnamese don't like them and the North Vietnamese Army (NVA) force them to carry their equipment, etc. The Montagnards have always been friendly to the French and U. S. troops, especially our Special Forces troops who had worked closely with them for many years.

Before my eyes was a picture that would forever be inscribed into my brain. It consisted of men, women and children all closely grouped together. Most had their heads broken open from bullets and their hair was wet from brain fluid. Total silence ensued as we all were stunned by the visual sight. Rain began coming down very heavily, breaking some of the silence; you couldn't tell if faces were wet from rain or tears as we tried to comprehend it all. There was a distinct odor about the scene and someone broke the remainder of the silence to ask, "What's that smell?" Our medic or someone else said, "Brain fluid." It was a very distinct odor—one I had never smelled before but would never forget. Most had been struck by several bullets and all were carrying something on their backs. The men had baskets of rice and the women had small children strapped to them. We began searching the area for weapons but all we found were a couple of crossbows, some arrows and sickles. As our search began we heard a baby cry; we started turning the dead bodies of women over, looking for survivors, and found four children ranging in ages from one year to perhaps four. They had survived because their mothers, who were directly facing us at the time, had acted as human shields, protecting their children from the grazing fire just a few inches above the ground. In retrospect, although they must have heard the sound of our machetes, it appeared they had continued toward us, perhaps thinking it must have been some of their own people. They didn't seem to have approached cautiously by sending in only one man, but instead had approached with the whole group. They must have believed no one but their own people were in that area, just as we thought only the enemy existed there.

    We re-distributed equipment for those that were carrying the children because we were returning them to our Company CP after our medic had examined them. Remarkably, none of the little ones had a scratch on them. I was weighted down with extra equipment for the return trip. Chaplain Bowers was right behind me the whole way and he carried the biggest child. I offered to give him some relief, but each time he declined. He carried that child for hours until we finally made it back to the rest of our company. Private First Class Tom Joyce carried another child all the way and I can't recall who carried the others. It was stop and go as we had to cut our way through the jungle. It also continued to pour down rain on us for a good period as darkness fell upon us. The company sent out a patrol in our direction to find us. That patrol fired a shot in the air and we were able to link up and close in on the company perimeter. The children were flown out by chopper the next morning to an orphanage; we never heard anything after that of their fate. Those that carried the children all pretty much ended up with lice afterwards. To the best of my knowledge I don't believe they were ever recognized for having volunteered to carry the children, for the strength and endurance they demonstrated, or for the compassion and comfort they provided to those children, who so needed it at that time. Thanks guys, for an outstanding job! I have to believe that because of the children's young ages, they grew up without ever knowing or remembering the incident; we, however, would not be so fortunate.

Chapter 6

Collateral Damage

In World War II, incidents like these were an acceptable part of war. Since then the military has come up with the political spin to call it collateral damage. In the upper echelons of the chain of command, it's an acceptable fact and part of war, but down at our level, we are the ones that must bear the results—it's never an acceptable outcome. There's a myriad of reasons for collateral damage; however, it can best be summed up with "Murphy's Law," which states; "If anything can possibly go wrong, it will."

Anti-war civilians would have you believe this sort of thing is intentional, but that's far from the truth. Do we intentionally kill our own troops? Oh yes, shit happens! Collateral damage isn't a one way street, as the anti-war crowd would have the uninformed believe. They are so prejudice in thought and nearsighted in vision, they don't see the forest for the trees. We do just as much if not more damage to our own forces in comparison to civilians.

Following this incident a month or so later, while assaulting a village, our own mortar platoon dropped a round in the middle of our platoon. No injuries occurred as it was a dud, and the incident was due to the inaccuracy of the maps we were using. On hearing the round come in and land in the paddy, I saw it smoking and buried halfway in the mud. I froze and thought it was going to explode any second, but luckily it was a dud. Later, through aerial photography and a continuation of the war, maps were updated and proved to be more accurate. After that incident, I don't ever remember using our mortars again. We used almost entirely 105mm artillery because it was much more accurate and more powerful. Later, our 81mm mortars at company level were done away with, as we continued to tailor units for the conditions we encountered. I remember going on a helicopter assault and prior to loading, a sergeant gave me an 81mm mortar to carry. I placed it under my web gear straps, in front of my chest, in order to carry it. Man was I glad to get rid of that! The weight of their base plates and ammo in this environment just wasn't feasible, the men of the 4.2 mm mortars primarily ended up providing direct support for the Battalion CP. Our own 81mm and weapons platoon became another maneuver element as a line platoon, but also provided security for the Company CP and a natural reserve force when called upon.

During one incident, we were strafed by M-60 machine guns from a helicopter gunship. Then during the battle of My Phu, we had a 2.5mm rocket fired at us. Our luck continued to hold until the battle of Dak To in

June 1966, when the Company Commander called in helicopter gunships for support against an overwhelming enemy force. They shot up the company, killing a lieutenant and wounding twenty-six troopers, to include all the medics.

On 28 October 1965 our Battalion suffered the loss of six men killed and four men WIA (wounded in action), all members of the Battalion Recon Platoon (Tiger Force); this was the result of friendly artillery fire, along with other occurrences described later. In a war like Vietnam, the sheer number of decisions being made on any given day is phenomenal. Consequently, Murphy's Law is bound to come into play...or as they say, "shit happens!" One of the problems with leaders is, despite having similar training, they're not all created equal in regards to proficiency. It is somewhat like knowing your Doctor might have graduated last in his medical class.

In the Gulf War of 1991, which lasted a month, the combat death toll was 148 KIA (killed in action)—24 percent resulted from friendly fire. An additional eleven more men died from unexploded allied munitions, thus raising the percentage to 31. Prior to the Department of Defense and Army taking over promotions in the early 1970s, the old Army adage for promotions was, "Being in the right place at the right time." Collateral damage could be summed up as being in the wrong place at the wrong time. No, collateral damage isn't an intentional act of war, but it is a reality of war!

Chapter 7

Rocky

Top left: Raymond T. "Rocky" Ryan, Graduate from Jump School.

Top Right: Newly assigned to ABU. Courtesy of Rocky.

Bottom left: Christmas 1964, Ft. Campbell, KY. Courtesy of John C. Haughain

Raymond T. "Rocky" Ryan, of Chadwicks, New York (which is near Utica), enlisted in the Army at the age of eighteen, continuing a long family tradition of serving America's military. Rocky's father, Joseph, and his uncle, James, served in the Navy during the 1940's. Rocky's stepbrother, Arthur, served in Korea from 1951 to 1953. His brother, Edward Charles, served in the Air Force from 1959 to 1962. Rocky's other brothers, James Joseph, Patrick John, and Joseph Wesley, served in the Navy during the 1960s. His brother Dennis served in the Marines during Vietnam and Helen, one of his three sisters, also served in the Navy during the late 1960s.

Soon after completing Jump School, Rocky was assigned to Abu Company and it wasn't long before troopers started calling him Rocky. Some say he was a spitting image of the famed World Champion, professional boxer Rocky Marciano. Rocky's favorite past times were drinking beer, fighting, smoking cigars, and chasing women while not necessarily in that order. He epitomized what a typical paratrooper was in those days. No one ever messed with Rocky or his beer, without having a serious situation on their hands. Young troopers were taught back then at jump school and also their units that they could whip any three legs (non-airborne soldiers), and some in believing that, would go to town and get their asses kicked. Rocky was one who could actually accomplish such feats and didn't need any ignorant oil (booze) for encouragement. Rocky stood 5 foot 10 inches, weighed 195 pounds, and was hard as steel. Others say his nickname came from knocking out men that fooled with either him or his beer; regardless, it was a most appropriate name and he had earned it.

Soon after becoming an Abu, he caught the eye of Platoon Sergeant Humphries who made him his RTO (radiotelephone operator) and the platoon armorer. As platoon armorer, he was responsible for all the equipment in the arms room getting cleaned, or he had to answer to Platoon Sergeant Humphries and he wasn't about to do that. If a trooper's weapon was dirty, Rocky would send him back to clean it after inspecting it. If the trooper disagreed with him, Rocky would invite him into the Arms Room and close the door, where a severe ass-whipping would take place.

He sort of had a way of fixing things or breaking them, such as a dud or slacker in the platoon, while a smart-ass would get knocked out faster than a Cobra strike and left feeling like the Abu mascot had just jumped in or on his chest.

At Fort Campbell, Rocky would travel to Nashville, Tennessee to party on the famed street of Printers Alley, considered the hottest spot around. Rocky returned one Sunday morning around 0530 hours. At about 0600 hours, the CQ (charge of quarters) came through the 3rd platoon bay waking up troops for police call. The CQ was Sergeant Robert Turner, AKA "M-17", as tagged by new members of his squad before deployment to Vietnam, because Turner looked just like an M-17 protective mask.

Abu Trooper wearing an M-17 protective mask. Other troopers prepare for an operation in the Iron Triangle by refitting their masks. November 1965.

Rocky and Turner sort of had a love/hate relationship going. It also existed with Turner's peers or whoever had to work with this numskull. M-17 made the mistake of putting his hand on Rocky and shaking him to wake him up; Rocky immediately hit him with a roundhouse, knocking him completely out and he fell into a wall locker. Nothing happened to Rocky because

ROCKY

M-17 had made the mistake of putting his hand on him, which was a no-no even in those days. They could kick the bed, bang on the bed, shake it, or simply make a lot of noise, but touching was against Army Regulations. This author believes M-17's education level was about one point above a wilted carrot at best, while Rocky was greatly admired by all and even more so after this incident.

 Rocky was always seeing the Company Commander, Captain Donald C. Hilbert at that time, or First Sergeant Duane E. Finley, for fighting or raising hell. Note: soon after our arrival in Vietnam, Captain Donald C. Hilbert was promoted to Major and moved to the Battalion Staff. He also is another Abu who had a distinguished military career and went on to become a Major General before retiring.

 Rocky snuck some beers onboard for the trip to Vietnam on the luxury cruise ship known as the USNS General LeRoy Eltinge. He occasionally would drink one, however he ran out. After about three weeks we pulled into Subic Bay in the Philippines and they let us off. Rocky tried to make up for the beers he missed by trying to drink all the San Miguel's on the island. Of course he snuck some of those San Miguel's back on the boat for the remaining trip.

 After landing at Can Rahn Bay a few weeks prior, Tom Joyce, myself, and a few others, bought some local beer by the name of Tiger, from a couple of kids. We called it Tiger Piss, due to its not being cold and tasting very bad. Well M-17 caught us and proceeded to give us a lecture on how it could be poisoned. We couldn't have cared less, as combat instills a "live for the moment, not tomorrow" type attitude, and the longer we were in combat the more that philosophy became fertile in our minds. M-17 had us dig a 6 x 6 foot hole in the sand. It was one shovel out as two slid back in. Rocky told me Platoon Sergeant Humphries asked him if he bought any beer and Rocky said; "No, I wasn't about to tell John T. yes!"

Around this same time Rocky was on radio watch at the Platoon CP and received a call from First Sergeant Finley who asked, "You have any beer there?" Rocky lied and said, "No!" First Sergeant Finley said, "Come get it at the Company CP." Rocky took the initiative and placed himself in charge of the beer rations without telling anyone of the radio call. He got with fellow trooper Specialist Fourth Class Rodney C. Eades and together they borrowed a jeep and headed out to the Company CP about a half a mile away. Now the foxes were really in the henhouse. After picking up two cases of beer, they made a couple pit stops on their return. Rocky was driving and upon arrival at the Platoon CP, fell out of the jeep. Platoon Sergeant John T. Humphries was not a happy camper. I told Rocky many years later,

"No wonder I never got any beer in the field, except one time." We couldn't stop laughing. They had us climbing mountains to get acclimated and the following day, while coming down off a mountain, Rocky says to John T., "I can't wait to get down and have a couple beers." John T. replied, "You had yours!" A Colonel hearing this told Rocky he did an outstanding job on the radio and asked Rocky, "Is there anything I can do for you?" Rocky said, "Sure, can you get me a couple beers?" The Colonel replied, "You got 'em." I'm sure John T. had murder on his mind about this time.

In early September, the 3rd Platoon was conducting a patrol in the jungle north of the An Khe Pass searching for the enemy, while controlling the area to prevent the enemy from using it as a staging area for attacks against the 1st Cavalry Division as they moved in to establish their base camp. The enemy used mines and booby traps for several reasons, such as to provide early warning to allow their escape from an area and to slow us down where as we may not find their caches. For psychological reasons, by not killing and just wounding or maiming forces, a unit is forced to use men in the treatment of the wounded, therefore taking them away from their primary mission of finding the enemy. We had been humping almost all day in the hot humid environment; men were tired, thirsty, and looking forward to an end of this mission.

We made contact and during the incident Sergeant Paul F. Wolfe sustained an injury to his right hand and was WIA, while Rocky apparently had stepped on a mine, severely injuring his right ankle/leg. "Doc Staley" (Sp/4 Raymond R. Staley), the senior medic of Abu Company, immediately began treatment. Our medics had long before given up carrying stretchers because in the jungle a six foot stretcher seemed to get caught on every vine. We used a machete and quickly cut down two small diameter trees to use as poles, and made a poncho litter. Rocky's equipment was redistributed and a new RTO by the name of Private First Class Ashley Stetson, Jr. was designated. Rain began to come down as the field expedient litter was being made.

We continued through the jungle with the point man hacking his way forward to get someplace where a dust off/medevac (medical evacuation) could get in for Rocky's pick-up. As we began movement I was one of the pole bearers and Rocky was dropped a few times. He said, "If you drop me again I'm going to knock someone out!" We looked at each other knowing he meant every word of it. Each time he was dropped it caused severe pain because the morphine shot hadn't kicked completely in yet. Rocky was no lightweight either, but the real problem was the pole bearers were all different sizes, causing Rocky to roll off the poncho litter. We changed some pole bearers to get rid of the

ROCKY

short lightweights and chose some men that were about the same height. As we moved along, the rain that showed up on a daily basis continued to fall, making the ground and the poles slippery. We dropped Rocky another time or two, but by then the morphine had kicked in and Rocky was in a much mellower mood. We also switched off pole bearers as we trudged along on this laborious task. I mainly carried load bearing equipment from other pole bearers to lighten their load as they didn't want to rotate and switch off.

After what seemed like forever and a day, we made it back to the remainder of Abu Company where Rocky and Sergeant Wolfe were medevaced. I never saw Sergeant Wolfe again and didn't see Rocky until over forty years later when he filled in all the blanks regarding his experiences after being WIA. Back in the States, Rocky spent about three years in and out of hospitals—Valley Forge Army Hospital, Pennsylvania, St. Albans Naval Hospital on Long Island, and Syracuse Veterans Hospital in New York. All the doctors wanted to amputate his leg just below the knee, but he kept asking them not to, so they gave it more time, honoring his request. In all, Rocky had twenty-seven operations and wore a cast for about three years until completely healed. He still has his leg, however it is 4 1/2 inches shorter than the other and he now wears a special prosthetic shoe to make up the difference.

While in the hospital the doctors kept him sedated on drugs, primarily morphine, while also administering penicillin and streptomycin, for a total of ten shots a day from September 1965 when WIA until January 1966. He lost about seventy-five pounds. Finally he told the nurse, "No more morphine!" They weaned him off gradually with less powerful drugs.

Rocky said he was honorably discharged in November 1966 and received a 100 percent disability rating from the Veterans Administration (VA). Although discharged, Rocky remained in a long leg cast for three years and was in and out of VA hospitals during that time. Then about eighteen years later, the VA reversed its decision and downgraded him to 40 Percent disability. Rocky put in an appeal of their decision, hired an attorney to argue his case, and over two years later they reversed their decision, restoring his 100 percent disability rating. However, unable to work to pay bills, Rocky's debt accumulated and his credit rating plummeted. Rocky's marriage went to hell and his wife divorced him. He also almost lost his home due to being unable to pay the mortgage. This was obviously a piss-poor decision made by some bureaucrat doctor or doctors that were probably getting a bonus for the dollars he saved the VA. While overall the VA does one heck of a job, there's always that 10 percent and they need monitoring as this battle continually rages long after the

ROCKY

combat zone. Today Rocky does exactly that by helping other veterans with claims, as he enjoys the golden years with his second wife.

Looking back I'm not sure why Rocky and I hit it off, but we did. Perhaps from our bunking near each other in the platoon bay barracks, or maybe my having been in the Army over three years may have had something to do with it. After all, no one had to tell me how to clean a weapon and I developed soldier skills from a unit with very high standards; therefore I fit in very quickly. Rocky hung out in Nashville but my favorite hangout was Hoptown (Hopkinsville). Perhaps it was from our mutual dislike for M-17, regardless, we bonded immediately from the beginning of my assignment to Abu Company. Rocky wasn't a Sergeant however he was a bellwether within 3rd Platoon, and because of his wounding probably missed his calling with a military career.

FATE UNKNOWN

Chapter 8

Hard Times

The jungle had the strangest creatures, the ugliest bugs...and, how could I forget the elephant grass that was taller than we were? If men had their sleeves rolled up to fight the heat, the grass would cut their arms worse than an army of ants with razor blades. Speaking of ants, the jungle has red ants that are huge compared to piss ants, about the size of wasps, and their sting or bite was just as bad. When they are on the ground they aren't a problem, but they also climbed up vegetation and trees, so that when a man brushed up against them unknowingly the ants would get all over him, stinging the hell out of him. All of a sudden if a man began un-assing all his gear and clothing while doing the fastest striptease ever, it was from red ants. Others would help in brushing them off as fast as could be done. Some of these men would have red welts all over themselves, while others would get an allergic reaction and have to be evacuated.

Anytime we spent in the stagnant water of the rice paddies, especially at night, the mosquitoes just swarmed over us as if we were the only meal within miles, biting through our fatigues as if we were naked. The insect repellant that we carried and used worked great, but we were only supplied with a couple ounce bottle of the stuff. What we needed was a five-gallon can of it, plus take a bath in it to stop these bumble bee sounding little bitches. Reflecting back, I see a little humor in it now, but trust me, at the time this stuff wasn't the least bit funny…except to Sergeant Clio Johnston, who found humor in everything and always had a shit-eating grin during tough periods.

Sgt. Clio Johnston, Squad Leader of 3rd Platoon and Boat Trooper.

HARD TIMES

Sgt. Clio Johnston, in a graveyard near Qui Nhon, October 1965.

One night in particular was so bad that the whole patrol violated security by breaking out our ponchos in order to stop the mosquitos. Ponchos weren't allowed in an ambush site, as they were noisy and, if too comfortable, the men would fall asleep; however, we kept all our gear with us in case we had to move. On many other ambush patrols, we would lie all night in the rain and wouldn't dare think of putting on a poncho. I have never been in a place, to include the rest of Vietnam, where the mosquitoes were that bad–probably due to the stagnant water of the paddies. Only the Anopheles or female mosquitoes bite, because a blood meal is necessary for reproduction, and there were literally thousands of females buzzing about the area instinctively sensing a feast. Oh, there was no doubt these bitches were dominating this battle. If not for the ponchos, our weapon of choice, I'm sure it would have been death by a thousand bites in the form of malaria, dengue fever, and other diseases. Which environment was the worst? I have no idea, take your pick, none of it resembled home, but the grass always seemed greener where we weren't standing.

Once in the An Khe area while out on patrol we crossed a stream that was about chest high deep. After arriving on the other side we posted security out, refilled our canteens and as usual dropped an iodine tablet in for purification. By then Kool-Aid had become all the rage, and the men were demanding at least one packet minimum per letter to kill the taste of the iodine tablets. Those who were fortunate to have one dropped a package of Kool-Aid in with the tablet, which really was going first class. It is just truly amazing, how one can take an ice cold glass of water for granted. Private First Class Jimmie L. Stacey (Stace) took off his fatigue shirt and was wringing it out when I noticed something black on his back, which turned out to be a leech. In a matter of maybe five or ten minutes, they were on us and some were already gorged with blood. Hell, we

HARD TIMES

never felt a bite. Everyone began stripping down, which was a show in itself, because no one wore underwear. They had long ago ditched them due to heat, rashes and the fact that those Indian shorts were always sneaking up the crack of the ass and attempting to wipe us out. Security sort of went to hell with the men more concerned with leeches than with the enemy. We tried insect repellant on them but quickly found the lit end of a cigarette worked the best. So there we were, Private First Class Richard R. Taft, Private First Class David T. Rogers, Specialist Four John E. Petty, Specialist Four Charles E. Griffin, and Private First Class Clarence E. "Griff" McKinnis, to name a few, but essentially the whole platoon, having a leech burning party. They were worse in tight places like around the waist and ankles. I teamed up with Stace for the extermination party; if he hadn't taken off his shirt to wring it out, who knows what the outcome may have been, from diseases they may carry and so forth.

We were one of the first units to arrive in Vietnam and the supply boats were obviously slower than the USNS Eltinge that we had arrived on, that broke down in route. We had no base camp and everything we owned was carried on our backs. Essentials only were the priority; anything else was a luxury, due to weight. Everything was just about impossible to keep dry; however, we did hump and keep a few of those precious letters received from home that were re-read more than once. Men were even turning down c-rations (canned food) to lighten the load. Most days were spent humping all day, pulling 50 percent watch at night...that is if we were lucky enough not be sent out on an ambush patrol at night, which required 100 percent alertness and no sleep. We were functioning on about four hours of sleep a day. Some days we actually fell asleep while walking through rice paddies or if we stopped for more than five minutes. That pace pretty much continued throughout my tour, and it's truly amazing what the human body can adapt to and how it can endure on three to four hours sleep a night.

Hard times were made worse by the environment, along with elements a trooper had to endure, and the conditions changed daily, if not by the hour. A comfort zone seemed either to be non-existent or lasting only for short periods of time. We were always hot, at times cold, wet, thirsty, tired, sleepy or dealing with creepy crawlers ranging in size from the bad ass red ants to python snakes. The harsh environment took a greater toll and turnover rate than the enemy was inflicting on us; men succumbed to malaria and other diseases. Some troopers, like Private First Class James D. Hawes from Waycross, Georgia, died from illness or disease, while others from the 101st even drowned. Then again some illnesses didn't show up for years

HARD TIMES

later, such as diabetes and other related illnesses due to Agent Orange. The heat and wetness was the perfect breeding grounds for infections. Germs were the only happy campers around here! The bath situation consisted of washing from a steel helmet, or once in a while from a stream if leeches weren't present. It was seldom, however, because it was a security risk, we weren't about to get caught with our pants down, and because most of the time our units were on the move. Rain cleaned much of the dirt off and good old sweat, which was in abundance daily, cleaned the pores. We had been in the country about three months while occupying a defensive position, when Platoon Sergeant Humphries said, "Get them up Robbie." In addition, Staff Sergeant Billy R. Robbins said, "Saddle up…we're moving out." My first thought was what else is new, when Private First Class Tom Joyce asked, "Where we going now Sarge?" Sergeant Robbins replied, "To get that dirt off your goat-smelling ass." After which Tom and I looked at each other with bewilderment, or a "you got to be kidding me" kind of look. Tell no lie as it turned into reality when we arrived at a stream where the Engineers had set up a shower point complete with tent, soap, warm water, and the works. Upon coming out the other side, we received a towel and gave our sizes to receive new jungle boots, jungle fatigues etc. This reminded me of when I received my first issued clothing in reception, upon entering the Army. These items were much lighter and thinner and dried out much more quickly. That slow ship must have finally docked, but at least the Army had its priorities correct with beans and bullets.

Not long after, we received word that the 1st Brigade(S), 101st Airborne Division was establishing a base camp in Phan Rang, wherever that might be located! Not that this did us much good, as the routine was constant humping, searching for Charlie (slang for Viet Cong guerrillas), kicking ass, adapting our tactics to the environment and anything else that was thrown our way continued to be the norm. Personnel in the 3rd platoon, along with those in Abu Company, began to turn over. This was not only from enemy contacts with KIA and WIA, but also from a host of other reasons as well: malaria; foot problems from constant wetness; infections, as small cuts turned into major infections; boils on the butts (in which case I learned to sit on my steel pot rather than the ground); dysentery and fevers.

On 21 September 1965, Private First Class Manual F. Fernandez of New York City, New York, became the first Abu to be KIA. He was clearing fields of fire to the front of his foxhole when he struck a mine in an old unmarked French or VM minefield. We had already been in this area for a few weeks on both sides of Highway #19 at the top of An Khe Pass in the form of two U's, with the open end of the U's adjacent to Highway #19 and the rest of the U's formed the forward edge of the battle area (FEBA). We rotated in and out of there going on different missions, sometimes for days, and the unopened part of the U actually became a worn path from position to position. No one had a clue until this fatal incident made us aware of the dangers that lurked there. Some engineers were brought in with mine detectors to sweep the trail; they laid out white engineer tape, which is made of a heavy cloth material, and this allowed us to hold our positions while continuing the mission. This wouldn't be the last minefield we'd encounter or which would claim additional causalities.

On 27 September 1965, the third day of a search and destroy operation, Abu company began setting up defensive positions for the night. Platoon Sergeant Humphries and Staff Sergeant Robbins observed the CO (Commanding Officer) and his headquarters group setting up in a sparsely overgrown area of an old destroyed hamlet. The time was approximately 1900 hours when they observed the company clerk, Specialist Fourth Class Thaddeus Zajac, sit down and an explosion take place, startling them—it was obviously a grenade type booby trap or pressure detonated mine. The result was three causalities: the Artillery Forward Observer (FO) Lieutenant James P. Kelly, his RTO,

Halford Logan, and Specialist Fourth Class Thaddeus Zajac were KIA. Specialist Fourth Class Charles Lostaunau (Charlie Tuna) and three others were also wounded. The LT died in Charlie Tuna's arms. The medevac request was sent in at 1900 hours, but was denied by the 1st Cavalry Division due to rainy weather and night approaching. Company A, 502nd Aviation Battalion responded in their usual dedicated and professional manner by taking the mission and picking up six extremely urgent cases. They arrived at 2010 hours, after two men had already bled to death. It was becoming unsafe to take a step or even to sit the hell down. These are just some of the reasons, as a complete laundry list for the attrition would be exhausting and overkill.

There were some shit birds we were glad to see gone, such as my squad leader, Sergeant Robert C. Turner, nicknamed M-17, so called because he looked just like one and was one ugly piece of shit. Dumber than a box of rocks, the whole squad was damn lucky that we weren't killed during his tenure. He was replaced by my fire team leader, Sergeant Clio Johnston, who had his shit together–along with great common sense and always a calm demeanor. M-17 was scared to death of his shadow and was always nervous. If taking a crap, he would probably forget to put asswipe (toilet paper) in his hand. I suppose one can tell I had absolutely no respect for him; however, my attitude wasn't the exception, but pretty much a consensus among the squad and platoon. It was the highly respected fire team leader Sergeant Clio Johnston who was keeping it all together anyway.

At a reunion many years later, Lieutenant Howard told the story of when Sergeant Johnston had come in drunk one night and at the time was rooming with M-17 in a two-man room. Sergeant Johnston actually pissed all over M-17 as he slept. Naturally a fight ensued and Lieutenant Howard had to report in to take care of the situation, which eventually was handled by the NCOs (noncommissioned officers) of the Company. Apparently M-17 must have gone too far with Sergeant Johnston about something, as he did with everyone on a frequent basis. I don't recall how or where M-17 went, but no one gave a shit. One thing for sure, it was a beautiful day in Vietnam that day. We hated to see the squared-away troops depart, no matter the reason, as we were greatly dependent on each other for survival. The new guy was arriving at a fast pace.

FATE UNKNOWN

Chapter 9

Mama-San
By Staff Sergeant Billy R. Robbins

Sergeant Billy R. "One Zero" Robbins, Weapons Squad Leader, Ft. Campbell, KY. Courtesy of "One Zero."

We off-loaded the choppers in the Qui Nhon (Quinn Yon) area and were met by United States Marines. They immediately led us to their defensive positions as both units conducted a relief in place. Our new mission: Secure and maintain this area for the arrival of the Korean White Horse Infantry Division, who planned to establish their base camp in the Qui Nhon area.

Then came the bitching! "Here we go again! Nobody secured our base camp! We haven't even used our base camp yet! When are we going to get some new clothes and boots? We're always moving, like a bunch of damn gypsies. Moving, moving, all the damn time!" "Shut up! Ya' volunteered for the Army… and Airborne…huh?" Someone said, "Oh shit, don't let the first sergeant see that Marine vehicle; he'll have us dig it out so he can trade it." The Marines had left a large boat-looking vehicle, with large wheels stuck in a muddy rice paddy. The Marines called it a "duck," and they would return and recover it when the water recedes. Our Company CP was on flat ground adjacent to a dirt road, at the bottom of a large hill. The next morning, it was clear and hot. First Sergeant Finley gave Heavy-Drop Jim Wagoner and me a wad of Vietnamese money and sent us into town in the company's ¾ ton truck to purchase ice, beer and soda-pops.

MAMA-SAN

We stopped at a shop in Qui Nhon and I bought 10 black pistol belts with holsters, made from elephant hide, for each of my men in the M-60 machine gun squad for twenty dollars. After we bought the soda pop, beer and blocks of ice, Big Jim drove that truck like Dale Earnhardt Senior drove a race car, because it was hot and the ice was melting. The heavy volume of slow traffic didn't help our cause, but Jim zigzagged through it, constantly blowing the horn as we passed heavy laden, slow carts being pulled by a water buffalo, with slow, loaded buses, and mopeds on both sides of the road.

By the time we returned to the company CP, the mess tent had been erected and Staff Sergeant Jackson, the company mess sergeant, had his portable field stoves roaring with blue flames. The cooks were working-out and preparing food, while the aroma of fresh coffee was drifting through the company area. The spoons (cooks) grabbed the ice, beer and sodas and dumped them into a ¼ ton jeep trailer. I waited until the first sergeant walked over to the mess tent, then I slipped into the back of his tent to repay a debt and left a case of Coca-Colas, with a M-16 bullet on top and a note: PAID-N-FULL! When we were back in An Khe I was sitting in the first sergeant's tent, waiting for a debriefing from a patrol, when I spotted an ice cold cola. As I walked closer to the soda–pop, the first sergeant said, "One-Zero, don't mess with my soda. Get away from it. My rifle may accidentally discharge and you might be down range, and there won't be a purple heart!" "Top, I ain't going to mess with your soda-pop, I don't even like Coca Colas, and if it disappears, don't-chu go blaming me." "One-Zero, if my soda disappears, I'm going to send your ass on a one man patrol to Hanoi!" After being debriefed by the commander, let me flat ass tell you right now, the only thing on my mind was that iced cola and I was damn sure going to confiscate it. In return, I left an M-16 bullet in its place.

1SG Duane E. Finley (sitting) with his ¼ ton Jeep Trailer filled with free ice, cold beer and soda.

The 3rd Platoon was in company reserve and although the Marines told us that this was a secure area, we still placed out LP's/OP's (listening post/ observation post). The troopers were sitting around cleaning weapons, writing letters, shaving, washing clothes, playing cards and catching up on some sleeping. Lieutenant Howard and I were laying in the shade under my poncho lean-to, waiting to eat, and laughing at John T. using an aluminum pan of water to take a whore's bath.

The 1st and 2nd Platoons were conducting small security patrols around our company CP area. The 1st Platoon was on a reconnaissance patrol mission; they were moving along a dirt road that was flanked by flooded rice paddies, checking out a supposedly abandoned village, about a mile away, and then were to return to the CP for supper.

About 1600 hours, we started smelling steaks, chicken, and fresh vegetables being cooked. Good God Almighty! Oh man! That food smelled fantastic! The troops always reacted happily about hot meals in the field. Slowly, troopers started edging closer to the mess tent, volunteering for KP, savoring that wonderful smell of food being cooked and coffee being perked. Our lounging around was rudely interrupted by the company commander hollering, "3rd platoon–saddle up! 1st Platoon was just ambushed!"

Someone hollered, "God damn it! What about the food?" John T. began grabbing his clothes and kicked over his pan of water, while Lieutenant Howard and I were laughing our asses off at him. John T., a Korean

War combat vet, didn't have to think about what to do. He hollered, "Robbie, round them up, full combat gear...moving out in ten minutes!" I told Lieutenant Howard, "LT—go check with the CO!"

By the time Lieutenant Howard returned from the CP tent, the 3rd Platoon was ready to rock and roll. Lieutenant Howard gave the platoon a frag order: "1st Platoon was ambushed at the edge of a village and is taking casualties. Order of March: 1st Squad right side of road, 2nd Squad left side of road, 3rd Squad bring up the rear, an M-60 with 1st Squad and one with 3rd Squad, single file on the red-ball (road). Robbie take the front left file; I'll be front right! John T., bring up the rear. Move out!" Usually, when a reserve unit is deployed, it means serious things have happened, or about to happen to the element being reinforced.

In Abu Company, the SOP was thus: when a reserve unit is deployed, it usually carries everything available, including the kitchen sink. In Abu's order of battle plan, when going into action from a reserve unit status, be prepared for the worst, be loaded for bear, taking extra ammo, grenades, M-79, M-72 LAW's (light anti-tank weapon used on bunkers and concentration of troops), water, food, medical supplies, the whole nine yards to re-supply the engaged force plus for ourselves, and the 3rd Platoon used the code of XE...Extra Essentials...warring toys so the unit in contact can also be re-supplied…today was no exception.

As we hurried along the hardened dirt road, we passed the remnants of a small, abandoned hamlet on the right side of the road. "Clank," the distinct sound of an M-1 rifle bolt slamming home rang out. If you've ever heard that sound, you'll never forget it. It seemed like every trooper in the platoon reacted simultaneously, just as they were trained, hitting the dirt and immediately crawling into water-filled ditches, assuming an all-around defensive position, observing, listening, ready to unleash a heavy volume of fire, and a lot of grenades. Lieutenant Howard asked, "Anybody have a location?" About thirty men pointed to thirty different directions.

After maneuvering fire-teams and squads through piles of debris, and after surrounding the area and checking it for about ten minutes, we didn't find anyone. I guess the enemy had disappeared…if he was ever there. Most of the men in the platoon heard the sound of an M-1 bolt slamming shut. Was it a sniper, imagination, or perhaps nerves? Combat will do that to you!

The VC/NVA are experts in the art of initiating ambushes on a relief force/reserve unit that was rushing forward to help a unit in contact, or pinned down. And sometimes the enemy attempted to confuse their opponents by using a ruse to delay the reinforcing unit until the pinned down unit is annihilated, or until their comrades can escape.

Later we learned from captured enemy prisoners of war and documents that revealed the fact that the enemy tried to avoid contact, if possible, with "American soldiers with a black and white bird on their uniform, and carrying a little black gun." The enemy wanted no part of the "Screaming Eagles." But, if necessary and under the right circumstances to their advantage, those little bastards would fight their asses off, displaying unbelievable courage and tenacity.

I said, "LT! We gotta go. We gotta move it." John T. walked up nonchalantly and said, "Good reaction, now on your feet, we have to move out NOW! First platoon is pinned down and being flanked. We have to get to-um fast!" After we were back on the road, we started running toward the village as a strong wind began to blow and I could see a sheet of rain coming across the water covered rice paddies toward us; then a torrential monsoon rain engulfed us. We disregarded the rain as no big problem, but later we found out that the rain would definitely be a big damn problem.

The battle din rode the wind right through us and I could smell the cordite from the powder of gun fire and grenades, and it sounded like we were in the middle of the battle. A medevac chopper had landed on the road in front of us and had departed by the time we arrived at

MAMA-SAN

that location, successfully evacuating some wounded troopers. As we ran along the road, we passed patches of blood, first aid bandages, clothes, and equipment lying in the road, which was picked up as we ran by. Lieutenant Howard was in the middle of the road and in the lead and I was right on his ass. I looked to the left edge of the road and saw a civilian AM/FM portable radio. I never slowed down as I scooped up the radio. Written on the side of the radio was, Sgt. James D. Mullins, Abu Co., 1st Platoon. To me, it seemed like time stood still and took forever to run that last quarter of a mile to where the 1st Platoon were pinned down in the water behind rice paddy dikes. As we neared the village, I could see the lead squad of the 1st Platoon on the left side of the road, pinned down in the edge of the village, and the rest of the platoon was pinned down in waist deep water behind rice paddy dikes on the left side of the road about one hundred feet from the edge of the village. They couldn't enter the village on the road because a tall wooden gate blocked the village entrance.

As the rain fell harder, hitting my helmet with loud sounding splats, I could see the rain hitting the water in the rice paddies so hard that the water was uplifting in grey/white spurts similar to water white-capping. I could also hear the closeness of the sharp-cracking M-16's, popping of M-79 grenade launchers, and the automatic distinctive sounds of the enemy's AK-47's, (standard weapon for NVA) and the ka-booming of hand grenades, along with shouting from the pinned down troopers.

Over the radio, the 1st Platoon informed us that the enemy in the north side of the village had pinned down their lead squad at the edge of the village, and the rest of their platoon in the water filled rice paddy, while the enemy in the south side of the village was attempting to flank the rest of the 1st Platoon.

As we meshed with the 1st Platoon in the water, we were told to hold up until their FO called in artillery fire. The FO, an artillery second lieutenant, along with the 1st Platoon, was down in the water, peering over the road, shooting an azimuth with his magnetic compass and reading his map. He planned to place a barrage of HE (high explosive artillery shells) rounds to the right of the road in the edge of the hedgerow and in the water filled rice paddy on the southwest side (right side of the road, our side) of the village. The FO was attempting to blow an opening in the thick hedgerow that grew atop the embankment that surrounded the village, hopefully, to facilitate our entry into the village, and then the FO was going to lift that fire and walk the artillery to the east and south sides of the village. The FO couldn't place supporting fire on the enemy in the northwest side of the village confronting the lead squad because the combatants were within close proximity of each other.

I saw red and green tracer bullets streaking at each other in the northwest side of the village. Green (enemy) tracers bullets were also streaking, zipping, and popping over our heads as we huddled in the dirty stinking water of the rice paddies by the road embankment. Then I heard the artillery shells overhead, whistling and roaring, and sounded like a freight train. Then I saw huge geysers of water, mud, tree limbs, and other debris rising upward as black and grey smoke billowed upward, then the debris fell in slow motion, as the wind blew the smoke through our position. Then I saw black and grey smoke, orange-red flames dancing in the edge of the hedgerow and in the edge of the village.

Immediately after the first volley of artillery rounds splashed down, I heard a second freight -train passing over head, landing in the village farther to the east and to the south. The FO began walking the artillery eastward as the artillery shells exploded with deafening sounds. I thought, "Man! That FO has his shit together." I smelled and tasted the cordite on my lips from the exploding shells, which always did get my adrenaline flowing.

John T. hollered, "Move–out!" We were on the road again, running. As we closed on the village, the strong distinctive cordite smell, and the popping of weapons made me run faster…I think? We were in a flat-ass foot race toward the village, and I don't even remember being tired; I guess my adrenalin was really kicking in now.

Zoomed in picture of Mama-San Village with entrance/ gate on right side, just prior to receiving fire.

Approaching the big wooden gate with a large sign that had a white background and black lettering above the gate, I could see large plumes of white, grey, and black smoke rising up through the trees in the village. Parts of trees and houses were being blown up into the air, then like before, the debris fell slowly to earth. The artillery was on target and really tearing up the village. I could hear people hollering and shouting amongst the battle din.

I forgot that time was also on the move, and the heavy rain and clouds was causing it to get dark sooner. Yet, I saw Sergeant Paul Shamp, Jr., and his pinned-down fire team laying in the edge of a hedgerow on the left side of the road. Shamp hollered, "One-Zero! Take the path to the right—outside of the hedgerow. Get

MAMA-SAN

some!" I hollered at Lieutenant Howard, "Run! God damn it, run!" We took off running to the right along the path headed south along the outer berm of the hedgerow. I was about ten yards behind Lieutenant Howard. We were looking for an entrance in the thick hedgerow, so we could enter the village.

I heard a loud whistling sound getting closer...like it was drilling into my head. In the mud on the side of the hedgerow, I saw a splash! Then I heard a sizzling sound, announcing that an over-head round had landed on the side of the berm right between Lieutenant Howard and me. We both froze! The 4.2 mortar round was apparently a short round and also a dud. Thank the Lord for duds, sometimes! About six inches of the round was sticking out of the mud as gray smoke rose, and the hot round was sizzling like fat-back being fried in hot lard on a red hot wood stove. Some people later said it was a 4.2 mortar round from our battalion's mortar section, however, I don't know where it came from, and all I thought about was getting out of the area.

Lieutenant Howard looked at me. We stared at one another, and then looked at the mortar round sticking out of the mud, then looked back at each other. I can close my eyes now and still see that picture as clear as the day it happened. I can't erase it from my brain. It's stuck there forever. I didn't get scared then, but later I started shaking all over, uncontrollable—it scared the shit out of me to the point I couldn't even talk.

    I hollered, "Run! God damn-it! Run!" We ran about ten steps and found a gaping opening blown through the hedgerow. Lieutenant Howard knelt by the opening as I ran through it firing my M-16 rifle on fully automatic, extracting and flipping my two magazines that were taped together, reloading, and continuing firing, spraying the area in front of me. Lieutenant Howard directed troopers through the opening, left and right of me...while some of the troops stepped on me and tripped over me in the semi-darkness, while I was cursing at them to get off me and spread out. They fanned out and hit the prone position and began firing on fully automatic. Realizing we weren't taking any fire, I hollered, "Cease fire!"

    The enemy had disappeared. Like they always did, which always made me think that they could see in the dark and could fly...well not really fly, but it seemed that way because they could get gone so damn fast...day or night.

    As the rest of the platoon rushed inside the village, stepping on and tripping over us, the men lying prone were hollering and cursing. It was funny as all get out. I told the LT, "Get some illumination flares popping so we can see how to set up a platoon defensive position!" John T. arrived and said, "What the hell are you all bunched up for? Move!" Someone said, "We can't see, Sarge." "Crawl...move it...move it!" They began crawling forward and outward from his barking.

POP! An illumination flare high above us turned the darkness into something like a football field at a Friday night football game back in the States, but brighter than daylight. I was amazed to see how torn up the village was; the artillery really messed it up. John T. said, "Look at you! If people back home could see you all now. Get up and spread out—one grenade will get you all. Squad leaders organize your squads. Make a hasty upside down U position around the platoon CP, which is right here. 1st, 2nd, and 3rd Squads from left to right! M-60 with the 1st and 3rd Squads! Move it!" About thirty five men sprawled all over each other jumped up and ran to whatever cover they could find.

After staying there for about ten minutes, Lieutenant Howard received a call from the Company Commander, Captain George Shevlin, to secure our position and tie in with the 1st Platoon on our left flank and that 2nd Platoon had returned from an uneventful patrol and was now the company reserve back at the company CP. I immediately thought...oh shit! They're eating our steaks and chicken. What a bummer!

"Robbie, take the platoon CP group, while pointing at a nearby house, and check out that house for a CP. The squad leaders and I will make defensive positions, place out OP's /LP's and tie in with the 1st Platoon on our left flank. Lieutenant, keep those flares on station."

I took four men and occupied the house. It had a covered porch over a cemented floor raised about two feet above ground level. The house had two rooms; the front room had two side windows; and the rear room didn't have any windows. The windows were quickly covered with ponchos, candles were lit, and C-4 (a plastic explosive) fires were boiling water for coffee. John T. arrived and checked the house. Specialist Fourth Class Ashley Stetson, Jr. held a cracker can filled with boiling hot coffee by the opened lid and handed it to John T. Upon grabbing the can, John T. hollered and dropped the can of coffee, saying, "As a waiter, you're fired!" Someone offered John T. another can of steaming coffee, and he said, "Put it on the floor."

Lieutenant Howard and I perused the map; John T. finished his coffee and a stinking Camel cigarette and then told us to follow him. We walked the platoon's defensive lines as the rain continued to fall. The men were digging-in quickly and erecting ponchos over their positions for protection from the rain. Lieutenant Howard and the 81mm FO, Staff Sergeant Bobby R. Salt, plotted defensive fires. I checked my two M-60 teams, and as always, they were ready to put some hurt on the bad guys.

MAMA-SAN

According to Platoon Sergeant Press, late in the afternoon his platoon pushed through the village until they reached the flooded river that ran through the village. He could see san-pan boats that were docked on the far side of the river that the VC used for escaping. His men were firing wildly, fully automatic, into the village on the far side of the river, spraying everything, wasting ammo. Press said he hollered, "Hold your fire. Cease fire...you numb-nuts!" Then I launched into a scene reminiscing of Fort Campbell when I taught marksmanship training classes. "You're wasting ammo. You act like there's a supply sergeant behind every tree with a re-supply of ammo! Get behind a tree, a hut, or a mound of dirt and take up a good firing position and focus on a specific area, and when one pops his head up, take well aim, squeeze the trigger, one shot, and you'll have success...like this." I got behind a mud hut and aimed at a certain spot...and, right on cue, a VC slowly raised his head and I shot him right between the eyes. "See, that's how you do it!" I looked over to my left and I saw my M-60 machine gun squad leader, Staff Sergeant Noe Quesada, standing behind another mud hut, his face was depicting a smile of approval at my fortunate deed.

    I began to chew the asses of some of my men because they were standing up openly, uncovered, walking around like a walk in the park. I instructed them to get down and use cover and concealment. About ten minutes after I finished my lecture, I heard a shot from across the river and since I thought I heard the bullet go out into the rice paddy to our rear, I didn't really pay much attention to it. Then I saw Private First Class Charles (Charlie) Jones fall—he had been gut-shot. We didn't have a litter, so some of the men ripped a door from a hut and Charlie Jones was placed on the make shift litter. I looked down at Charlie and I saw blood, feces, meat, and intestines hanging from his stomach and dripping off the litter and I thought he's not going to make it. Charlie was medevac by an H-34 chopper. That was the last I saw or heard of Charlie…until about four months later when someone in the company received a newspaper from Fort Campbell. The Courier Journal's front page was adorned with his photo—a smiling Charlie Jones, with a big smile that engulfed his entire face. Charlie Jones had survived. You never know.

Lieutenant Howard and I walked to the road that ran through the middle of the village and talked with Sergeant Shamp. Then we walked over and coordinated with the platoon leader of the 1st Platoon and his FO. Their CP was in a mud house with one large room with no windows. There was a small wooden bed over in the corner covered with dried blood, and French cigarette butts, dried blood and bandages littering the floor.

MAMA-SAN

Apparently, some wounded enemy soldiers had recently occupied the house, and the room contained a strong pungent Vietnamese odor, which was about to gag me. In a dim and flickering candlelight, the artillery FO pointed out his artillery plots/targets and Lieutenant Howard marked them on his map.

About an hour later we returned to our CP; the oscillating overhead flares caused eerie shadows to dance throughout the village as the rain continued to fall in sheets. The temperature was dropping, getting chilly, and we were all wet and shivering.

I prepared the after action report and the re-supply request and gave it to John T. for approval. I also set up the radio watch between Stetson (platoon RTO), Salt's RTO, a runner, Salt and me, one hour apiece from 2200 hours to 0400 hours. I took the last watch, with stand–to at 0500hours, which meant 100 percent awake and ready for a possible enemy attack. John T. told Lieutenant Howard to sack out on the wooden bed in the back room, and told the rest of us, "If you all have to fart, go outside; don't be cutting any damn stinking C-Ration farts in here!" However, John T. farted all night.

While I was on radio watch, about 0430 hours in the pitch-black room, I heard a familiar sound coming from where the lieutenant was sleeping. About five red-filtered flashlights clicked on and reddish beams of light shown through the pitch-black darkness, creating weird shadows on the walls and ceiling. The lieutenant was hollering, "What the hell's going on?" We jumped up and ran to the door of the rear room and shined our flashlights inside the room, as the wooden bed rose and began wobbling, then started moving toward the doorway as Lieutenant Howard fell off the bed onto the cement floor and said, "Damn, that hurt!" The bed banged against the door frame as we jumped out of the way. When the bed reached the big room, the bed crashed into the radios, then fell over onto the floor, as a big, white ass, sway-back sow wobbled out the door snorting and grunting.

Everybody started laughing, except the lieutenant, who said, "It wasn't funny!" I said, "Right LT, it wasn't funny! It was hog-larious! You are now Abu's champion hog rider. If I had made a movie of that ride, I'd get rich!" Everyone started laughing again, including the LT. He said, "John T., when you get back to the States, and you're ready to retire and purchase a house; hire a professional house finder instead of a wise-ass Staff Sergeant! If you don't, you might wind up with a house full of hogs!" Everyone started laughing again, including LT Howard. Lieutenant Howard said, "Sergeant! Since you thought it was so funny, you can spend the rest of the night on radio watch."

"No sweat LT. It's stand-to time anyway." John T. always had me pull the last shift of radio watch, and then wake the entire platoon for 100 percent stand-to for a minimum of about one hour prior to first light or BMNT (before morning nautical twilight, which begins when the sun is rising and is twelve degrees below the horizon) and for stand-to at EENT (ending evening nautical twilight, which means until the sun has set and is twelve degrees below the horizon). Usually, those are prime times for the enemy to attack. "LT, if you go back to sleep now, that damn hog might return looking for her sleeping spot, so you might as well stay up with me." The LT just stared at me and then walked outside, mumbling something about a sergeant.

I walked to each squad to ensure they were all awake. About an hour later, at first light, John T. and Lieutenant Howard began walking the platoon line, checking the platoon's positions, and then they were going to visit the 1st Platoon. When John T. returned, he said that the LT stayed with the 1st Platoon. I was off radio watch, and everybody had moved outside under the covered porch in the daylight to cook C-Rations, heat coffee, and eat. I flopped down on the bed to take a nap.

I woke up with the feeling that someone was looking at me. The little hairs on my neck and arms rose, and I felt my skin tingling a little. I kept blinking my eyes, focusing in the early morning twilight. I was staring straight up at the ceiling when I saw an eyeball blink through a cigarette size hole. The blinking eyeball looked as big as a horse eye. "God damn" I thought, as I attempted to get up, trying to grab my rifle, steel pot, and run all at the same time. I guess I turned into assholes, elbows, kneecaps and all thumbs; because all I could manage to do was fall off the bed onto the hard cement floor, scraping the skin on my elbows and knees, while jumping through my ass trying to get up. I started hollering and cursing, and moments later Stetson and the medic started running into the house through the open doorway, as I began running out the same doorway. We all three met in the open doorway, and all three of us were knocked on our asses, as our rifles and steel pots went flying. John T. was sitting on the cement porch making coffee, laughing his ass off at us.

I began hollering, "Somebody's in the attic!" "Robbie, did you have a bad dream? Here, take a sip of hot coffee. It'll clear your head." I then began shouting, "John T., somebody's in the attic, somebody's in the attic!" I haven't had a bad dream, and I don't drink coffee. I don't even like people who drink coffee. Coffee will rust your pipes anyway. Listen to me John T. I know damn well that I saw someone looking at me. I saw an eyeball blink through a hole in the ceiling. Stetson and the medic started rolling on the porch, laughing like crazy. I said, "Knock it off, shit birds! God damn it—get up, grab your weapons and come with me, NOW!" We walked back into the house and I pointed at the little hole in the ceiling, and said, "Right there! See that damn hole! I knew I saw an eyeball looking through it, blinking!" We searched around inside the house, but couldn't find any opening in the ceiling. My mind was racing...and then it hit me. "Entrance to the attic is outside."

I whirled around and started running back through the doorway, only to meet the rotund John T. in the middle of the doorway and he knocked me on my ass. Stetson and the medic started laughing, and the medic said, "Hey Sarge, you want me to medevac you? Maybe you've lost it, have combat fatigue or hog fever." "Shut up, damn it, and come with me." John T. said, "Robbie, you've gone crazy."

I jumped up and we ran around the house looking. Then I saw a little wooden louvered vent on the rear gable end of the house. I grabbed the canteen of water the medic was getting ready to drink from. "Hey, give me my canteen back!" Too late! I threw the canteen at the vent. Whack, sounded the plastic canteen when it hit against the wooden vent. I hollered in Vietnamese language, "Lai day, do tay len!" which is supposed to mean, come with me, hands up. Nothing happened, not a sound came from the vent.

John T. hollered from the other side of the house, "Robbie ain't no Vietnamese going to understand your southern lingo shit for the Vietnamese language—its piss poor." I jumped on top of a small wooden table resting against the house and climbed onto a cement wall, and smacked the vent with the butt of my rifle. The vent fell to the ground, revealing the attic. Again, I ordered any occupants to come out with their hands up or I would shoot. I heard some noise from inside the attic. The medic also heard the noise, and as he unholstered his 45 pistol said very excitedly, "Damn, Sarge, someone is in the attic." "Hold on doc, don't shoot! I see fingers on the vent sill!" Stetson hollered, "Yeah, me too, Sarge!" "Come out…fast …hands up," I said again in Vietnamese.

"I'll be God damn," I shouted, as a little dried up woman about eighty to ninety years old stuck her hand out, and after feeling the rain, jerked her hand back inside. I hollered at her again. She started climbing out of the vent hole and stood on top of the cement wall. She then squatted at my feet, her thumbs were raised upward, and started jabbering, praying and spitting red beetle nut juice from her toothless mouth as rain water splattered against her brown weather-beaten face, and ran along the deep wrinkles etched into her face.

I jumped onto the ground and motioned for her to come down from her perch. The old woman slid off the cement wall and landed on the ground squatting in front of me—jabbering and praying again. Then I crawled up on the wall and entered the attic with my pistol in one hand and a flashlight in the other hand. Damn! A strong odor of human feces, body odor, odors from other moldy and spoiled items hit me. All I found was bedding, clothing items strewn about, pots, pans, and some beef jerky hanging in the pitch of the attic with flies swarming on it, some black bananas, and a few coconuts. I didn't find anything of military value. The stench took my breath. I couldn't get out fast enough. Whew! I was gasping for fresh air so hard and quick, almost like I was biting the air. I jumped down where the woman was still squatting on the ground jabbering, praying...and now soaking wet.

John T. walked around the corner of the house to see what the commotion was about. "Where did you find your girlfriend, Robbie?" "In my dream, John T.! She was hiding in the fuc-n attic, like I told you." With a concerned look on his face, John T. said, "You mean she was up in the attic all night?" "Is water wet? Hell yeah, John T.! Maybe she was watching you. She could have shot your dick off while you were sleeping!" Stetson and the medic started snickering, then laughing real loud. John T. gave them a strong stare; they stopped laughing and then hurriedly moved to the front of the house. John T. turned and said to me, "Nobody likes a wise-ass Staff Sergeant, and especially, talking about me being dead...or losing my dick!" "Think about it

John T., all night long! Remember, you picked the house! And think about this…you thought I was dreaming, huh?"

John T. said, "Take her over to the 1st Platoon for interrogation." (They had a Vietnamese interpreter assigned to them.) Then he walked into the house. I told the runners, Specialist Fourth Class John L. Toney and Private First Class Joe G. Salinas to tie her hands, blindfold her, and take her over to be interrogated. About an hour later they brought her back. Salinas, explained what she told the Vietnamese interpreter—she owned the house and hog. She also said the NVA took over her house, made her cook for them, and told her they were going to kill her hog. She said when the NVA departed last night they took her husband, her two young grandsons and her dog. She further said that yesterday when the big booms (artillery) barked, the rest of the NVA rode san-pans (small boats) across the river. She said that the NVA told her the Americans with the chicken on their uniforms (they had no word for Eagle) and with the little black guns would rape her, then kill her; and if she told the Americans anything about them, they would kill her family, the dog, and then return to eat her hog and kill her.

It kept raining and at times, it poured like you were directly under a faucet. On our side of the river in the village, water was really overflowing its banks, and the flooded rice paddies were nearing the top of the hedgerow berm. Like most small villages surrounded by rice paddies, this one was built up about two or three feet above the top of rice paddy dikes. Most of the floors of structures in the village were also built up by an additional foot or two above ground level. A lot of the houses like the house we used also had a cement patio type porch. We kept shrinking our platoon defensive position as the water rose and inched toward the center of the village.

We began running patrols every day, all day long, for about a week and employing ambushes every night. The rain continued to fall, and the water continued to rise. The mosquitoes ate our asses up, day and night, and the leeches kept swimming toward us. It came to a point where we had to use the tallest men to go on patrol. So of course being the tallest squad leader, I was that damn bug again. I had to take out a patrol each day, and out in the rice paddies the water was up to the middle of my chest. Back at the platoon CP, the water was slowly inching toward the top of the porch, as the little old Mama-san was running around with a straw broom continually sweeping the water off her porch, like a crazy person.

We gave the women a case of C-Rations and she was happy, happy...happy as a pig in mud. She boiled water for us all day so we could make coffee and co-

coa. At night Mama-san would crawl back up into the attic to sleep. When she crawled down in the morning, she brought down some chicken and duck eggs and dried meat. She would then take our C-Rations and mix them together in a big pot and cook it on a kiln. However, the medic wouldn't let Mama-san add her dried meat to the food. Mama-san cooked all day long for the platoon. Old Mama-san became pretty damn good at cooking C-Rations.

Troopers continued to bring her unwanted C-Rations. By the time we left the village, old Mama-san had enough food to last her for a year. The men gave her some socks to wear on her feet and hands at night because it was so damp, and at night it was chilly. Mama-san was smiling all day.

Then one day she started crying, worrying about her family, and because she was so short, she couldn't wade through the water to look for her hog. By now the men were fond of her. The medic checked her out and placed ointment and Band-Aids on her scratches and sores. Mama-san walked around very proud, displaying her bandages to all. Other troopers fussed over her, attempting to learn some Vietnamese words and trying to teach her some English words, but she continued to speak Vietnamese and French.

I still had the portable radio that also contained a cassette tape, and we played it every day for morale boosting. Mama-san would squat right in front of the radio, listening to the tape playing soul, rock n roll and whatever else was on the cassette. When someone turned the dial and picked up a Vietnamese station, Mama-san would go crazy. The 1st Platoon's ARVN (Army Republic Viet Nam) interpreter said that Mama-san thought the "black box" (radio) had spirits inside. She had never seen or heard spirits coming from a box. That old woman couldn't get over the radio. At first she was a little leery of it and she refused to touch it. However, when the troops woke up each morning, Mama-san would nudge the nearest troop to the radio, then point to the radio. She squatted in the Vietnamese traditional style, about a foot in front of the radio, staring at it intently—listening and watching the radio as if she was expecting someone to jump out of the radio. When the announcer would say the word Saigon, or another well-known Vietnamese city, she would beam with pride, smiling and displaying her reddish-black gums, and dancing around like an American Indian performing a rain dance. Some of the men helped her like she were their own grandmother, and they kept telling her that probably her hog had found some high ground out of the water and was waiting out the flood. She smiled, happy again.

When I was told to take out another patrol, I asked the LT, "Why do we have to run these stupid patrols,

Sir? The Gooks are much shorter than us. They can't walk through that deep ass water!" "The old man (Company Commander) said so, Sergeant. The NVA can use san-pans to move around." I could always tell when the LT was pissed at me—he'd call me Sergeant. Other times, he'd call me Sarge, or Robbie. And when he was really, really pissed off at me, he'd ignore me, or walk away from me without uttering a sound. "Well, why can't we use san-pans LT?" Well that did it! The LT became madder than hell at me. He was obviously pissed at something else too—maybe he had discussed these nonsense patrols in the deep water with the company commander and the answer had been to keep running the damn patrols. If a patrol got into trouble or made enemy contact, it would be extremely hard to assist the patrol. I said, "Ok LT. I'll see if I can find that big, fat-ass hog and bring it back so you can learn to ride it without falling off."

That broke the ice. The LT laughed and said, "Find some dry, high ground so you can observe a large area, and report any enemy activity directly to the old man. Then inform me." Then I became pissed off, "Lieutenant! Where the hell am I gonna find high, dry ground? All I'm gonna see are cruise ships. Have you checked the weather lately? It's still raining. It's been raining for two weeks!" "Well if it'll help, I'll go with you." "LT you can come if you want, but your presence won't part the water, and it won't lower the water level—if anything, it will cause the water to rise. We departed on patrol without the LT.

While on patrol, wading through the deep water, a little puppy came floating by and clinging to a small tree branch. I reached out and scooped up the puppy and placed her into my left front breast pocket and named her "No-Nuts." Most of the morning as we walked around on patrol, No-Nuts kept her head sticking outta my pocket, looking around and looking up at me, yawning. No-Nuts would fall asleep and slide down to the bottom of my pocket. Sometimes water would get into my pocket and No-Nuts would come up for air, sticking her head up outta my pocket, sputtering as water flew out of her mouth; then she would shake water from her head.

It took us until midafternoon to conduct our slow, short patrol. I'm six two, and most of the time the water was up to the middle of my chest, until I stepped in a depression and the water was then over my head. What a damn joke. Shorter troopers were really having a hard time walking. Sometimes a man would trip and became submerged—then thrash around, flapping in the dirty, muddy water like a hooked catfish on a trot line. The closest man would fish around in the water and drag the floundering man upward, lifting and carrying him to water not over his head. We didn't see any dry, high ground or Gooks. However, we saw plenty of water...water, mosquitoes, snakes, and leeches floating by us. The point man carried a bamboo pole to aid walking and to check the depth of the water, and every time an unwanted guest would get too close, it would get whacked with a bamboo pole. If the enemy was watching us, they probably thought we were crazy. I thought we were too. When I returned to our platoon CP, I gave the puppy to Mama-san; she had a fit and became very excited. She carried that puppy with her all the time, even sleeping with it.

About a week later, the rain slacked off a bit and the water began receding. One day M-17 approached Mama-san; she grabbed his hand and rubbed on it with her hand, as if to see if the black hue had rubbed off of M-17's hands. M-17 flung his hands and arms as if to shoo her away, saying, "Go hed-on fu-uul! Get away frum me...you old bitch! Ya ain't nutin but ah old ugly Gook no-how!"

The batteries in Moon-Mullin's (Sergeant James D. Mullins) radio had died. Mama-san kept staring at the radio, picking it up, shaking it, holding it up to her head as occasional static and vaguely, garbled noise emitted. Mama-san placed the radio on the porch, walking around it like it was the end of the world for her, albeit, that had already occurred when the NVA took her family. I told one of the runners to take the radio over to the 1st Platoon and give it to Moon-Mullins and tell him we found it on the road.

Mama-san sensed by our activity that we were leaving. I could tell she was worried, yet her body language was trying to present an attitude of denial of the inevitable. Mama-san just squatted, holding her puppy, looking at us. She knew something was up; Mama-san looked very concerned. Each day troopers visited her and fed No-Nuts and that puppy acted like she recognized each trooper. I guess because each had a distinctive strong odor. But on this day, no one had time to feed No-Nuts, and the puppy was squirming, yapping, and running around in small circles. The little dog also sensed a change of routine, she knew something was up.

About midmorning, we started walking out of the village through the open gate. Mama-san stood by the gate crying, and sometimes, running around in little circles as the puppy ran after her jumping, yapping and wagging her tail. As Abu troopers walked passed her, they said, "good-bye Mama-san…good-bye No-Nuts." Most of the men lightly tossed cans of C-Rations at Mama-san's feet. Mama-san was running around, squatting down, trying to pick up all of the C-Rations before other Vietnamese could grab them. She was dropping them, standing up, and wringing her hands, crying, as red beetle nut juice ran out of her toothless mouth.

As Abu's exited the village and passed through the gate, Mama-san would run after them, grabbing their arms, trying to prevent them from leaving. I was the last Abu to exit the village, and No-Nuts ran behind me jumping and yapping. After tiring, No-Nuts lay down in the road, resting her head on her front paws, and her eyeballs looked like they were going to roll out of her head. No-Nuts lay on the dirt, whining. I stopped, walked back and knelt in front of No-Nuts and rubbed her head, picked her up, and pointed her in Mama-san's direction and gave her a little shove. No-Nuts walked about four steps, stopped, turned around and flopped down in the dirt, watching me as I walked away.

Vietnamese women going to market near Qui Nhon, in October 1965. Where are the men?

Chapter 10

Meet The FNG

In the military, one thing soldiers learned fast is that they have an acronym for damn near everything. Such as FEBA for forward edge of battle area, DZ for drop zone, and perhaps the most infamous one used by non-lifers or non-career men, FTA or Fu-k The Army.

Being in Vietnam quickly brought on a slew of new ones such as, VC for Viet Cong or Victor Charlie, which were a local enemy guerrilla force, and NVA for North Vietnamese Army, which was a highly trained regular structured military force much like our own. One of the more interesting ones to quickly come along was FNG, which stood for fu-king new guy, a name that was given to anyone new to Vietnam or the unit. Why? Well, a new guy was totally unpredictable, with most of them running around with their heads up their asses while making numerous mistakes. To have a chance at survival in combat requires great common sense, ability to think and perform under intense pressure while experiencing the fastest learning curve known to man. This situation also was compounded by units receiving men fresh out of jump school or training with as little as four to five months in the military. Many experienced men still bit the dust by running into overwhelming odds, with lead flying all over the place. After all, this was combat.

A new guy was closely scrutinized and posed unimaginable additional problems that one had to contend with on a constant basis. The thought process by all was that if I'm going home in a body bag, it's not going to be from a new guy. No one wanted to become a casualty by a FNG, which was a controllable fate, unlike the enemy situation which was never controllable. It was a classic Catch 22.

"The enemy is anybody who's going to get you killed, no matter which side he is on."
~ Joseph Heller, Catch-22.

No way is this meant as a negative to any new guy, although it does explain the Catch 22 we were in, and after all when it comes to combat weren't we all FNG's at one time?

We were operating around Qui Nhon (Quinn Yon), a coastal town, after securing the An Khe area for the 1st Cavalry Division. We relieved a Marine unit and were told the area was secure. The CO however still sent out two platoons to check the area. We were kicked back in reserve, getting some sun, drying out our feet and we had built some hooch's for shade with our ponchos. The mess hall set up and was cooking our first hot meal

MEET THE FNG

since arriving in July. The Marines left a vehicle that they called a "Duck" because it was stuck in the rice paddy mud and they would return for it later. Good paratroopers never let anything go to waste and made use of whatever they could find. Stealing? Hell no! This wasn't stealing at all and was known as a "Midnight Requisition" among troopers. It really wasn't as cushy as Private First Class David T. Rogers portrays in the photo with the nice chair that he borrowed from the Marines. The vacation was interrupted because the 1st Platoon was ambushed and we quickly moved out to assist them. That first hot meal would have to wait several weeks until Thanksgiving in November.

Author eating a can of c-rations while catching up on the latest news from Stars and Stripes.

FATE UNKNOWN

After helping the 1st Platoon, we occupied a village located next to a river. The rainy season was beginning to set in, which is named the monsoon season. People in America have absolutely no idea what rain is until enduring a monsoon season in Southeast Asia. The drops are huge and an inch of rain can easily occur in a few minutes. As the season progresses, the length of time that it rains lengthens to where it can rain twenty-four hours a day for days.

Also during this time, we received a new FNG who had just recently completed jump school at Fort Benning, Georgia. My first impression was how this could be possible, as the new guy stood out by the massive amount of baby fat he was hauling around on him. When I graduated from jump school, not an ounce of fat existed on me and I had a twenty-eight inch waist. In a regular airborne unit, troops were lean and mean, and ran many miles while conducting a grueling session of PT on a daily basis.

The weather was downright nasty during this period because it was raining for hours on end, some days your thoughts of building an ark didn't seem like such a bad idea! We were conducting patrols in this environment with the water up to our chins and over our heads in places, while holding our weapons overhead in an attempt to keep them functional and not submerging them. The short troopers were put behind taller men so they

MEET THE FNG

could climb on the back of the man to their front, horseback style until their feet could touch the ground again in more shallow places. The worst were the non-swimmers, who feared drowning more than the enemy. Naturally the snakes had nowhere to go so as we patrolled, they would swim by and troopers would push them away with the barrel of their rifles. They were intent on going in a certain direction, toward us for some unknown reason, and then when pushed away, they would come right back. Believe it or not, snakes were the least of our problems. We were smart enough to figure out that the enemy, who were much smaller than us in height, couldn't operate in this situation without scuba gear or a sampan boat. Now if we could just get the powers that be or chain of command to realize it.

101st Airborne Troopers patrolling the flooded rice paddies near Qui Nhon, October 1965.

During the period that we occupied defensive positions in the village, it continued to rain; our perimeter kept shrinking to avoid the water. The flooding of the river from the monsoon rains was the main reason the water was so deep. The Vietnamese go through this every year. They mound up their villages so that the center is the highest point. The 1st Brigade (S), 101st Airborne Division was rumored to actually have had several troopers drown during this period. It's a long damn way to come and drown is all I know!

The powers that be finally had an epiphany and the patrols stopped, perhaps because of the drownings. Who knows? Our biggest concern was that if the damn place was going to flood completely, they better come up with some boats to come save our asses. The flooding caused a halt to our operations, which resulted in a very relaxing period for the most part, except for some occasional sniper fire from across the river. This time gave us a chance to catch up on letter writing, sleep and allowed the body time to heal. For the most part, we were wet and cold but used some Vietnamese huts for shelter. Mama-san, an old Vietnamese woman that was about ninety-years old, was hanging out at the platoon CP. The CP was occupying her house and there were a few other Vietnamese in the village that mostly consisted of women and small children.

MEET THE FNG

Lard-ass was a typical new guy who asked too many questions and could have learned a lot more by observing. He asked me once what to do if we receive fire. I told him to immediately hit the ground, observe everyone else, and follow them. In jest, I also added for him to keep his big ass down or he'll get it shot off. Despite numerous questions, everyone helped him to get it together as their life also depended on his reactions. Had this been in the States, they would have left him out to dry, so to speak, after too many questions.

After several days of damn near twenty-four hours of rain, it suddenly stopped and the water began to recede. It still rained for shorter periods, but not with the same intensity. After a couple days, the water receded completely and we returned to the company CP for a day or so. Then it was back to the norm on 27 October 1965 with a helicopter assault across the Song Am River, into the rice paddies, on a search-and-destroy mission. Later we called this area "sniper valley."

The Marine chopper pilots missed LZ (landing zone) Alice completely for Abu Company; landing us on two different LZ's and splitting our company force in two. Our LZ was still a hot one, though. Bullets were cracking and zinging overhead while most seemed to be coming from a small village about 200 yards away. At the time, I carried an M-79 grenade launcher, which wasn't worth a shit in the jungle because the round had to travel about 10 meters to arm, but was excellent in rice paddies. I placed a few rounds on the edge of the village, plus where others called out targets for me. I remember one round hitting two VCs with a direct hit and that spot became quieter than a graveyard. I'm not sure if the enemy knew of the M-79 that early in the war, but if not, they must have wondered how someone could have thrown a grenade that far…well not them, but their cohorts.

As things started to calm down, I observed Private First Class Jimmie Lee Stacey jump over a rice paddy dike and immediately jump back over into the paddy with us. It happened so fast, one would have thought "Stace" had spring-loaded combat boots on his feet. Stacey was a hell of a trooper from Arizona who came over on the boat with us, a highly likeable guy that everyone respected. He was always clowning around without taking too much seriously. After landing, he was on his knees and trying to get his weapon clear since it appeared to be jammed. He was in a panic like I had never seen him before and hollering, "My weapon…my weapon!" Apparently he tried to fire his weapon and it jammed. I said, "Stace, relax you got water in it. Break it open and drain it out." He did it. Now, all of a sudden, the Stacey I knew came back and spoke: "Gooks! Gooks! I jumped right on top of their heads." Someone asked where and Stacey said, "Right over the dike."

MEET THE FNG

Someone said, "Drop a couple grenades over the dike!" Every weapon in that paddy was now pointing at that spot; Stacey took a grenade off his belt, pulled the pin, moved back over to the dike, dropped it, and then scrambled back away. When it exploded, a VC flew over the dike approximately three feet or so to about where Stacey had been fumbling with his weapon along with black mud and water. Another grenade or two went over for good measure and that problem was solved. Later whenever that story was told, Stacey would just smile that shit-eating grin he always displayed. That was the only time I ever saw Stacey shook, but he regained his composure and acted with valor and no doubt prevented further casualties. After a few days he went back to the smiling, game-playing of old and remained that way. When Tom Joyce tried to make contact some years after the war and found his mother, she stated that Jimmie Lee had committed suicide after suffering from many personal problems in coping. She said he had displayed many of the symptoms that are known today as severe post-traumatic stress disorder (PTSD). Stacey was the last trooper that I would ever think for suicide, based on the demeanor he always displayed. Obviously stress was taking a toll that none of us could observe...so tragic an ending. Even the most expensive watch can break if wound too tight. Stacey was survived by a son.

On right PFC Jimmie L. "Stace" Stacey with another unidentified 3rd Platoon member on left. Taken near Qui Nhon in October 1965.

Abu Company moved forward and separately proceeded from their LZ's along route Adolph, with all units linking up at the village. While advancing along

MEET THE FNG

route Adolph, Abu Company had killed twenty seven, verified by body count. After entering the village, Sergeant Larry Trowbridge passed by us with about twenty POW's whose hands were tied behind their backs. Also they had a rope tied around their necks linking one to another. Ropes were carried for repelling if needed. They were definitely VC or NVA clad in black shirts and pants. They were all strong, young looking men and appeared to be well fed. The looks on their faces was rather serious—they seemed like a bunch of unhappy campers. Normally only old men, women, and children are found in villages.

Later that day, after the LZ had cleared up and the village was taken, we moved out and came upon a river that had to be crossed. A rope had been taken across for men to hold onto while crossing, as some could not swim. The river was a little more than waist high or three and a half to four feet deep with good movement to it. Specialist Fourth Class Tommy G. Campbell, an M-60 machine gunner, was moving rather slowly as if afraid of the water. Some men began calling him "Grandma" and getting on him. Campbell turned around and was hollering back when a sniper fired, hitting him. The bullet knocked him down and his arms were thrashing all over. He appeared to be more worried about drowning than being shot. Immediately, the nearest men helped him to his feet. The round went right through both cheeks of his face while never touching a tooth or his tongue. Campbell refused medevac and the medic put a Band-Aid on each cheek; he continued humping around like that all day carrying his M-60. Now that's a hardcore trooper.

We continued moving through the rice paddies on a search and destroy mission when we received sniper fire again. Everyone hit the mud because this damn sniper was good and seemed to hit someone every time he fired. Then a second sniper round fired, after which we heard "Medic!" As I looked back, here it was the FNG, and of all places, he had been hit smack in the ass. We all talked about how lucky he was after only being with us about ten days and in the first day of some real combat gets the million-dollar wound for a trip back to the world. Meanwhile, we had been there for months and at best, our fate would remain unknown.

About eight months later, after getting out of Valley Forge Hospital in the summer of 1966, I was assigned to Fort Dix; I was the NCOIC (Noncommissioned Officer in Charge) of a rifle range and observed one of the unit cadres with a Screaming Eagle combat patch adorned on the sleeve of his right shoulder. Not many were combat veterans at that time and I made it a point to speak with him. I go over, and low and behold, it's the new guy! Now promoted to corporal, he was doing quite well. Of course, our reflections were much

MEET THE FNG

less serious than the atmosphere at the time. Naturally, I had to remind him that he was one lucky bastard! I never quite understood why troopers right out of jump school were assigned to fill our depleting ranks. There were, after all, two Airborne Divisions back in the states with at least twenty-five thousand men in them; they were much more experienced after having gone through extensive training at Fort Campbell and Fort Bragg. Leadership positions were filled somewhat in the same manner, which resulted in more costly mistakes as the war progressed. In 1968, after a few years of war, one could get assigned to Fort Bragg and find NCOs that had never been to Vietnam, while others had received orders already two or three times—we called this group "Homesteaders." On my second tour in Vietnam with the 173rd Airborne Brigade (S) we had many instant NCOs which had been identified early in basic and advanced infantry training, sent to a leadership school, promoted to sergeant with only about five or six months service, and then ultimately sent to Vietnam. They quickly became known as "Shake and Bakes" while 95 percent of them were useless screw-ups. Rather than the Department of the Army handling reassignments, they should have been handled internally by the 101st Airborne Division, which would have allowed for a much higher continuation of efficiency of combat units and unity of command. The way the reassignments were handled hindered the continuity, cohesion, and unity of effort—this resulted in the loss of hard-won combat knowledge that was paid for with blood.

After taking the hamlet, we moved out, sloshing through the rice paddies. Every time we came within three or four hundred meters of a small hamlet, we encountered sniper fire. These snipers were pretty good marksmen though, hitting the new guy and a couple others. As we were being fired upon, we would deploy and conduct fire and movement to close with the sniper and enemy. Upon reaching the hamlet, all we could find left were some old people as the snipers withdrew to the next village. This was very tiring—running, hitting the water and mud of the paddies to close with the enemy only to have them escape, very frustrating as well. Then as we departed one hamlet, the sniper shot at us again when we were about 200 meters away. How had we missed him? He either returned after our departure or was very well hidden underground while we were actually there. I'm thinking, "Man this shit is getting old and here we go, back again plopping down in the water and mud." Meanwhile, I could visualize this sniper laughing his ass off, and every time he fired was like cracking the whip on our ass. The company command group was near us and I heard Company Commander Captain George Shevlin giving a report of the contact to battalion and asking permission to use artillery, which must

MEET THE FNG

have been granted because next thing I heard was a fire mission being called in on the hamlet. The rounds were adjusted from the far side until it hit the hamlet—then a fire for effect was given. We continued, and received sniper fire once again from our right front about three-to-four-hundred meters away. Artillery was called again to quell the sniper and that was the last time we were bothered that day or the next by snipers. Perhaps we killed him, or he couldn't take some return fire that had to be smoking his ass. The solution was effective, while preventing further casualties...I tucked it away in my book of hard knocks.

Results for the two days of fighting in sniper valley were 57 enemies KIA and approximately 25 suspects captured, most of which came on the first day from the village that was surrounded by rice paddies and had been effectively cordoned off preventing their escape. After suffering heavy causalities and having their fate sealed, the remaining VC surrendered. Abu Company incurred 10 WIA and 2 KIA, Private First Class Daniel E. Allum age 20, from Dilliner, Pennsylvania, and a new replacement that wasn't there long enough to even learn his name. As Specialist Fourth Class Joseph Czarnecki of 1st Platoon, weapon's squad, recalls: "After exiting the Marine chopper, we were running in waist high water in the paddies. Bullets were splashing all around me, so I dropped down to my neck in the water to make myself a harder target to hit. Private First Class Allum was nowhere in sight. Me and another trooper went back to look for him. There he was, face down in the water. He had a small hole in his left side under his arm. A few nights before, we had a long conversation about his wife and children who lived in Pennsylvania. He also came over on the boat with us and was a real nice guy."

Additionally, Tiger Force assumed a blocking position on the other side of the village and had six troopers KIA from friendly artillery fire. My luck continued to hold out as there were three men wounded right next to me, one being a medic to whom I administered first aid.

Chapter 11

Phan Rang: Our New Base Camp

Author standing next to Abu Company sign, Phan Rang Base Camp in November 1965.

Thanksgiving approached and we proceeded to Phan Rang for the holiday after nearly four months of straight combat in the field. Big General Purpose (GP) tents were set up for us with army cots to sleep on.

That slow boat carrying vegetables and other fresh food hadn't docked yet, but once again the chain of command had their priorities right with real turkey to compliment the rest of the meal. The remainder of the food came from five-in-one rations, which were large gallon cans of food similar to c-rations, but of a different variety, such as pancake powder and powdered eggs. After eating c-rats for nearly four months, getting this stuff was like dining at a five-star restaurant in a secure atmosphere. To die for! Well not quite, but very good, regardless. I was in the chow line one morning when some FNG behind me made a remark about how nasty the powdered eggs looked and said, "Who ever heard of green eggs?" I turned around and said in a loud voice, "Wait until you eat c-rations for about four months then tell me how they look, in fact, give me yours, I'll eat them!" He complied and I scoffed them down. Damn FNG! The canned peaches and pears were unbelievably good, and had a slight chill to them as I remember.

First Sergeant Duane E. Finley had set up an area that had a parachute above to provide shade over a jeep trailer that was loaded with beer, soda and ice. A person just cannot realize the importance of how the simple

PHAN RANG: OUR NEW BASE CAMP

things of life such as a cold soda, cold beer or a shower, let alone safety and security can become so meaningful. The mess sergeant, along with the cooks, were to be commended for doing such a great job under much less than ideal conditions; many troopers thanked them as they were going through the chow line. Speaking of cooks, there was this small, skinny cook who was a Specialist Fourth Class and some thought was always mean and nasty to the guys going through the chow line. Then we heard one day he placed an M-16 under his chin and blew his brains out. Rumor had it he had received a Dear John letter from his wife. Another shot himself in the foot with a .45 caliber pistol to get out of Vietnam while we were at the Phan Rang base camp. These were hot topics for a day or so; one quickly moved on, because to dwell on stuff like that would spell trouble for our own fate. Every day presented new challenges for the mind to conquer and we were in the zone—always knowing the boundaries to never step out of the zone. The stress of duty in Vietnam and combat were having an effect on all regardless of one's role. At Fort Campbell there was the sick, lame and lazy squad, so called because going on sick call was frowned upon no matter what was wrong. Even if it was a sprained ankle from a jump, or they were ghosting in any way and not pulling their load or share, they would receive the wrath of their peers. The axiom was: take two APC's and drive on. An APC was another acronym which stood for All Purpose Capsules, or just plain old aspirin. It's obvious that with this type of attitude ingrained in airborne troops, particularly in the leadership we had little sympathy for a suicide or someone that shot themselves in the foot to escape the future we had to endure.

General William C. Westmoreland conducting a T.V. interview at Phan Rang Camp Base, November 1965.

PHAN RANG: OUR NEW BASE CAMP

General Westmoreland showed up with an entourage of reporters, brass, etc. I watched as he conducted an interview with a CBS correspondent. Soon after, we were loaded on a C-130 aircraft, moved a few hundred miles south and eventually to the Michelin rubber plantation, where the South Vietnamese 7th Regiment, 5th Division was overrun by the VC 272nd Regiment. Most of them were killed, along with five U.S. Advisors. Apparently, they had all been asleep that night. Operation Checkerboard included the 173rd Airborne Brigade, 1st Infantry Division, Australian troops, and ARVN. We went into the Iron Triangle, which was a well-known enemy stronghold, to conduct search-and-destroy operations, or hunt-and-kill. Prior to this, any unit entering the Iron Triangle was met with fierce resistance and essentially kicked out of there. For the most part, the enemy chose not to fight us, but we found large caches of rice, small arms ammo, and a hospital. They left pretty damn quick too, as many cooking fires were found with hot coals and freshly cooked food. Even with little contact, we still found numerous enemy booby traps, and every step taken by any soldier could have been his last. We were living through each day in constant stressful conditions. Does that mean we thought about every step we took—absolutely not—otherwise, we would have frozen in place and never taken a step forward. The thought of potential danger, however, always lurked somewhere in our minds and never completely went away.

On 24 December, we departed to Phan Rang for the Christmas holiday; it was pretty much like the Thanksgiving excursion. I do remember lots of mail. Every trooper in the company received a package with goodies, such as cookies, that had been donated by church groups and other organizations. The men were appreciative for their caring. This is where I developed a fondness for fruitcake. As most disliked it, they were either trying to trade it or give it away.

No one could ever forget Chaplain Bowers, who in this God forsaken place had come up with a Santa Claus outfit and worn it for the troops. Chaplain Bowers conducted services for all the KIA, and was highly respected among the troops, as he literally walked in their footsteps. Chaplain Bowers walked the walk, while humping all day through the jungle with the 3rd Platoon in the heat and rain, on the day Rocky Ryan was WIA. He made the rounds with all the units, when he probably could have been a REMF (Rear echelon mother fu-ker), had he so desired. Chaplain Bowers would later be awarded the Silver Star, earned for acts of heroism while out with one of our Battalion units. Praise the Lord and pass the ammo!

I was made aware of General Westmoreland presence when a trooper remarked, "The Red Cross worker is here again," in reference to him. Normally a Red Cross worker was the bearer of bad news, and it seemed like every time "Westy" showed up it meant we would be leaving soon for somewhere new. The following day, word came that the Brigade was moving out to to a place by the name of Tuy Hoa (Too-ee Waa)—a new and exotic adventure to another unheard of, God forsaken place. I would never return to Phan Rang during the remainder of my tour; my total time in the rear was perhaps two weeks after over 10 months in country.

FATE UNKNOWN

Chapter 12

Promotion

Sometime in early January 1966, the 3rd Platoon received a new platoon leader named Lieutenant Eugene R. New, who was originally from Alabama, to replace Lieutenant Howard, who transferred to Tiger Force. As I compared the two men, my first impression was that the two men were total opposites in all aspects. Lieutenant Howard, who was not long out of West Point, was in his early twenties and looked like a teen. On the other hand, Lieutenant New who was older, perhaps in his late twenties, was more muscular and already had the face of a hardened WWII Marine. Lieutenant Howard was a non-smoker, while Lieutenant New smoked these huge cigars whenever a feasible situation allowed it. Later, we were surprised to learn that despite his appearance, Lieutenant New was actually an OCS (Officer Candidate School) graduate and prior to that, had been a Staff Sergeant with quite a few years in the Army. This was not a typical Army Lieutenant.

Lieutenant New sent for me one day, so I headed to the platoon CP. Upon my arrival, I noticed that Staff Sergeant Perkins had a c-rat can of coffee and Lieutenant New was smoking a humongous cigar that looked like the size of a large Cuban cigar. There was laughter and both seemed to be in a good mood. Lieutenant New said, "Mitchell I have some good news for you." My mind immediately received a visual of Australia…women, beer, and R&R (rest and recuperation), which normally lasts seven days. The thoughts lasted about seven seconds, when Lieutenant New interrupted and said, "You've been promoted to Sergeant." Huh…a sergeant? What is he talking about? Someone had mentioned putting me in for sergeant a month or so prior, but I hadn't given it a second thought. Unlike the sergeants that were around who had come over on the boat and had over ten years in the Army, I only had four years of service. I thought that someone was just trying to make me feel good. Then Lieutenant New said, "I want you to take the weapons squad," and my thought process was, "take what?" Quickly, I informed him that my only experience had been in rifle squads and that I knew nothing of a weapons squad—to which he replied, "You'll be alright, and I think you can handle it." I understood from the tone in his voice that I really had no choice but to accept my promotion as a new sergeant. At this point I'm thinking, "Has he been talking to Perkins?" That confidence in me is much more than I had in myself. My reply was, "I'll do the best I can, sir." Later I learned that no one had wanted the weapons squad because the life expectancy of machine gun crews in a fire fight is about a minute, and they are the enemy's number one target. Therefore everyone had turned it down. The weapons squad consisted of two M-60 machine gun crews, which are the most important weapons in the platoon. Bear in mind, this job normally fell to the most senior sergeant in the platoon...they all out-ranked me. Later I found out that Staff Sergeant Robbins, the regular weapon squad leader, had departed for the States on emergency leave to attend the funeral of his father. I would not see him again until about forty years later. My base pay was now $261.60 a month...no great sum, especially considering all the additional responsibility I had for the lives of the men under me and for the decisions I had to make. We were only a heartbeat away from our own possible death, and hostile fire pay (combat pay) was a mere $65 a month. Obviously none of us were in this for the money. Even if we received $65 a day, we would still be underpaid.

    The following day I'm traveling with the lead gun, when the point man comes up on two trail watchers (provides early warning for their main force). As they spot each other, both open fire. I immediately deployed the M-60 on line on the left side of the trail and had gunner Private First Class Pedro Jaime, Jr. of New York City, New York, rake the front left to right about six inches above the ground with approximately a hundred rounds, then cease fire. We moved forward on line through some thick bamboo to find one enemy wearing black pajamas and armed with an AK-47 rifle. He looked like a pretzel—his arms and legs going in every direction but straight—obviously broken from M-60 rounds, and I could see wounds in his chest and torso. I issued the order for someone to pass the word back for the Doc to come forward. Upon his arrival, I asked him to examine the VC to see if he could do anything to help him. Doc checked him out then stated, "This one will never make the chopper ride." He bit the dust faster than a speeding bullet, in what seemed like a heartbeat.

    We continued paralleling the trail, and a short distance later received fire again from a single weapon. Once again we deployed, returned fire, began fire-movement, and soon came upon a couple of huts. The point man yelled, "He ran in the hut." And in response I said, "Throw a grenade in." As everyone quickly scattered, they went down in the prone position and took what cover was available. In mere seconds we heard a loud explosion, and we quickly advanced; however, on arrival we couldn't enter the hut because of all the smoke billowing out of the entrance. Shortly after, two or three of us entered the hut; we observed a VC in black pajamas—he was on his knees, plastered up against and facing the wall of the hut, with his elbows out like a chicken man, while his hands were concealed in front of his chest. He was bleeding from the ears from the concussion, but appeared not to have any other wounds. Nearby him lay a mangled AK-47 rifle. I wondered to myself what he had been thinking when he decided to go into a hut that had only one way in and no dugout bomb shelter. The only answer I could come up with was that he must have been trying to conceal the weapon in the thatch of the hut. My thoughts were interrupted when I heard the Doc say, "He has a grenade!", and then I saw someone run out of the hut. Just as I'm thinking, "Oh shit I never thought of that," I heard a gunshot as the Doc shot the VC in the head with his .45 caliber pistol. By now the hut is clear, except for the Doc and me. We cautiously pulled the VC away from the thatched wall to check for a grenade. We also looked for documents and discovered he had no grenade; however he was riddled with shrapnel from the grenade and had already been dead. Apparent to me was why they like to wear black pajamas as he appeared to have no wounds or a drop of blood on him with the exception of that coming out his ears. But the truth was that his clothing, although camouflaged by the color of black, was actually covered and soaked with blood. This gave the enemy a tremendous psychological advantage in combat. I heard, "Make way," and a none-too-happy Lieutenant New entered the hut. After having heard a single shot after several minutes of calm, he was thinking we had deliberately killed the VC. Lieutenant New asked, "What's going on here?" I explained everything that happened to Lieutenant New; he said in a stern voice, "I'll have a talk with you later, Sergeant Mitchell!" As he walked away, he gave the Doc a seriously bad look. By now I figured my first day as a new sergeant wasn't going to damn well, and surely not as well as I perceived it to be, though Lieutenant New never mentioned it again.

Being a weapons squad leader came natural to me, kind of like a hard dick in a whorehouse—I just kind of fell into it. By this time, my combat experience was greater than most in the platoon. My good observations of the best leaders, had served me well, not only then, but throughout my military career

Chapter 13

Tuy Hoa (Too-Ee Waa)

Located a couple hundred miles north of Phan Rang and south of Qui Nhon lies Tuy Hoa. This is the rice bowl for Vietnam, with its boo koo (beaucoup/many) miles of fertile rice paddies as far as the eye could see. Our first mission was to protect the rice crop from the enemy, who traditionally took 80 percent of the crop from the farmers to feed their forces. It didn't take a dumbass to figure out that the enemy would fight hard to protect his dinner table.

Rice paddies in full bloom with a new crop.

The landscape was beautiful—a lush green, with the rice in full bloom. The tops of the rice plants were bending and swaying with the gentle breeze. The terrain was very open, only sprinkled with small hamlets and sparsely populated villages that consisted of: women, young children, and elderly people, but absolutely no men of military age (between the ages of 12 and 60).

The men from the villages essentially were forced into fighting for the VC or would be killed if they refused. Now there's a choice one can believe in! Of course, if asked by our interpreter where their husbands or sons were, their natural response was that they were away fighting with the South Vietnamese Army. At the edge of the paddies, there were mountain ranges of dense jungle that our intelligence sources said contained the regimental headquarters and the 95th NVA Regiment, made famous in the book *Street Without Joy*, by Bernard B. Fall.

On or about 6 February 1966 Abu Company had a mission to search and destroy that area. As we headed across the rice paddies, the company was well dispersed with men from the 1st Platoon in the lead. When nearing the base of the mountain where the rice paddies turned into jungle, a loud explosion occurred. The point man had stepped on a mine, and as three others went to his aid, they also stepped on mines, with all four losing legs

TUY HOA (Too-ee Waa)

from about the knee down. These type mines maim and have a psychological effect, while other types of mines have a sole purpose...to kill. Screams for "medic" and shouting of "mines" filled the area...repeated...and then silence seemed to overtake us. Believe me, everyone froze in place in an instant; not even an ice pick could have forced any movement. Frozen for what seemed an eternity, orders started coming for us to face toward the center, break out bayonets, and probe our way back to the center and into a single file. We had practiced probing in prior training, and it is pretty much the only choice the infantrymen has in this situation. It can best be described as delicate, because done improperly, from a squatting position with a mine in the ground it will mess up a pretty face rather quickly, while the best-case scenario will result in the loss of the family jewels.

It was every man for himself in their effort to get to the center, and upon reaching it, felt as though an eternity had passed. I felt a little relieved once we arrived; however, I realized it wasn't over when one man said, "These crazy mother fu-k's are still pushing on through to get into the jungle." The closer we approached the jungle, the more soggy and swampy the ground became, due to run off from the mountain. We focused and never took our eyes off the area of ground where the man in front of us first lifted his foot, so that we could step in the same exact spot. The going was very slow—as they probed with bayonets up front and as I watched that spot on the ground, it would begin to fill with water when a man lifted his foot. I knew exactly where the spot was though, until my foot landed on the same point. Occasionally, if a man was following too closely, you could see him struggle to keep his balance, especially if the man in front of him started and suddenly stopped. It was truly amazing how the men of Abu company handled this situation without panicking or doing something stupid. I firmly believe it was a classic case of mind control, which paratroopers go through on each jump. That training allowed us to overcome this situation, and it was much like taking that first step toward the door of an aircraft after which you heard, "See you on the ground." Once they probed some area and took that first step, they were ok. But when we talked about it afterwards, they would reply, "It ain't nothing but a thing sarge." Yeah a humongous thing!

After forever and a day, we made it through that bullshit. The WIA in the minefield and those who lost their legs from the knee down were: Sergeant First Class Donald E. Emel, Sergeant Carlos Torres, Sergeant Williams, and Private First Class James J. Nowlen. Sometime later I was asked how the wounded had been taken out, and I honestly don't know. Combat is like playing football where the guard or tackle is so concen-

TUY HOA (Too-ee Waa)

trated on his area or job that he has no idea what the end or the quarterback is doing. Leaders are like quarterbacks with more training that allows a larger visual of the field. Another way of putting it is: a peon and a Lieutenant could both be under fire while each having a completely different perception of what is taking place, so consequently each will make totally different observations of the same event. I was with one of my M-60 crews as usual. The immediate concern for them was the part of the minefield where we were standing and the area we had to probe.

We went through that same mine field a second time, when our mission was to conduct a bomb assessment after an Arc-light strike (B-52 bombing). It was a sight to behold one morning, in the area of the suspected NVA Regiment Headquarters. This time we were issued Bangalore torpedoes (a WWII weapon that came in approximately three-foot sections) for breeching an obstacle like a minefield. Amazing how the Army can come up with stuff from nowhere. They were assembled, fired and blew a path about two to three feet wide for us to cake-walk through it this time. The bomb assessment indicated pure destruction—with huge craters, down trees, and splinters which caused a total mess to the terrain. Checking it out was like going through the largest obstacle course known to any military. We were only able to search a small area because of the difficulty, so the number of enemy KIA was unknown. I could work with some arms, legs, heads, or an eyeball or two; but for me, the destruction resembled a billion pieces of a jigsaw puzzle, and any enemy was just a part of it. I doubt it killed too many, as the AO (area of operation) remained hotly contested with large numbers of NVA. At least this would be my assessment, or SWAG (scientific, wild-ass guess).

The minefield turned out to be an old French minefield that was unmarked on any of our military maps. Later in my military career, while attending Land Mine Warfare School, I learned that any obstacle, to include all minefields, can be breeched or negotiated. They're only effective if covered by fire. Had the NVA been that smart and had it covered by fire, well I can picture that outcome. Can you?

The 3rd Platoon also once checked out an area in those mountains that was completely defoliated and had a reddish-orange powder on the ground. Nothing else was in that area; however, many years later many of us found Agent Orange the hard way…one of the now known causes of diabetes, prostate cancer, heart problems, and a host of other associated diseases.

Chapter 14

Nasty Rumor

The landscape of Tuy Hoa South rapidly changed from our first arrival. The rice harvest was complete, which made the paddies more open, and the dry season was setting in. The civilian population was gone, run off by fire-fights, fear of the NVA and the ROK (Republic of Korea) soldiers who swept through the valley one day and didn't leave anything alive that breathed. The area was very much a depiction of war, with dead enemy bodies strewn all over, dead water buffalo, bomb craters and destruction everywhere.

On 7 February 1966 Bravo Company, along with Tiger Force, engaged a Battalion of the 95th NVA at My Canh (2) that was fought in hand-to-hand combat. It resulted in 105 enemy KIA and Lieutenant James A. Gardner, Commander of Tiger Force, receiving the Medal of Honor. Our battalion had 24 KIA on this day. Note: a couple of enemy bodies were burned for sanitation reasons, but this practice was quickly abandoned when not enough gas or diesel fuel could be obtained or brought in, so the rest were left to rot.

On the night of 10 February 1966, two men from the Mortar Platoon of Headquarters Company were KIA from a grenade, while they were on an OP/ LP.

When the area was immediately checked, a lit cigarette was found on the ground—a deadly mistake. Also KIA was Private First Class Warren G. Peterson from Stanwood, Washington, and Private First Class John S. Voegtli from Madison, Connecticut. In that same area, our company occupied a dug in defensive position and about four positions to my right (or about 30 meters away), received probing all night by hand grenades. The next morning, we located three unexploded (duds) Chicom grenades, one being only three inches from the hole, as well as several marks on the ground all around the foxhole from exploded grenades. The two men in that hole had been unharmed and were glad to see daylight. Whereas we previously looked forward to nighttime to escape the heat, humping etc., this was no longer the case since as we were now the prey. We smokers received a reality check that smoking does kill!

The 95th NVA Regiment was a unit proving to be a tough foe and was challenging us every day in some way, even if it was just sniper fire. Prior to here, we were hunting the enemy, where as now we became the prey and were keenly aware they were observing us at all times. The 95th NVA Regiment was well trained, disciplined and led by good experienced leaders who had so much confidence, that we caught them several times walking around at sling arms (weapons over their shoulder)…just walking around like they owned

NASTY RUMOR

the place. Every day was a game of cat and mouse, trying to surprise while not getting surprised. Why move us after the rice harvest to look for the enemy when we had all we could handle right here? Around this time, a nasty rumor was circulating faster than a bullet, something to the effect that all tours of duty would be 18 months in lieu of 12 months. This rumored extension had a terrible effect on morale of the troops and I myself became devastated by the prospect of it. I had about 7 months in country when this occurred, therefore I could see some light at the end of the tunnel and end of my tour. The turnover rate was rapid, while the intensity of combat was steadily increasing; there was no way to survive 18 months on line in this shit. I was in some serious depression for about three days, pushed almost to the point of tears, when through channels the word came down from the powers that be, that it was untrue and just a nasty rumor. The asshole that started it, probably some REMF, should never make it out of Vietnam alive. Morale quickly went back to normal, and once again I felt invincible. At the young age of 21 years, that's exactly how one feels. Men would say, "No bullet out there has my name on it," meaning those bullets are for someone else. I truly believed it also, and it was reinforced all the time as I saw men get screwed up all around and near me, like for example, when some men smoked at night. Sure, there are times of overwhelming odds and some things are out of our control or influence, but an awful lot is contributable to dumb-ass decisions and failure to prioritize things in the proper order of importance, like cleaning your weapon before any personal hygiene, and not smoking at night.

Chapter 15

Lieutenant New's Old Indian Trick

2nd Lieutenant Eugene R. New, 3rd Platoon Leader of Abu Company. Courtesy of Major New (USA Ret.)

On or about 21 February 1966 around 1600 hours, the 3rd Platoon stopped to prepare for nightfall. We frequently would to accomplish necessary tasks prior to darkness, such as cleaning our weapons, chowing down and taking care of our feet. These are noisy tasks that if done during darkness would draw incoming grenades like a baseball to a catcher's mitt. Before darkness, that M-16 or M-60 had to be oiled, cleaned, and functional. And no one would think of taking his boots off at night. Many times boots never came off during the day, as we had to be ready to saddle up at a moment's notice, but changing socks, applying foot powder, and allowing our feet to air dry was important. There were many men who, because of their lack of foot care had developed some serious infections, and had to be evacuated. If staying the night, there were a host of other tasks to accomplish, but we weren't booking this hotel or NDP. (Night Defensive Position) Only 50 percent of the unit would participate at any one time, as 50 percent security remained at all times. I insured that only one machine gun was broken down at any one time for cleaning, and I coordinated the tasks or priorities.

Where we stopped was just off a cart track, as it showed on the map; but, in actuality was a dirt road around 12 feet wide, consisting of a reddish, dirt-like and hard-packed clay surface, which was raised a couple feet or so above the rice paddies that were all along its route. The road connected small hamlets and villages, while meandering for miles throughout the valley as a major artery. The road had single banana trees here and there along the sides. We nicknamed it the Banana Trail

LIEUTENANT NEW'S OLD INDIAN TRICK

and used it frequently for navigation purposes to return to the Battalion CP/FSB (fire support base) or to enter the part of the AO which was always active with a lot of enemy activity. To walk on it would invite an ambush, as the NVA had defensive positions in the form of spider holes, which were one man round holes in the ground, at different areas along its route. We noticed quickly that these holes were bigger than any previously seen in Vietnam. Most were big enough to accommodate us, as well as the NVA being killed who were much larger than the typical South Vietnamese or VC. Many were as big as us, obviously well fed while no worse for wear, after coming down the Ho Chi Minh trail to counter the U. S. buildup-taking place. I always pondered if they were Chinese troops, but what did I know? I was only a grunt!

Lieutenant New was airing out his feet and smoking the stubbed end of one of those big ass cigars while studying the map, which I presumed was for a NDP. He then called a squad leaders' meeting to give us the mission; we all looked at each other in total surprise. We continually evolved by adapting our tactics along with other units of the 101st; such as, stay behind ambushes and night movements, while mainly operating as a platoon. We were issued Starlight's, a crude night vision devise by today standards, which was dependent on light from the stars and batteries that were in short supply, plus we were told at all costs, not to allow it to fall into enemy hands. The mission was to move three to four hundred meters to the northeast to set an NDP, and then as soon as darkness fell, return to this location and set up a platoon size ambush. That old Indian trick of doubling back on them had not yet been tried and had a chance of success, especially knowing they were always watching us for weaknesses, and tracking our whereabouts. Next, the ambush site was prepared—every position was selected along with fields of fire, so that every man knew exactly where to go, what his area of responsibility entailed, and all fires were interlocking for mutual support. For the most part, the men were already in position. A few adjustments for security to the flanks and rear were all that it needed.

We headed out around two hours prior to darkness and set up; this included putting out claymore mines and conducting our normal practices, such as stand-to, which means 100 percent alertness with all equipment on an hour prior to darkness and continued for an hour after darkness—the same for daylight—as this is when most attacks take place. After darkness had completely fallen, we headed back to the ambush site, moving in smoother than a newborn's ass. We were only in the site about an hour, when an alert by our left flank security got passed down the line…my heart started pounding to where I thought it could be heard. Then, visible in the moonlight, came figures walking down the road and moving from left to right, with their weapons hung on their shoulders at sling arms. Upon reaching the center of us, they stopped, looked around. Then the signal was given to spring the ambush. The shit hit the fan as claymores went off, M-60s and M-16s opened up, and a few grenades were thrown in to the opposite side of the road to prevent escape. A cease-fire was called and slowly it stopped. Men were excited and anxious to check the kill zone to claim their prize; they were like animals with a tasting for blood. Their adrenalin rush was interrupted when Lieutenant New ordered us to get our men together for a tactical withdrawal to our previous NDP—an excellent call—as they may have just been a point element for a much larger force. The return to the NDP and the remainder of the night went without incident.

The next morning consisted of stand-to, then a move back to the ambush site where four dead NVA lay in the road with four AK-47 rifles, one of which was mangled all up. Each had approximately two or three magazines, or about 90 rounds per man, and a couple grenades apiece on them. In addition, they were wearing black pajamas. One had a bunch of small red flags with many political papers on him, and we believed he was some sort of political cadre or VIP (very important person). The most significant thing was they were all wearing NVA belts with a red star on it, indicating they were probably four officers. At the time, it didn't register, but later as events unfolded, I believe we killed four high-ranking officers who had themselves been conducting a reconnaissance for an ambush.

Lieutenant New was a calm, calculating, tough-ass paratrooper whose experienced call that day made all those lonely, wet, sleepless nights on other ambushes, with no results, all worthwhile. His old Indian trick of doubling back would be entered into the book of hard knocks for reference in future operations.

Chapter 16

Ham and Lima Beans

On 26 February 1966 after stand-to, we prepared to leave the Battalion base camp and to move out into the AO; this was becoming all too familiar to us. Company C had been attached out to our sister Battalion, the 2/327 Airborne Infantry, for some time. Abu and B Company were alternating providing security for B battery 5/27 Artillery, which had about six 105 howitzers, plus the Battalion CP, while the other company was conducting operations in the part of the AO where the enemy was constantly being engaged. This switching had become the routine about every four days so that the artillery pieces and Battalion CP remained protected. Because of re-supply issues, it was limited as to how long the other company could stay in the AO.

Each man was issued a case of c-rations, which consisted of 12 meals, or 4 days of rations, and weighed close to 25 pounds without the cardboard case. This always caused a flurry of activity, as every man was trading to obtain his favorite meals or cigarettes. Every man had his own way of dealing with this situation; some would just return most of the food to avoid humping the weight. However, if your ass didn't carry it...well...your ass didn't eat. The size of the man was never a consideration, whether small in stature like Pedro Jaime of New York, or solidly built like Private First Class Warren R. Newton—every man carried his own weight and sympathy just wasn't a known paratrooper trait. I won't go into all the other stuff we carried, except to say that the best description would be considerable and heavy. After months, the whole process had actually become an art—like placing cans in socks and then tying the sock to our gear to carry them, and eating the big cans first to lighten the load. This may sound like a lot of food, but with what our activity entailed, even if one were to eat it all, no one ever gained weight.

My personal dislike, along with many other troopers, was ham and lima beans, or more commonly known as ham and mother fu-kers. The cans were big (more weight), tasted like shit, and the more they were cooked, the more grease floated to the top. They were good for medicinal purposes if you had constipation, but then again, some men loved them. Go figure!

One such trooper was Private First Class James D. Wilson Sr...and for good reason. Wilson was an M-60 gunner for Tiger Force on 7 February 1966, at the battle of My Cahn (2), where 24 Above-The-Rest troopers were KIA. During the assault, Private First Class Wilson charged forward while firing his machine gun, and was hit by enemy fire in the area of his pistol belt, knocking him to the ground. Thinking he was wounded, he looked down and noticed that the rounds had actually struck the extra canteen cover in which he carried a c-ration meal. The meal of ham and lima beans had served him well by stopping the rounds intended for his body. Wilson looked up and sighed, "God bless ham and limas." Wilson also recovered two WIA Tigers from the open rice paddy on that day, while exposing himself to intense enemy fire, and dragged them to safety behind a rice paddy dike. Wilson was awarded an Army Commendation Medal with the V device for valor for his bravery and heroic actions under fire. Wilson also fought at Dak To in June 1966, when Tiger Force was completely surrounded by an NVA force with far more men than they had, and was threatened with being annihilated. Abu Company broke through to reinforce, stabilize the situation, and allow for the evacuation of casualties. Wilson remained in the Army, where he had a successful military career and retired as a Master Sergeant. Above the Rest!

FATE UNKNOWN

Chapter 17

MIAs

While out in our AO (area of operation), we received word to be on the lookout for two men from Tiger Force, our Battalion Recon element. Tiger Force was originally formed from the Anti-Tank and Recon Platoons, while the Radar Section merged with the Recon Platoon in Headquarters Company. The Anti-Tank and Radar Section really didn't have much of a role or mission in a counter-insurgency war like the Vietnam War. Volunteers were taken from the line companies to beef up their numbers as they formed a reinforced platoon consisting of an Alpha Force and Bravo Force. Lieutenant John Howard, our original platoon leader of the 3rd Platoon, left us to lead one of the Tiger Force's units.

They were the eyes and ears of the 1st/327 Battalion; they gave the battalion a maneuver advantage and provided other tactical actions that could be executed against the enemy once they were found. To the best of my knowledge, this concept began in our Battalion and quickly spread to the other 101st units. They were so successful, that these type units became a part of all battalion size units and above during the conduct of the Vietnam war.

FATE UNKNOWN

At dusk, on 25 February 1966, two small teams of Tigers, consisting of about seven men each, were inserted. Lieutenant John D. Howard led one team and Staff Sergeant Smith led the other. The remainder of Tigers would be conducting other missions. They would be several miles apart and wouldn't be mutually supporting each other. It takes special men to operate in this manner, even more so knowing the AO is infested with hardcore NVA regulars.

Two men from one of the patrols led by Staff Sergeant Smith were sent out on a recon, or an OP / LP, on the morning of 26 February. They never returned and all contact with them was lost. No shots were heard or reported...they just seemed to vanish. MIA (missing in action) was 23-year-old Sergeant Donald S. Newton from San Pedro, California, and 21-year-old Private First Class Francis D. Wills from La Plata, Maryland.

The search was on to find the two missing troopers, and I remember looking for a reported POW camp in the mountainous jungle. During the search our platoon was conducting, we came upon a four-man Tiger Force team who were also involved in a search. They were well camouflaged and stealthy. Upon my noticing them, they just smiled and waved. It was sort of a brief, I-got-you...no I-got-you...moment. Actually we had not been informed of their presence in our AO. We exchanged information about areas that had been searched and then moved on with our missions.

If any of us were fortunate enough to locate the missing Tigers, we all wondered about how we could rescue them without causing them more harm, since the Tigers would most certainly be with the NVA. We had also heard rumors that one of the men was being paraded through the villages with a rope around his neck and his hands tied, while being used for propaganda purposes. Unfortunately, we never found them; but, there were lessons to be learned from this incident...like being disciplined about noise levels, never going far from the perimeter to take a crap, and other basic lessons. When tired, men tended to get slack and thus put others at risk. Also, we used OP/LP's in the day and at night on a daily basis. The 95th NVA, who could not be underestimated, was challenging us every day for control of the area. I gained great respect for their abilities and learned that to underestimate them would be at our own peril.

Only those men who were actually there could ever give an actual accounting of what had taken place or why they had gone MIA, but I think it safe to say their position had obviously been compromised. MIA Private First Class Francis D. Wills was declared dead a year later, while Sergeant Donald S. Newton was carried on the MIA rolls until 20 August 1974, when he also was declared dead. Neither trooper's remains have ever been recovered.

Author's note: Many Abu's would make the Army a career and have success in doing so. Their success was attributed to the caliber of men within the Abu unit, as well as those in the Tiger Force. Lieutenant Howard was yet another who had a distinguished military career and rose to the rank of Brigadier General.

Lt. John D. Howard,
original 3rd Platoon Leader & Tiger Force Leader.
Courtesy of BG John D. Howard (USA Ret.).

Chapter 18

Doc Jackson

Upon leaving the Battalion Base Camp on the 26th of February 1966, a new medic was attached to 3rd Platoon. His name was Private First Class Arthur James Jackson from Los Angeles, California, and his parent unit was D Company, 326th Medical Battalion of the 101st. He had only been in the country about four months. He was a tall and lanky, 24-year-old black soldier, standing approximately six-foot, two inches tall, and weighing about 160 pounds. Doc Jackson was non-airborne qualified (commonly referred to as a leg) and was to my knowledge the first leg assigned to an airborne unit. We asked him how in the world he had ended up with us. He told us that he had heard about the 101st, so when he was in replacement depot and they asked for volunteers, he knew he wanted to join us. Traditionally, airborne troopers back at Fort Campbell would start a fight with a leg for no reason whatsoever, just because they despised legs. Medics were worth their weight in gold, but it seemed for one reason or another 3rd Platoon couldn't keep one very long. I presume it was the same all over the Brigade. This was one man the troopers never screwed with, as they were aware their life could depend on his actions. The leaders wouldn't tolerate it either. The issue never had to be addressed though, because...hell, we were happy to have him with us. Most medics were called Doc to the point most men could not tell you their real name; however, it was different with Jackson. Everyone always referred to him as Doc Jackson right off, or he quickly corrected them.

My first encounter with Doc Jackson was on 26 February, down around the My Phu area where we had stopped to chow down. I had gone just outside of the perimeter to take a crap, when as I pulled up my pants and turned around to bury it; I noticed these white things moving all around in the pile. I immediately thought of worms! "Damn!—I have f-ing worms, and no wonder...living in this filthy, shit-hole of a place." Observing Jackson nearby, I said, "Hey Doc, got a minute?" Sure, he replied. I asked him if he had anything for worms. Doc Jackson said, "What makes you think you have worms?" Then I ran it down to him as to what had happened while I was taking a crap. He asked if it was still there and I told him yes. He said, "Show it to me." Doc looks at it closely for about a half a minute and then says, "It's not worms—its maggots." "Maggots," I replied. "You mean to tell me I have maggots coming out my ass?" Doc stated, "No it's the flies... watch, there's one." As I observe this pile of crap, a fly lands on it and lays a larva maggot right on top...it immediately starts crawling around, happier than a pig in shit. I believe they were hitting the shit even before it ever smacked on the ground—not because they were faster than Superman looking for Lois Lane, but because there were so many flies from all the piles of dead enemy bodies in the area. If you have ever smelled the stink of one dead animal, you can imagine the odor of this area. I told Doc Jackson I would inform my M-60 crews and asked him to inform the men as he went around, because it was pretty unsanitary eating c-rats where the flies were going from shit or dead bodies to their food. If anyone opened a can, the flies were on it faster than a speeding bullet. My thoughts, while proceeding to bury that crap, was that Doc Jackson knew a thing or two about excrement. Upon returning to the platoon CP, I informed Lieutenant New that this new medic had his shit together, so to speak. When he asked, "Why do you say that?" I simply replied, "He's good, that's all," and let the rest of that story go untold. Now if you're laughing, let me just tell you that every word of this account is true, and while looking back now it seems somewhat amusing, trust me, at the time this was serious business and no laughing matter.

FATE UNKNOWN

Chapter 19

Water Re-Supply

Early on 27 February, 3rd Platoon was moving into the mountains, south of where the minefield had been, toward an area that provided quick access to the valley and where a lot of enemy activity was occurring. As we got to a stream, we stopped to allow everyone the chance to refill their canteens prior to entering the jungle of the mountains where there would be no water re-supply, except off the land. I was with the lead M-60. I filled up my canteens and dropped a water purification tablet (iodine tab) in each one. The platoon saddled up and continued to travel along the left side of this stream; after about 75 meters, we found a dead NVA lying in the stream, He was all bloated, to the point that his stomach was beginning to bust, and his skin was a yellowish-tan in color. I'm sure the sight bothered no one, but the thought of filling up canteens just downstream from the body was a mind blower. We moved on another 75 meters or so, crossed the stream, and then stopped—the platoon was now on both sides. I'm figuring that Lieutenant New had seen the same thing we had, and was stopping to allow us to refill upstream from the dead NVA. Just about the time I had gotten my canteens out of their covers, the man to my front started moving out before I could even refill them. Separation in the jungle can occur very quickly, so we had to move out. The only thing Lieutenant New stopped for was a compass bearing, or quick map check. As we moved out, a trooper behind me said, "I'm not drinking this shit." In response, I quickly turned around and jumped in his shit saying, "Put another tablet in it and drive on." In other words…man the hell up and shut up. But, after I put another tablet in my own canteens I thought to myself, "I'm not drinking this fu-king shit either." I never heard another word or bitch about the water.

Chapter 20

Meanwhile Back In The Jungle

It felt good to get back into the jungle; it was shaded and much cooler than being out in the direct sun in the valley. The vegetation provided concealment...an area where I no longer felt eyeballs all over me and a big bull's eye target on my back. Shortly after entering the jungle, we came upon a trail that was like a major highway. It appeared to be used so much that the roots from trees which crossed it were flattened from wear and the trail was worn down into the ground, causing it to be deeper than the surrounding terrain.

Private First Class Blair A. "T-Bird" Funderburk of Lebanon, Tennessee was on point, as he frequently was for the platoon. Some of a point man's duties are: to detect the enemy before they detect our unit; find booby traps and trip wires; detect snipers in trees; and to look for signs of recent enemy activity, to include broken vegetation on bushes, or moss missing off rocks in a stream bed, which indicated someone had walked over those rocks; and bent grass that was flattened to the ground, which indicated both the direction and time of someone's movement—since as the length of the day increases the heat forces the grass or vegetation to stand back up. A good point man must know what's natural in order to detect the unnatural and have some tracking skills. Not long after our arrival we had a couple dog teams with us for tracking, and the men handling the dogs impressed the hell out of me with their ability. I tried to learn all I could from them in the few days they were with us.

**Blair "T-Bird" Funderburk,
after completion of Basic Training in April 1965.**

Blair A. "T-Bird" Funderburk
Photo taken in 2010 at the Airborne Museum, N.C.

As we travelled on the trail that day, T-Bird's keen observation skills really paid off; he found a chewed-up piece of sugar cane which was fresh and wet with saliva. It was passed back to each man so they would be aware of the situation, as were arm and hand signals alerting the men to remain extra quiet and very observant. As far as I'm aware, T-Bird was one of only two men from 3rd Platoon that completed a tour in the field by always walking point—the other was Tom Joyce. Point men generally didn't survive long, yet not once did I ever hear him bitch. T-Bird was small in stature, and although he was a quiet man, he had nerves of steel. He was very well liked throughout the platoon. His attitude, as well as that of most point men, made him and the others better suited to walking point. Because of their lead position out in front of everyone else in the unit, a point man's survival rate was about as long as that of a machine gunner. Nonetheless, their degree of competency and pure luck seemed to have a direct effect on their survival.

The men knew there were large enemy forces inhabiting the mountains, and things became even quieter after the sugar cane was found...in fact so quiet, that about 35 men made less noise than a three-man recon patrol. We slowed down considerably, following the trail upwards until we reached a plateau at the top. The trail continued on, but we established a platoon perimeter with three OPs, using the clock system with twelve o'clock being the direction of travel. The first OP was located at the six o'clock just down the trail from where we had come from; the second OP was located at the ten o'clock and was positioned on a ridge of high ground; and the third OP was located at the twelve o'clock position further down the trail that we were following. I emplaced an M-60 on the trail and deployed another on the ridge leading to higher ground. We settled in, and about ten minutes later, the forward OP shot an NVA he had seen coming up the trail with his weapon slung over his shoulder. One shot...one kill.

Chapter 21

Staff Sergeant Ira H. "Perk" Perkins, Jr.

SSG Ira H. Perkins, Jr.
Courtesy of Dominick "Nick" Fondo, Jr.

Lieutenant New received the situation report (sit-rep) on the OP, then called a squad leader's meeting and stated he wanted one squad to go on patrol. Staff Sergeant Ira H. Perkins, Jr. immediately interjected saying, "My squad will take it." The mission was to check out the area using the hour numbers of a clock. Lieutenant New designated twelve o'clock as being North, with the patrol going from six o'clock through three o'clock and around to twelve o'clock. Lieutenant New said, "Sergeant Mitchell, send one gun with Perkins. Move out in ten minutes." Perkins was a career soldier, with about eight years in service, some of which was spent in the motor pool working with vehicles. He had recently received a promotion to Staff Sergeant and had been with the platoon only a few months. "Perk" was from Calais, Maine, and was married with a couple of kids. Perk's appearance was deceptive in that he appeared a little overweight, even after being in the country a few months. Regardless, he could hump all day, keep up with anyone, and seemed to have an endless source of energy. Perk was also very ambitious; he was telling everyone that he was going to win the Medal of Honor. I once said, "Perk, do you know most men that get it are KIA?" His reply was, "Yeah, I know, but it makes no difference. I'm going to get it!" He conveyed this also to his squad members, who were beginning to think he was Dinky-Dao (pronounced Dinky Dow), Vietnamese for crazy. Well, Perkins wasn't a crazed nut job, just an aggressive, hard-charging, fearless, and no-nonsense sergeant that felt invincible. Once something was in his sights, fixation took place and he could go from 0 to 100 miles per hour in about a second. Perkins was also fulfilling a duel role as the Platoon Sergeant and a Squad Leader, mostly as a Squad Leader. As leaders, we spent an awful lot of time together and expressing our inner thoughts. We became quite fond of each other, even though we were somewhat like opposites. We were like that old bull joke where Perk would say, let's run down there and get one (cow), and then being the old bull I'd say, let's walk down there and get them all. I was the same way once; however, on my first day as a sergeant Lieutenant New had slowed me down and I became more calculating. Experience also does that.

I went over to my gun position on the trail, to inform them of the patrol, and my M-60 Gunner Tom Joyce said, "We're not going." I said, "What?" He repeated, "We're not going." I asked him what was going on, and shortly after he started to explain, the others began to chime in. Apparently, they had been talking to a member of Perk's squad who was present at the gun position. He was telling them that Perkins was a nut, that he was going to get everyone killed, and that he didn't know what he was doing. Tom Joyce was the kind of soldier who could be easily pumped up by another. I said, "I'll tell you what...I'll go with you." They all looked at each other, and one of them said, "I'll go." Then the rest of the gun crew chimed in, while Perk's squad member kept quiet. I knew my men very well and knew the member of Perkins squad was stirring them up—causing the type of problems that we damn sure did not need. Then I told my M-60 crew,

"I'll be back as soon as I get my shit." I went to get my load-bearing equipment, and when I returned they were ready to hump. Private First Class Mattson from Perkin's squad moved out with us and I guess he didn't have the balls to tell Perkins that shit or me directly. I just knew from that day forward I needed to keep close observation of him.

The patrol then began to haul ass down this trail like a bat out of hell, sacrificing security for speed. I passed word up the line for everyone to stop, but it seemed to take forever. Once stopped, each man alternated facing out to the flanks. I proceeded up to the front and found Perkins in the lead without a point man. I called him over to the side and whispered, "What the hell are you doing?" He just looked at me with complete surprise, as he did outrank me. Then I whispered to him that he knew the area was loaded with NVA, reminded him that we had just killed one, and that it was important for us to get off the trail and parallel it. I went on to tell him to slow down before we walked into an ambush and got everyone killed. Perk said, "You're right." Then I said, "Hey, we have all fu-king day for this shit." Anytime we can detect the enemy before being detected, we gain the advantage because it allows us time to access the terrain for cover and concealment and insight as to where to maneuver. We moved out with stealth, and shortly after found an abandoned large base camp built in a draw that was not visible from the air due to triple canopy jungle. We stirred up an NVA at about the three o'clock position when as we were crossing a dry (Damn!) streambed, just about everyone but the M-60 opened fire on. The stream had some huge boulders, as much as four feet high in it, like the size of a Volkswagen; however, this NVA ran down it like it was a paved highway—his name must have been the Roadrunner, because we felt like Wile E. Coyote! We couldn't believe he had escaped so much fire, but we were on him like bloodhounds. A search of the area only produced some blood plus an AK-47 rifle. We returned to the platoon from about five o'clock position, after looking for the wounded enemy without any luck, since we had lost the blood trail in the jungle.

Lieutenant New said we would remain there for the night and called in some artillery smoke to mark some plots at about the one o'clock position up the ridge to higher ground. We conducted stand-to and to our front when Roadrunner, the NVA started moaning rather loudly. Surprisingly, he was not far from our perimeter. I guess it did get on someone's nerves when he hollered out loud, "Someone shut him up." Or maybe they thought the NVA would draw attention to our location. Well, no one was going outside the perimeter or going to fire and give away their position. The moaning seemed to go on forever through the night...a somewhat eerie sound in the quiet of the jungle night. The sound grew fainter and fainter as the night grew longer.

At about 1900 hours, another Abu Platoon observed an enemy force, consisting of approximately 20 NVA, in the open rice paddies just west of My Phu. They called artillery into the area to engage them. The result—four NVA found KIA, one suspect captured, three AK-47s along with ammo and several grenades were recovered. The enemy probed the Battalion Base Camp/FSB at 2400 hours—otherwise, the night was uneventful.

Chapter 22

Perkins Brew

On the 28th of February, immediately after stand-to, a patrol took off to check out the high ground in the form of a ridge not previously checked at the one o'clock position on the clock. I went with the M-60 crew and found another major highway of a trail with a few mass graves along its side.

I had been drinking canned fruit juice to sustain my liquids as much as possible, but when I returned to the platoon CP I made a cup of coffee. Yes, it was the same damn water I swore I wouldn't drink...one can only go so long without water, especially while constantly out on patrol. I only hoped the two purification tablets and boiling worked. Perkins sees what I'm doing and states, "You don't know anything about making coffee, Mitchell. You're an amateur." I reply, "What's wrong with it?" Perk says, "You see all those golden brown bubbles around the outer edge of the can?" "Yeah," I said. "Well, that's coffee that's not dissolved and where the entire flavor of the coffee is." This wasn't the first time we had this discussion; we had gone back and forth about it before. Perkins says, "I'll show you how to make a real cup of coffee—Perkins brew." In addition, with that Doc Jackson jumps up and says, "Sergeant wait for me, I'm gone to get my stuff." Doc Jackson was a noticeably very polite and respectful individual. He returns with his stuff and Perkins breaks off a piece of C-4 explosive and rolls it into a ball. We had learned this trick back in December in the Iron Triangle from the engineers attached to us, as a means of exploding booby traps we encountered; after that we always tried to keep some on hand by begging, borrowing or stealing. C-rats are a lot more palatable when hot! He lights the C-4, which sputters, spits, and then begins burning, giving off intense heat as they placed their cans of water over it. Perkins is holding court and Doc Jackson is duplicating every move…I'm sitting on my steel pot drinking my coffee…and Lieutenant New is checking his map. Perk drops in the contents of a coffee pack, begins to stir it, and says, "This is the key: take the spoon and smash those golden brown bubbles around the edges into the side of the can, stirring it until it's all gone."

Perkins didn't take any cream or sugar with his; however, I had to have some sugar. Perkins finally won me over, and during the rest of my 20 years in the Army whenever I was in the field, my method of choice to brew coffee was the Perkins brew technique. No man ever mentioned a word of the NVA body in the water, at least not to me.

Later that morning when the opportunity was right, I informed Lieutenant New of the men refusing to go on patrol. My opinion was their morale was poor because of fatigue. They were getting less sleep and rest while incurring the stress of additional combat, plus our AO was loaded with NVA, and it was taking its toll on the men. In addition, Perkins was volunteering his squad for every patrol or ambush. Meanwhile, the other two squads were doing nothing as far as sharing the load, while getting over like a fat rat in a cheese factory. It's a delicate balance, but when lives are on the line and important missions are at hand, leaders tend to go with their best. Lieutenant New never said too much as he wasn't one for a lot of words...but he listened. I never said anything about how the patrol went, not being that type of an individual. Besides, it turned out to be a great patrol with the situation defused and the mission accomplished.

On this day, I spent some time with Private First Class Clarence E. "Griff" McKinnis and Private First Class Harold Mattson who occupied a position together near one of my M-60's. The three of us sat around bullshitting about home, girls, and the goings on. One thing about Mattson was he mostly spoke his mind and never held anything back. He was always an up-front, tell-it-like-it-is soldier from Minnesota; however, he never mentioned a word the day before about not wanting to go out on patrol. I guess he perceived me to be stupid; believing he had nothing to do with it and I guess he wasn't as up front as I thought, but I was a step ahead of this trouble maker and planned on staying a step ahead. Clarence "Griff" and I had come over together on the boat; we had seven months in country. This common bond was becoming an extinct thing because of the rapid turnover rate of the men. We had endured experiences together that a newbie couldn't relate to, and in turn, I gravitated to old friends or men that had some time there. I found it difficult to warm up to men that had only a month or two in country. Much later I learned about survivor guilt—a defense mechanism for when some men survived and others were KIA or severely injured—it was easier to deal with if a personal friendship or relationship was non-existent. Therefore, I started to become somewhat aloof, and aware that being a sergeant had a role unto its own.

Chapter 23

Reality Check

At about 1500 hours on 28th February, the platoon saddled up with Private First Class Funderburk "T-Bird" on the point. This was our third day out and was time to start working our way back. It didn't take long to know I was back in the valley as we followed a small foot path. About 20 or 30 meters ahead lie a NVA who appeared to have been recently shot; I thought he might be alive because it seemed like his stomach was moving up and down, As I approached and got a closer look at him, I realized this was far from the case; he was definitely dead and his stomach was so swollen that it had split open and had hundreds of maggots moving all over it. This likely from a distance made him appear to be breathing. The fresh air of the jungle was gone and the flies were feasting at the dinner table with bibs on—holding a fork in one hand and a knife in the other—or so it seemed. In all seriousness, they were the only thing thriving in this valley of death. Maggot expertise could now be entered into my military records or future resume.

After doing a reality check, my mind quickly moved on; you couldn't dwell on this kind of stuff because combat requires one to be in the moment at all times…not the minute…but now! Today in sports, it's called "in the zone." Fact of the matter is walking around with your head up your ass is a recipe for disaster to take place…with suffocation as the best-case scenario. The enemy was funny in that he would go to great lengths to carry off bodies if possible just to prevent us from making an accurate assessment, but once we knew or had them, they couldn't care less about them. The psychological effect for them as they observed all this must have been tremendous; however, they must have still felt invincible because it never deterred them one bit as they continued to challenge us for control while refusing to concede the valley to us.

Chapter 24

Red Rain

At about 1700 hours, we stopped on the east edge of a village, in the vicinity of My Phu, to chow down and prepare for the next night phase that was approaching. When checking to insure the guns were cleaned, I observed Tom Joyce, Harold Matson, and Robert R. Papesh eating some c-rat, totally oblivious to the flies, with an attitude of...if they're not off my spoon fast enough, they'll be eaten. The guys wouldn't waste the energy to shoo them because as quickly as they did, the flies returned. At one point Tom Joyce called out, "More meat!" and we all laughed. He had a point—screw it; flies were the least of our worries. I returned to the platoon CP, broke down my M-16, and began cleaning it. Meanwhile Lieutenant New had his boots off and Doc Jackson was working on his feet.

Sergeant Perkins came to the CP around 1800 hours and informed Lieutenant New that some of the men had spotted people approximately 300 to 400 meters out into the rice paddy. Lieutenant New said to send out a patrol to check it out and Perkins said, "I'll take it." To which Lieutenant New replied, "No, stay here, just send a fire team of three or four men with a radio." Perkins departed to issue the order. Meanwhile I broke out my binoculars to check it out and observed 3 to 4 people in black pajamas, however, I couldn't tell if they were civilians or what—no weapons were visible. Generally, all the civilians from the area were gone and no sense could be made of the enemy in the open like that. Perhaps some farmers had returned and were working the fields. Lieutenant New called artillery in on a point 400 meters or so to the east of the suspected enemy, toward the jungle, to have a marked plot or concentration point of adjustment if needed later.

A short time later gunfire occurred, and immediately a frantic call came over the radio. "Help, we need a medic!" Doc Jackson threw the medical stuff that was on the ground into his aid bag, zipped it, then threw it on his back and took off toward the incident. I quickly started assembling my weapon while Lieutenant New was throwing on boots and shouting out orders: "We're moving out. Get your shit together!" Lieutenant New was calling in artillery toward the sighting and behind it to the wood line. Squad leaders gave him an up for readiness. All this took no more than 2 or 3 minutes for us to be gone.

Doc Jackson had a few minutes head start on us when we took off at a full run for the contact area to our recon element. After going some 200 meters, or about half way, we heard small arms fire cracking overhead...the all too familiar AK-47 rifle...which probably meant NVA regulars. No sooner had we hit the ground, we heard a chopper, but didn't know if it was a medevac chopper. We looked to our left rear and observed a Huey chopper quickly coming up on our left rear flank with both door gunners letting their M-60's continuously rip. These babies will fire 550 rounds per minute if continually fed; choppers are capable of doing this with continuous linked belts. Every fifth round is a red tracer used to adjust fire. They were coming right for us and all I could see was the sky full of red raindrops falling to earth, saturating the area around us. Lieutenant New grabbed the hand mike of the radio and began shouting, "Cease fire...cease fire. Stop that fu-king chopper firing—you're shooting us. Cease fire!" I thought, oh no, and tried to crawl under my steel pot while placing my hands over the steel pot. We were absolutely caught in the open with no rice paddy dike close for protection, nor time to do anything, including saying a prayer. I heard the chopper cease fire and a few seconds later it whizzed by us. I wasn't sure, but didn't think I had been hit, but I figured the platoon had to be massacred. I looked around and surveyed the scene; I was astonished that not one man had been wounded or killed. How, you ask? I have absolutely no clue, except perhaps luck or divine intervention. To this day on reflection, it's as clear as yesterday, yet I still have no explanation.

After waiting for a cry for medic that never came, we looked at one another in amazement and shocking disbelief. The platoon closed with the enemy by fire and movement which limited our exposure time. Upon reaching Doc Jackson, we learned that he was KIA, the result of small arms fire to the head…shot through the front teeth as he made one continuous run to render first aid to his newfound Abu friends. Without stopping or limiting his exposure time, and forsaking his own personal safety for his brothers in arms, Doc Jackson had made the ultimate sacrifice. He forever dispelled that myth about legs—I would remember this for the remainder of my career and life.

I moved my two M-60s to the right of the platoon where there was a small knoll, and deployed them in pairs. I had never done this before and I was not quite sure how I ended up there. Perhaps the platoon shifted left, but the location was excellent. It provided a clear field of fire across the entire platoon's front that could provide sustained fire from a slightly raised position that put their fire above the rice paddies' walls and dikes. I looked to the rear and the jungle was about 150 meters or so behind us; this concerned the hell out of me when I realized I was on the flank without security. We had to provide our own security—I ordered the ammo bearers to drop their ammo and move out about

50 meters, while also telling them to maintain a constant watch on the wood line to protect our rear.

PFC Phillip "Tisch" Tischman, Jr., M-60 Machine Gunner of 3rd Platoon. Phan Rang Base Camp, December 1965.

On the guns were Private First Class Phillip "Tish" Tischman, Jr., a massive soldier that came to us in October, and Tom Joyce, who came over on the boat with us. I wanted Tish to join me in the weapons squad and the Lieutenant gave him to me. Both of these men were well experienced, excellent gunners.

PFC Thomas R. Joyce, M-60 Machine Gunner in a rubber plantation.

The NVA began popping up to the platoon's front, about 100 meters, and the first M-60 fire I directed was Tish's until the tracers were going through him as he fired 15 to 20 round burst. I had him stop when another popped up just to the right of the first one. I told Tish, "To your right," and he quickly got on him as he now had the range. Once again I saw tracers going right through him, but he didn't seem to go down. Further to the right another popped up; I had Tom Joyce engage that one and he quickly adjusted his fire without having to be told and was on him. Again, I'm observing tracers going through the sons of bitches, thinking are they doped up and not feeling this shit. We had heard rumors they would dope themselves up prior to battle. Two more came up on the left and right and each gun took one. Then I noticed every time we ceased or shifted fire, they dropped. Now I'm thinking, after three to four tracers they had about 20 rounds hitting them and it was actually holding them up somehow, perhaps pinning them back against a paddy wall or something. I did know one thing; the bastards weren't surviving that shit. I realized also there didn't seem to be any incoming fire and I don't remember one round coming in our direction, which seemed odd as they always went for the guns. Tom Joyce took down another and by now I'm thinking this was strange, almost like being on a firing range with pop-up targets. They continued to pop up with both guns engaging targets and I kept shifting them as targets appeared. The multiple targets and excitement of the situation to kill them caused me to lose count after around ten. They slowed down in coming up and when they appeared, didn't seem to fire or stay up but for a second or so now…then down before we were on them, whereas earlier, they seemed to stay up longer. They adapted damn quick, but the guns were smoking their asses and dominating the situation.

    The platoon was gathering up the wounded and Doc Jackson while this all was taking place, and the sun was beginning to set. Lieutenant New ordered the platoon to withdraw back to where we had eaten—about 400 meters from our present location. A smart call to evacuate the causalities before dark and to break contact since night was quickly approaching. As the platoon withdrew, I covered their tactical withdrawal by placing fire on the area in the paddies where they had been popping up, and on the wood line to the rear of it, with short five-round bursts. After the platoon progressed about 50 meters, I explained to the gunners we were going to leapfrog the guns back 50 meters at a time and cover the platoon's withdrawal. Tom and his crew moved out—then set up and waved. We then displaced as he provided supporting fire. Upon reaching his position, I dropped off until Tish had set up another 50 meters back. I had learned this by observing the M-60 machine guns when they would leapfrog the guns crossing streams and danger areas, therefore I just reversed it. We repeated this but ceased fire after about 200 meters to conserve ammo while no fire was coming our way, and we continued to leapfrog until we closed in on the platoon location. The casualties…four WIA and one KIA…that all occurred on the initial contact, were evacuated. The platoon then moved out to a platoon-size ambush position, where we previously had passed through earlier in the day.

Perhaps the recon patrol had walked into an ambush, as all four were WIA and the enemy that had failed to flee was willing to take on a larger force. The remainder of the platoon came under fire just prior to the chopper incident, proving they were determined to stay and fight. There was also still a concern of the mine field which was somewhere in that area. Perhaps they were attempting to force us into that, or for us to maneuver forward, or maybe to the left into a larger ambush. Their action after the initial contact was suspicious and we failed to take the bait, primarily because darkness was approaching. If contact had been made much earlier in the day, we would have remained engaged with perhaps a totally different outcome. The total enemy KIA was 11 to 15. Soon after, I learned that the chopper crew was new to Vietnam and that it was their first mission. I learned many years later however, that they had been drinking with Major Hackworth the XO, back in the rear area when they heard the initial contact come over the radio. At that time they cranked up the chopper and then their drunken asses were off to where the real war was taking place. Damn REMFs! Hell, when someone can't identify their own troops in open rice paddies, there is a serious need to return to Charm School (orientation upon arriving in country).

FATE UNKNOWN

Chapter 25

Rotation

We followed the banana trail to the Battalion base camp on 2 March to rejoin the rest of Abu Company and assume security for the perimeter of 1st BN. (ABN), 327th INF FWD (Forward), CP located South of Tuy Hoa, while also protecting the FSB that consisted of B Battery and 5th of the 27th Artillery, who were in direct support. Bravo Company minus one platoon attached to A 2/17th Cavalry rotated out to conduct a four-day operation and C Company remained attached to 2nd/327. I'm sure the enemy had picked up on this as we were setting a pattern with the rotation; there are only so many ways to get to point A and return to point B. With one platoon attached out, B Company would operate at less than full strength in the same area we had just departed. The enemy doesn't miss much and knowing our whereabouts at all times was crucial to their survival.

We established seven LP's and two reinforced ambush patrols as part of the defense of the Bn. CP /FSB. Yep that's right, not much of a change, just a different place. During the night, the Battalion perimeter was probed by small arms fire about 2155 hours, with no casualties taken.

On 3 March a vehicle convoy was struck by mines resulting in four friendly WIA. Our First Sergeant Robert A. Press was one of the four, but he was only slightly wounded from some shrapnel. Meanwhile, Tiger Force and B Company made contact again down near the My Phu area killing 3 more. This area was burning up while hotter than a flamethrower for some unknown reason and the NVA were insistent on controlling it.

The Battalion urgently needed fortification material for its defense. Dug in positions existed; however, under any type of attack the artillery may not be able to maintain a supporting role.

Chapter 26

My Phu (My-Foo)

On the 3rd of March we received a new mission, which consisted of first conducting a helicopter assault and then attacking objective Bit at 1030 hours on 4 March with the LZ to be prepped with artillery and CS gas. It was pretty much standard procedures, with the exception of the CS gas part which was a new twist. Having trained with it before at Fort Campbell, I was well aware this was powerful stuff—much more powerful than the old tear gas that was only effective in a gas chamber that allowed for concentrated levels—in an open-air environment it wasn't effective at all. With one breath of CS gas, a man would fall to his knees and become incapacitated, struggling for a breath of air and not having enough air in his lungs to clear a protective mask, which took one breath. We had been hauling these damn M-17 protective masks around for seven months, the enemy had no chemical capability, the only use for them was for pillows, and troops stuffed them with their necessities. My thoughts were that if the enemy was there, this shit was bound to stir them up like a hornets nest. For once I really felt the scales tipping greatly in our favor. I ordered all my men to refit their masks and check them for serviceability. Using the issued grid coordinates, I conducted a map reconnaissance, studying our AO and scrutinizing LZ Abu and the surrounding areas. The AO was quite familiar as we had operated there several times before. The LZ was down around the My Phu area, very close to where Doc Jackson was recently KIA and where much of the contact was taking place. After securing LZ Abu, we were to conduct a coordinated attack on objective Bit, with B Company supporting us by fire.

Chapter 27

Objective Bit

On 4 March 1966, while smoking a c-ration cigarette and laid back on my pack relaxing, I heard a "whop–whop–whop–whop" sound in the distance—the familiar sound of helicopter blades cutting through the air announcing their arrival. I stood, kicked the feet of a couple catnapping troopers in my stick and shouted, "Saddle-up…Check your equipment!" When they were settled I ordered, "Get your masks on!" The choppers, bobbling and wiggling, slowly arrived. Nearing us, they appeared to be floating in air as they flared and landed. I was with the lead gun as usual and my stick quickly piled in and sat on the floor of the lead chopper. I sat in the right side door with my legs hanging out the door. The chopper swayed to the left, drifted to the right, and then moving forward with its nose in a slightly downward position, it began to gain altitude and air speed.

Co-pilot inside chopper and Door Gunner's M-60 machine gun, enroute to LZ Abu. (Back cover photo)

OBJECTIVE BIT

We departed, and the moving air from the chopper ride was very cool and refreshing compared to the hot air at ground level, even though it was only midmorning. I figured this was going to be about a two minute ride, but the choppers swung north away from our LZ because it had to wait for the preparation fires to complete their mission—timing here is critical. We were zipping along over a hundred miles per hour, with the chopper making a couple of sharp, quick, banking turns—I thought I was going to fall out. We didn't use seat belts in the choppers…just sat on the floor in the open door area, with our legs hanging out. Another chopper came alongside us about one hundred feet on our right flank and we exchanged greetings—a wave here, thumbs up there, a peace sign, and a few smiles along with the old middle finger being flipped back and forth as a term of endearment.

M-60 crew shortly after removing masks. Black smoke is high explosive (HE) rounds exploding to south of LZ Abu, 4 March 1966.

I could see the TOT barrage of gas and artillery preparations striking the ground off in the distance... something that many months ago was very impressive, but now no longer was. Seeing this for the first time gave one the impression and thoughts that nothing would be able to survive that kind of assault, especially when it's orchestrated to include TAC air and helicopter gunships. Then when we landed, it was a hot LZ with bullets flying everywhere. The little bastards seem resilient to almost everything, like cockroaches, short of a B-52 strike. This didn't impress me too much, and well, I suppose a FNG had a false sense of security when observing the show. By this time we had already made

OBJECTIVE BIT

numerous airmobile assaults using the same opening introduction, and sometimes even more destructive with TAC air. Although my expectations weren't any different this time, I was really hoping the gas would make a difference by incapacitating them and giving us a new edge in this landing. One big reason for a hot LZ after all that TAC air and TOT, is that once the enemy is forced to hunker down in their individual spider holes, they can't get up and run around, let alone leave. Though they're pretty much trapped in their holes, once we have made our landing their sense of self-preservation grabs hold of them...and then the fight is on. I was really enjoying the cool air and my jungle fatigue shirt was beginning to dry out...man, I could have ridden this bird all day...but the ride only lasted about ten minutes.

Our chopper suddenly banked sharply to the right and began a hasty decent into LZ Abu. About fifteen feet above the ground, the pilot flared the chopper and it felt like it had stopped in mid-air. The skids of our chopper never touched the ground; about five feet above the dry rice paddy my stick un-assed our ride in a blink of an eye. I quickly crouched down and ran away from the chopper to assume a defensive position and await the arrival of the rest of Abu Company.

FATE UNKNOWN

Shortly after landing, a trooper looks for the enemy while using a rice paddy dike for cover and concealment.

The 2nd Platoon landed prior to us into a hot LZ and quickly routed the enemy. Light gunfire could be heard to my left or south, but quickly dissipated. Our landing went smoothly for the 3rd platoon with us running and pushing out to secure the LZ. That little run and the increase in temperature from being on the ground, had caused my face to sweat; the water was rolling down my face and the lens of my mask were fogging up. I couldn't see through the fogged lens and the sweat was breaking the seal of my mask. I attempted to clear my mask and re-establish a seal to no avail. I then turned around to observe one of my men with his mask off. I asked him if there was any gas and he said there wasn't,

OBJECTIVE BIT

so I removed mine and determined there was no CS. Perhaps we were upwind, I'm not sure, but for whatever reason there was no CS gas present in our area. I gave my men an all clear signal. The CS turned out to be a bust, at least where we were standing. The artillery shifted to the south; I could hear their impact, plus I could observe some air burst rounds mixed in. The enemy was on the run and chose not to stand and fight.

Artillery air bursts of CS gas on LZ Abu. We landed upwind as the wind blew it east toward their mountainous hideouts.

Staff Sergeant Milton McQueeney and 1st Platoon took the lead on Objective Bit, our first objective, while 3rd Platoon brought up the rear in reserve. After a short hump, they drew automatic weapons fire from Objective Bit and deployed quickly on line. Platoon

FATE UNKNOWN

Sergeant Mac, a veteran of the Korean War conflict, encouraged his men to charge, by aggressively leading the assault toward the enemy, through a hail of bullets that kicked up dirt and dust all around his feet. Unfazed, he began leading his platoon and giving orders, maneuvering in an aggressive assault toward the enemy positions, as bullets zinged throughout the platoon. This combat tested NCO continued encouraging his men forward, effectively directing their fire and movement to assault until he was wounded. Several of his men said Platoon Sergeant Mac had given his rifle, ammo and grenades to his men and in an authoritative manner had urged his platoon to continue the assault. The contact only lasted about fifteen minutes; because of their fast response and the heavy volume of fire from the 1st Platoon, they were able to dislodge the enemy to take the objective. The results of the contact were: two enemies KIA (body count), six (est.) one WIA and six friendly WIA—most likely they hit a squad, because they had a machine gun with them. They were left behind to delay us while the main body escaped and withdrew. Perhaps it had been a company size unit, because the larger the size of a delaying force, the larger the main body that their protecting. A man or two would be more common or the norm. Additionally, they make contact then un-ass the area, whereas these stood their ground and had a machine gun indicating, that perhaps we just missed them. Hopefully the artillery shifting to the south to prevent reinforcements tore them a new asshole; we'll never know since the area wasn't checked by troops because all available men were committed. Nor was the area observed by air, besides if you're not on top of them and they have time they'll carry the dead away for burial.

SSG Milton E. "Mac" McQueeney. Courtesy of CSM Robert A. Press (USA Ret.)

One of the six wounded was Platoon Sergeant Milton McQueeney, who was shot with an automatic weapon in his arms and legs. First Sergeant Press caught up with the 1st Platoon, and then asked where Sergeant Mac was; he was informed that Mac had been hit, but had told the platoon to keep going. First Sergeant Press back tracked, and was stunned to find Mac sitting on the ground, propped up against a rice paddy dike, with a .45 caliber pistol lying across his chest and calmly smoking a cigarette. During his initial investigation, and while administering first aid to Mac, he reported: "I saw that he had been hit at least five times, and I asked, "Why didn't you call for a medic?" This experienced combat veteran paratrooper responded in a nonchalant manner, "Well, "Robert A," I knew the medic was busy taking care of others. The troopers were doing what they were supposed to do, and I knew that someone would be back for me, so I wasn't worried."

3rd Platoon takes up a blocking position during attack on Objective Bit. OP's/security is posted to rear behind small hamlet. (Front cover photo)

OBJECTIVE BIT

After starting treatment of Mac's wounds, First Sergeant Press determined that Platoon Sergeant Mac had been hit by nine separate bullets. Platoon Sergeant McQueeney, however, received only one Purple Heart. Combat is definitely unfair to an infantry soldier. As he was being loaded in a medevac chopper, First Sergeant Press told him, "See you in Clarksville." Realizing the severity of his wounds he replied, "Maybe!" His wounds were so severe that he was evacuated to the States, and spent about eleven months in military hospitals.

While moving to occupy a position to support this attack by fire, Bravo Company also made contact and killed two diehards.

FATE UNKNOWN

Chapter 28

Surprise Targets

We were proceeding to the next objective, while paralleling a stream on our left that was 10 or 12 feet wide with a pretty good flow. Actually it was more like a canal than a stream. The platoon received a radio call stating that a large enemy force had been spotted moving toward the Battalion Base/FSB and we were ordered to return to that location ASAP (as soon as possible). Lieutenant New gave the order out loud and we resumed movement at a quicker pace. My thoughts were...these sons of bitches are smart in that most of us are out here, and they are going to attack the artillery battery which is now lightly defended. I always wondered, if a large enemy force was spotted, then why the heck they weren't engaged. A loud volume of gun fire erupted to our left rear, several hundred meters away back towards the LZ area; it lasted about two or three minutes and then ceased all at once.

After moving a short distance, a great volume of gunfire erupted all at once on our left flank...it had to be B Company...and immediately all heads turned in that direction. The firing ceased almost immediately, lasting only about a minute. None of it was fired at us because not a round came our way or overhead. I don't know if they were ambushed or both groups of combatants just ran into each other. About 150 meters across the rice paddies there was a cut out or cove-like area that was clear, indented from the fringe line or where the paddies ended and sparse vegetation began. I could see two or three men of B Company lying on the ground that weren't moving at all, and one trooper with his upper body raised up from a prone position was waving his right arm back and forth at us. Obviously he observed us and was making us aware of their location, but was taking a somewhat protected posture—not completely raising or standing up. Was this man warning us? Did he think we fired on them? Having not fired, I thought it was some sort of warning to make us aware of their location so we didn't light their asses up.

We continued moving at a rapid pace; however, I kept a look to my left toward B Company. Seconds later, surprise targets of NVA enemy began running along this fringe line on the edge of the rice paddies in clear view, directly in front and right by the Bravo Company troopers. They were dressed in khaki uniforms, bent over at the waist, with vegetation on their backs for camouflage, and moving at a full run...hauling ass! They were hard core NVA and the most I had ever observed at one time in one place—approximately 50 to 75 of the enemy. Talk about a target rich environment...

this was it. I didn't need any orders to engage them and wasn't about to wait for any, so I immediately ordered the M-60 crew I was with into action. The gunner couldn't take up a prone firing position on the ground as is normally the case, because the growth along the stream was thick—at least knee high, as it usually is along waterways—and would have obstructed the gunner's line of sight. I told Tom Joyce, who happened to have the gun at the time, as the gun crew rotated the gun while humping, to put it on Private First Class Clinton E. Fluker's shoulder and get 'em. The fire initially was very high and barely left of the B Company men. I hollered out, "Left," and told Fluker to squat down. He began squatting and the fire went right on them. "Right there, I said." They began falling. I said to let it rip, and as I watched, I hollered to get the other gun going. By this time the other men of 3rd platoon also opened up with M-16 fire; the other gun opened up, but by then the enemy was gone. We watched some of the enemy fall, but the others kept hauling ass. After they disappeared, I allowed the guns to continue to rake the area and left of where they were last observed, as I figured they weren't too far…then gave a cease-fire. I kept looking to see, or really hoping to see, another wave run by, however, it never happened. This was a major disappointment. A strange thing about this situation was that as they ran by the Bravo men on the ground neither fired a round at each other. Normally after an ambush the enemy will run through the kill zone, finishing the job and policing up weapons or other equipment. They were in a large cluster fu-k at a full run doing neither.

Someone said, "See if we can cross here." Moreover, before I could blink, Private First Class Harold Mattson dropped his M-16 and jumped into the dark water. Mattson acted without hesitation and clearly felt a sense of urgency with the situation at hand, perhaps not felt by others. Mattson said it was too deep there, and with that, Lieutenant New said, "Move out and we'll find a place to cross." We started moving; meanwhile Mattson was still splashing around in the water. Toward the rear, Private First Class Ashley Stetson, Jr. helped him out because we had saddled up as that urgency became infectious. The NVA frequently shows a large force, which is the bait when they are setting an ambush trap for the reacting force in hot pursuit. Our inability to cross there probably was a blessing, as we would have been caught in open rice paddies at a distinct disadvantage—much like Tiger Force and Bravo Company were faced with on 7 February 1966.

Another significant fact that escaped me then, but became clear in retrospect, was that those Bravo Company men were near the Banana Trail in the vicinity where Lieutenant New had been successful with his old

Indian trick just a few weeks earlier. Perhaps they were on a recon patrol for today's ambush. The Company Commander called and instructed us to disengage and rush to help the 2nd Platoon. We moved maybe a few hundred or less meters when we came upon a very small foot bridge that 3rd platoon utilized to cross the stream/canal, then went southeast across the Banana Trail, staying to the right of the road but following it southeast to catch up with the remainder of Abu Company. We weren't able to search the area to the left or north side of the road where we engaged the enemy running away; and, as we moved along, found small groups of two or three men of Bravo Company in no particular military formation while seemingly scattered about the area with gaps between positions.

FATE UNKNOWN

Chapter 29

Rendering Assistance

As we moved further along, now closer to the road, I observed a man from B Company facing north in a kneeling firing position, with his rifle up to his right shoulder behind a large palm tree; he had short dark hair and I noticed his steel pot on the ground. He appeared to be about 35 years old and I believed he must have been at least a Platoon Sergeant; the strange thing was that he was alone with no other members of B Company close by, as if he was a one-man observation post or security. I thought this to be rather peculiar and asked, "You need any help?" He replied, "Hell yeah!" "Where are they?" I asked. The man said they were in the middle of the rice paddy—the 3rd dike which was 30 or 40 yards to his front. Meanwhile, since the platoon was held up, I grabbed two of my men and told him to fire some rounds to cover us. As he fired we ran across the road behind him and dropped down off the road, right into a rice paddy behind a dike located adjacent to his position. We proceeded to low crawl out into the paddy...I took a peek to locate the enemy and realized we weren't far enough out yet. I lowered my head and continued the crawl, when at that moment an AK-47 round zinged over my head. I crawled another

10 meters, took a peek, and determined our position was then good. I lowered my head...and just then, "Bam"...a round struck the paddy wall where my head had just been. Now I'm thinking: "This bastard is a pretty good shot and on my ass fast." We crawled to move back a short distance; I described to my men where the enemy was located in relation to us, and I told them that whatever they did, not to come up in the same spot twice. We all fired about three to four rounds apiece at the enemy; the enemy did not fire back. After this incident, we crawled a bit further and stopped. I told the man from B Company to take off while we covered him... He refused, saying that he had to stay put in his position. I couldn't believe what I was hearing; especially since my men and I were getting ourselves shot at so he could get out what I thought was a bad situation. After I calmed down, I advised him that we could no longer stay there and that we had to hook back up with our platoon, who by this time had departed. The three of us crawled back to where the dike met the road; I looked up and said, "Cover us." He fired at the NVA and we hauled ass up behind him, across the road, and then hit the ground below the road. No fire came our way—either B Company man had him pinned down, or the bastard was glad to see us leave.

RENDERING ASSISTANCE

We never saw the guy after that and no one of his possible rank was KIA that day, so I presume he made it. In thinking about this situation later on, I figured we had been really lucky that day because that location was like the middle of an hourglass where the road and village were only about 20 to 25 meters apart and the narrowest part. Had the enemy been there, they could have shot all of us in the back, including the man from B Company, and there wouldn't have been any place to go. As it turned out, the enemy had all been in the village, but perhaps not at that spot or at that time. Then again, perhaps they held their fire so as not to give their location away, especially if they had a machine gun at that location. If I had been the enemy, I would have had a machine gun there because it was the narrowest area of the village and the spot where the enemy was most vulnerable to be split in half and have their defenses breeched.

We hustled on down the road about 75 meters to catch up with the rest of the platoon who were stopped. We passed through them to the front, in order to catch up with Lieutenant New who was having a conversation in the middle of the road with Captain Albert B. Hiser, commander of B Company. I didn't recognize him myself, but clearly remember he was a new replacement to the Battalion and wore a non-camouflaged 173rd airborne patch. I'm not sure how long this conversation had been going on prior to my arrival, but as I got there I overheard Lieutenant New ask, "Where they at?" The Captain pointed to the area at the corner of the village of My Phu, located about 150 meters away, and stated, "Over there." Lieutenant New took a glance then said, "Let's go. We're moving out." Lieutenant New had previously received orders from the Abu Commander, Captain Hal Eaton, to conduct a coordinated attack with the 2nd Platoon, who he was traveling with. Their location was on the southeast side at about 5 o'clock—we were to attack from the west side from 9 o'clock. The 2nd Platoon was caught in the open when they assaulted the village, and they took heavy casualties. Captain Eaton's order was urgent and the order explained the first volume of fire we heard to our left rear shortly before spotting the surprise targets. The time was around 1300 hours.

Chapter 30

Assault

The 3rd Platoon moved out, dropping down into the rice paddy and I moved with the lead gun. Once the entire platoon had entered the rice paddies and the lead element was about half way across, machine gun and automatic weapons fire opened up on us. Immediately I set up my guns so they could cover the platoon that was now pinned down, with the trail gun pushing out to the left in order to cover the area of the village to our front and left flank while the lead gun covered the front and right. The platoon immediately took several casualties and they went right for my M-60 crews. With the gunner being hit, I grabbed the gun to continue placing some fire on the enemy so the platoon could advance. Meanwhile, rounds were whizzing overhead and hitting the area around me as the platoon was low crawling forward to close with the enemy. I jumped to my left over a rice paddy dike to get away from the enemy fire that was too intense where I was located. I could hear rounds going overhead then, but they weren't hitting around me any longer, while the lead element had reached a large dirt wall that blocked any visibility beyond. It had to take at least five minutes for them to reach the wall, but for some reason it only seemed like

30 seconds or so. I had Private First Class Tischman, Jr., who had been placing fire to the left into the village, displace and move forward to the wall with the platoon as we continued to provide cover. When Tischman's gun reached the wall, I applied some first aid dressings to a couple of men, told them to work their way back to the road where B Company was, and get to the other side of it, thinking that perhaps there was a medic there, as we didn't have one with us. I moved forward by low crawling with my M-16 for short distances, then reached back to get the M-60 which was hot, cumbersome, and a real bitch to move forward. I finally reached the dirt wall and took up a position on the right side. We were behind this area that was narrow—perhaps 25 meters wide—and from the paddy into the village, had this raised area to prevent water from coming into the village that consisted of a dirt mound in the shape of a wall or berm about two to three feet high. Once there I could easily see that we were in defilade (below ground level or dead space that can't be engaged with direct fire as we were shielded by the terrain) and the enemy fire after the initial bursts were ineffective. Unless I was past the wall to the right in the paddies, which was the best place to place effective fire on them to cover the platoons advance. If anyone was raised up in any way or to the rear of the platoon and not yet in defilade from the wall, their fire was effective. Every-

ASSAULT

one low crawled to move forward, as bullets were still flying overhead, to include rounds from our M-60s. No one had to be told to keep a low profile; it was similar to what every trainee went through in basic training during the infiltration course where machine guns fire overhead, except for there everyone knew that safety measures were in place while here none existed, not even with a prayer.

The enemy could easily have shot some officers with their RTOs on the road, however held their fire until they knew we were coming for them, most likely to conserve ammo, not disclose their position and more importantly, to hug our belt so that supporting fire was ineffective. How's that for discipline? Impressive as hell!

Lieutenant New gave the order: "Assault!" Everyone stood up, went over the small dirt wall, and began firing. Troopers started to fall all along the line. Private First Class Pedro Jaime, Jr., on the M-60, dropped the gun and was hit in the left side of the face. I grabbed the gun, jumped back behind the dirt wall, then reached up to grab Jamie by the ankles and pull him back down behind the wall. The fire was intense and we were unable to gain fire superiority; everyone realized this at about the same time, as they took cover back behind the dirt wall that afforded cover and concealment. The M-60 was shot up—the feed cover was all mangled up and unfixable, and now out of commission. I applied a first aid dressing to Jamie and his ammo bearer, Flucker, and gave them a morphine shot—we all carried ¼-grain morphine syringes with us in the field. Looking around, I observed several other wounded troopers.

During the assault, although only for a brief moment, I did get a glance at where they were; our position was only 40 to 50 feet from them. However, I still couldn't pin point their exact position since they were experts at camouflage, plus when you're in a hail storm of bullets, no one's ass is in a sight-seeing mode. The enemy was hugging us by the belt, a tactic employed by them which prevented us from using artillery and fast movers unless someone wanted to kill their own men—a smart, fast adaptation, even this early in the war.

Looking around I observed a tall palm tree about 40 feet high with another to the left, pretty much the only ones in the village and my immediate thought is snipers. I looked to my left towards Tischman on the other M-60 and said, "See that tree to the front. Put some rounds in the top of it." I turned back to observe and the whole damn platoon opened fire on it. Hollering for a cease-fire, I said, "Not everybody!" Then I designated a couple men to fire at the other palm tree. Nothing was in the trees, which was a big relief because we were sitting ducks if a sniper had been there.

ASSAULT

Lieutenant New was in conversation with a pilot who was flying overhead in an A-1E Skyraider, a single propeller aircraft that's terrific for close air support. I believe he was a Navy pilot. He flew around to survey the area and was telling Lieutenant New that he was aware of our location. Lieutenant New told the pilot that the enemy was about 20 meters immediately to our front. Next, the pilot made a run from south to north, threading a needle between us and the 2nd Platoon that also was to our right front of the village, to drop a bomb immediately to our front. All this was observable from the cover behind the wall and shrapnel wasn't a concern. My first thoughts were that this plane was pretty damn slow as it seemed to take a long time to make his run, then and after dropping a small bomb, perhaps a hundred- pounder, he started an immediate climb. The bomb landed just to our front, exploded with a very loud noise, and the earth shook. It felt good. I thought this would help big time, because it seemed he had dropped it right on them. He made a couple more runs and dropped some bombs further north in the village…maybe he had observed some better targets. Then he changed direction to make a run or two from north to south. After making several bomb runs, he made some runs firing his 20mm cannon; after which, he stated he was running low on fuel and had to leave. Lieutenant New thanked him and he wished us luck. Time on station was at least an hour or perhaps longer. One weird thing about it was that as slow as he appeared to be flying, I never heard the enemy fire on him nor saw any tracer rounds going in his direction. Either they didn't want to disclose their location or were hugging the ground talking to Budda.

Lieutenant New said, "Get ready to assault!" All the men took up an assault position, except for the wounded, and on his command to assault, we went over the wall, stood, and began firing. The incoming fire was just as intense as it was in the first assault and every one jumped back to seek protection as the unit suffered more casualties. To continue was sure death, even with the short distance needed to take the objective. Even after the Skyraider bombing and strafing, we still couldn't obtain fire superiority. The bastards were like cockroaches…hard to kill. If something didn't drop in their damn back pockets, they weren't going to be KIA or run off. We were all fighting for our lives like cornered rats, but their resilience and marksmanship made an impression on me. We had taken several more wounded and men went about giving first aid to them. My other gunner, Tischman, was wounded in the left arm; the enemy had been targeting the guns as their first priority. Now both were inoperable. These assholes were so well trained—they made the machine guns their first target and were aiming for the guns, with the

ASSAULT

rounds ricocheting off the guns and then hitting the gunner—essentially killing two birds with one stone. We redistributed what ammo we had left; Lieutenant New called for more ammo, M-60 gun replacements and morphine resupply.

As I looked around, I saw the wounded lying about with weapons on the ground, waiting for a chopper to get out of there as if the fight for them had concluded. For me the situation was looking pretty damn dire—most of the platoon was shot the hell up, we're low on ammo and because of the terrain, we were all forced into a small pocket of an area that no more than a squad should occupy, let alone a platoon. One fart would get everyone! An enemy assault...or if the NVA decided to start lobbing grenades our way...now that wasn't a pretty visual at all. I told the wounded to get their weapons and that if the enemy came over the wall, to be prepared to start shooting. They complied by picking up their M-16s and sitting up with their backs to the dirt wall. We were standing our ground and weren't backing down. If you were to look at the history of warfare, the force that holds on the longest is generally the victor, and sooner or later one of the combatants will fold. Even a cornered rat is looking for an escape.

FATE UNKNOWN

Chapter 31

Friendly Fire

Sometime later, a chopper lands about 150 meters to our rear, just on the other side of the road coming in from the south, to land facing north. And with the road raised above the paddies, I can see only the upper half of the chopper; I'm unable to really tell what they're doing, as the door on the right side was closed. I figured it was picking up some of the wounded, although this was not a medevac chopper. We were hoping he was bringing in some ammo. I observed the copilot on the right side turn his head to look in our direction, staring, as the chopper was probably being off loaded and loaded. Then it began increasing power for a takeoff, getting louder as it revved up. The chopper, instead of taking off north or turning left to the west, rose up about 20 feet or so, makes a complete 90 degree turn to the right to face east and our direction. He starts taking off and I can see his nose dip as he crosses the road; then at that instant he fires one of his 2.5-inch rockets, which lands about 30 yards to our rear. I see the friendly fire and the rocket explode—everything seems to be in slow motion to me. I observe all this black rice paddy mud go up in the air in the shape of an ice cream cone. Everything stayed in slow motion until the chopper flies over us and its noise brings me back to full speed. The mud was plopping down, splattering about, and its sounding like a heavy rain of mud. Oh man, what the hell is this guy thinking, I ask myself. Could this be the same crew that about a week ago had shot at us with their M-60's while we were in the rice paddies? I'm unsure if he was attempting to help us out or if once the enemy saw he was going to come their way, started firing at them. I never heard any rounds fired, but with the noise of the chopper plus the explosion, I may not have heard it. Perhaps he was asked to give us some support. I was able to quickly pass this off as no big deal since there had been no cries for medic or help after the incident had occurred. Besides, the remaining situation was of a much greater concern.

Chapter 32

Pucker Factor

Private First Class Tom Joyce and I were working on the guns, attempting to cannibalize the two guns into one working gun by switching out feed covers and other parts. My other seven men were all wounded in action; we were what remained of the weapons squad. While this is going on, First Sergeant Robert A. Press and Sergeant Johnnie K. Rogers had run, dodged, and low crawled their way to join us, bringing with them some much needed morphine and M-16 ammo. Johnnie K. (the only thing anyone ever called him) was passing out morphine and ammo. 1st Sergeant Press took up a position next to Lieutenant New on the right and I remained next to him on the left.

First Sergeant Press asked, "Lieutenant, what do you have?" With that, Lieutenant New began explaining the situation and how we were assaulting the village. As he did so, First Sergeant Press glanced to his left to survey the situation; as his head turned, I also looked left. As we were shoulder to shoulder, we observed the wounded strewn about in a small confined area—some with their shirts off so dressings could be applied, bandages on heads, arms, and legs. It seemed like more were wounded then were not. I noticed a look of fear on the men's faces...it had not been there prior to this moment. I'm not sure if it was the chopper incident that had given them a reality check that the situation wasn't over yet, but the look of fear became more apparent than before. They say fear is contagious, and perhaps there's some truth to that...all I know was that for the first time since I had been in Vietnam, an intense fear with the threat of death and helplessness, had grabbed hold of my ass. Everyone's pucker factor was such that someone couldn't get a stick pin up their ass and my asshole felt like a tourniquet was on it. Scared for the first time ever in the Nam, and while unscathed troopers were in short supply, fear was there in abundance.

> *"Courage is resistance to fear, mastery of fear—not absence of fear."*
> ~Mark Twain AKA Samuel Clemens, author, humorist & wit

Lieutenant New said, "Get ready to assault!" I said, "No-wait!" Lieutenant New said, "God damn it, Sergeant Mitchell...get your ass..." At that point, I interrupted saying, "Wait until we get the gun ready." He's thinking I'm refusing and I'm thinking of the gun. I know he can't read my mind and it's the first time I ever knew him to get excited; his pucker factor was up also from knowing the previous results. By this point of the battle, we had been locked up all day and pinned down for over 5 hours. Anyone without fear wasn't human, as death was no further than a moment away. First Sergeant Press calmly replied, "He's right, let him get the gun ready." For what seemed an eternity, my mind was racing with thoughts of stay, safety, assault, and death, but in reality was probably only a minute or so. I had just made up my mind I was going with my men when Tom Joyce said, "The gun's ready." No sooner had I told Lieutenant New, he immediately gave the order to assault. Every man who was not wounded went over the top of the wall again...into the same intense enemy fire as before...as the NVA continued to have fire superiority with automatic weapons. This online assault tactic wasn't working like it did in training—especially since the enemy had cover and concealment, plus an advantage of defense over us. At the exact same moment, everyone seemed to jump back behind the wall for protection. We took a few more wounded, with the platoon now having about 18 WIA or about 50 percent of the platoon at least shot up, and it was pure luck none were KIA. A short time later Lieutenant New said, "Get ready to assault." I heard First Sergeant Press say, "Lieutenant, I think you should hold what you have." Lieutenant New replied, "OK" and my thoughts were:

"Whew—that's a relief." I believe Lieutenant New would have continued if he had been the last man standing with one round left. However, everyone was glad to hear the bell in this fight. First Sergeant Press was one of the coolest men under fire that I had ever observed! That Korea War combat experience served him well and he set an example for all of us to emulate.

Paratroopers are always dealing with fear on jumps they make, and the one that says he doesn't is a fool, liar or full of it. Their ability to control that fear is what separates them from the average or normal soldier. This fear fluctuates in strength; no one really knows what the influences are that comprise it and there is no copyright or patent for the level of fear one encounters or how to deal with it. The quiet ones become talkative, the boisterous become passive, and the majority of them seem to be so relaxed they appear to be sleeping…they're really awake, however, and processing the fear to control it any time death or injury is a possible outcome. Once, while I was in the 506th awaiting for transportation to go make a jump, we had a trooper who we thought was choking. He was transported to the aid station/hospital, and upon our return after the jump, we learned he had died from a heart attack. The trooper was about 20 years old and was from Baltimore. He had made several jumps prior and also ran five miles or so a day. Whether real or perceived,

PUCKER FACTOR

fear is a dominant emotion, particularly in combat, that must be dealt with. Being a paratrooper with experience, youth, and training was extremely helpful in confronting this demon; however, there was no foolproof recipe and the difference between a coward and a hero can be measured in a single thought. There is always a trooper by the name of "Buster Bad Ass" who'll never admit to fear—but in combat and on the battlefield the question really isn't if you'll feel fear, but when. The greatest battle fought in combat and on the battlefield is fear within one's own mind.

"Courage is fear holding on a minute longer."
~ General George S. Patton, Jr.

It's difficult to say what the thought process was for each trooper prior to that assault, but I doubt it was discipline and the order given to make that assault. I believe we did it for each other and it was an all or nothing situation, or perhaps the only way out of the situation. There is a special bond that develops from teamwork in combat—simulated training can never totally duplicate that. Teamwork and that special bond overcomes daily physical adversity from bugs, heat, or sleep deprivation—to the mentally challenging thought that the next step or breath could be the last due to a mine, booby trap or a bullet with your name on it. Teamwork acquired by pulling tasks such as OP/LP together away from the main element or being in a two-man foxhole, develops through shared sacrifice. A trooper doesn't smoke at night or slack off when the going gets tough, which would expose their brothers in arms to danger. Through a shared strenuous barrage of hardships, men in combat develop a relationship and support system that they will do anything for each other, including facing death and giving up life for each other. I believe this is why they all met that challenge and made that assault. For those that survive the experience of combat, it becomes a rite of passage that never will be forgotten by those that served together. For those that didn't survive, we admire them for their great courage and we wish them eternal peace. Either way, brothers in arms are bonded together in a special way.

Chapter 33

Tactical Withdrawal

We continued to hold our position as darkness was approaching. By this time we must have been engaged or locked up with the enemy for seven or eight hours. I was zoned in to the moment...living for now...and I lost all perception of time. There is no conceptuality of the future, only the moment at hand. Additionally I don't ever recall taking a drink or being thirsty, despite temperatures well over 100 degrees all day. No one ate or even thought of food. Every second was consumed with combat...whether attacking or survival. As nightfall occurred we conducted a tactical withdrawal, allowing the wounded to move first while the rest of us remained in position to provide cover. This took some time to get all the wounded and their equipment moved. We were wondering what the enemy was doing and if there would be a counter attack. This was accomplished very smoothly, as if rehearsed. What we didn't know at the time was that the NVA were licking their wounds, so to speak, and doing the same thing. Darkness was like the bell ringing in a boxing match with combatants going to their respective corners for repairs and recuperation. We moved to a position to the south, only about 150 meters from our all day assault location.

FATE UNKNOWN

Chapter 34

The Grim Reaper

The battle on the East side of My Phu has been taken from the eye witness accounts of those that fought on that side and/or participated in the battle of My Phu. It's been a hard task to compile actual facts from combat troopers there that day on the East side, or to have them freely express their experiences. Many have since suffered from post-traumatic stress disorder (PTSD), especially the leaders who additionally must accept or account for their decisions that day along with the many deaths incurred by those decisions. Those leaders also have more awareness and knowledge of situational things taking place because of their knowledge and experience. In combat we must play the hand we have been dealt and deal with the situation at hand as idealism only happens in training.

On the other side of My Phu, the following took place sometime around 1130 hours. My platoon, the 3rd, led by Lieutenant New, broke off from the remainder of Abu Company and moved on an axis to the North and Northwest to provide flank security for the company and also Bravo Company. In the meantime, the remainder of Abu, the 1st and 2nd Platoons, and the command group, consisting of Captain Hal Eaton along with his

FATE UNKNOWN

RTOs, Vietnamese Interpreter, Forward Observer(FO), Senior Medic and others, stopped short of My Phu about 150 meters in a wood line and small hamlet and chowed down on some c-rations.

Lieutenant New received a radio transmission from Captain Eaton that a large enemy force had been sighted moving toward our Battalion base camp and artillery support unit, which was about three miles away as the crow flies. He was ordered to move to that location without delay. Bravo Company and the remainder of Abu also moved out to close in on the lightly defended Base Camp/FSB or find the enemy and trap them between two units with the lightly defended Base Camp acting as a blocking force.

When Abu Company moved out, they formed up into an assault line, which is normally used to attack an objective. It's unknown the exact reason this formation was chosen, as it wasn't a standard operating procedure to cross rice paddies—perhaps it was to move faster or they knew they were crossing a known danger area with the open rice paddies and wanted to cross it already deployed. Did they observe enemy activity prior or during chow time? When they moved out, the 1st Platoon was on the right flank and the 2nd Platoon was on the left flank with Captain Eaton and his command group centered between the two elements and slightly to the rear in close proximity. Bravo Company ing and constantly looking for a hidden enemy, this was like offering candy to a kid. We don't know if this was their overall plan or if they were dispersed by the gas and had set up hastily prepared ambushes and adapted to the situations that developed, as they were that well trained to execute this scenario.

1st and 2nd Platoon's Abu's continued their assault line formation, maintaining their intervals between men and attempting to keep the line dressed to the left and right, so not to shoot each other up. They crossed the last rice paddy dike which could provide cover and concealment and continued to the village of My Phu. In the meantime, the enemy was holding their fire and remaining in their camouflaged positions, allowing them to close in, a tactic called hugging the belt. By allowing them to close, they would make artillery and air power ineffective unless bringing friendly forces under fire and killing them. They were also observing, as trained to do, and picking out targets of opportunity with the M-60 machine guns being first priority, then RTOs, Officers and leaders etc. One of the problems with this hastily formed assault line was that each platoon deployed their M-60 Guns near the flanks to get the most fire to cover their entire platoons front from the guns; this put the left flank gun of the 1st Platoon in the center, the right flank gun of the 2nd Platoon in the center, and the Command Group in the center, making it one rich target area of opportunity to concentrate their fire.

On command, that's exactly what they did. All of a sudden when they were about 50 meters away, the enemy opened fire with all they had. We heard a loud volume of fire erupt around 1230 hours to our left rear or southeast, as we were proceeding to our Battalion Base Camp as ordered. Considering the direction, I believed it was Bravo Company and toward their AO. The volume of fire seemed only to last about two or three minutes—it abruptly stopped pretty much all at once, just as it had started. Lieutenant New immediately was on the horn (radio) to Captain Eaton, who told him they had walked into an ambush at My Phu and we were to immediately come help them by attacking My Phu from the West. Shortly after, while paralleling a stream/canal, we observed another ambush pulled on the lead element of Bravo Company and then engaged a large group of enemy NVA in the open making their escape. The NVA was executing an area ambush by conducting multiple ambushes to cut off avenues of escape and for reinforcements. I also believe the NVA thought they were engaging a Company size unit of ours, which typically operated in the area, and our platoon surprised them as they swept through the kill zone. Or maybe they had observed our presence beforehand. Upon realizing it, they immediately attempted to escape to My Phu and rejoin their other elements, leaving the kill zone, weapons, and equipment. The NVA ran through the kill zone without firing and made a hasty retreat having been made aware of our presence.

Others Abu's reflections from the My Phu battle follow:

Exhausted

SP/4 Joseph Czarnecki, M-60 Machine Gunner of 1st Platoon. Fought at the Battle of My Phu on 4 March 1966. Courtesy of SP/4 Czarnecki.

Specialist Fourth Class Joseph Czarnecki remembers: As an M-60 machine gunner with the 1st Platoon, I was carrying the M-60; as we came closer to My Phu, the shit hit the fan, with bullets flying everywhere. I was in line with the rest of the platoon and had to take cover in a ditch. I quickly returned fire and shortly after Captain Eaton gave the command to charge. As we rose up to assault, everybody around me was getting hit; the fire was so intense we had to get back down in the ditch. Staff Sergeant Bobby R. Salt, who was next to me, was hit in the left leg and he somehow made it to the rear for evacuation that night. I never saw him again. There was a small Spanish soldier, whose name I can't recall, that took a hit in the chest; I thought he was a goner when the medics later took him away. A couple months later he came marching back to the platoon like a proud peacock.

I was so happy he lived. During the charge, Captain Eaton, along with many men, was WIA. Many also were KIA, to include my very good friend from our weapons squad, Private First Class Phillip H. Clark.

Bombs were dropped on the enemy and it was so close that the ground shook and some shrapnel hit inside the ditch we had luckily landed in that gave us some cover. My ears were ringing from the bombs, they were so close. After it got dark, a few guys and I went to retrieve Clark and carried him to the rear where the medics were treating the WIA. I was then told to go back further to the rear to get some sleep. I was exhausted. I saw some guys lying down with ponchos on top of them; I joined them and pulled my poncho over me and went to sleep. When morning came and I awoke, I saw they were still there. I went over to wake them up, only to find they had all been KIAs from the day before.

God watched over me that whole year while in Vietnam, and he still does. I left the Army for four or five years, but for some reason I missed the excitement and rejoined on 11 January 1971, remaining until April of 1988. After leaving the military, I began a second career with the Department Of Corrections for the State of Florida. I had a good career in the Army and I'm proud of my accomplishments. I was extremely lucky to never have been wounded, but no one in combat can escape the mental scars and wounds that remain invisible to the casual observer. It was the worst year of my life!

Who Goes There?

PFC Gerald C. "Horny" Hornbeck with a puppy he named "VC" that wandered off after about a month. Courtesy of Horny Hornbeck.

As told to me by Private first Class Gerald C. "Horny" Hornbeck, a M-60 machine gunner with 1st Platoon: I was drafted into the Army Nov. 4, 1964 and was to serve two years; however, while in AIT, I extended eleven months for JFK Warfare School (Special Forces or SF) training. After MOI (Method of Instruction) training and while waiting for orders to Fort Sam Houston, I was visiting with a SF officer who informed me that if I wanted combat time while in SF I would have to reenlist for six years after my two years and eleven months. I left SF and was reassigned to the 101st Airborne Division at Fort Campbell, Kentucky. There I received orders to report to C Company, 2/501st. Once there I submitted paper work to volunteer for the 1st Brigade in South Viet Nam, and on the 25th of November 1965 I received my orders.

I arrived at Abu Company 1/327th Airborne Infantry at Phan Rang, South Viet Nam on 23 December 1965. Most of Abu Company was deployed in an area known as Bien Hoa and Bien Cat. Four other replacements and I reported to First Sergeant Finley who briefed us and asked if we would like to volunteer for the 1st Platoon's weapons squad. I liked firing the M-60 machine gun during training in AIT, so I volunteered—so did two other replacements. I know that you're not supposed to volunteer for anything in the military, but I was afraid I might be assigned to something I did not want or like.

When Abu Company arrived back to Phan Rang, we were introduced to 1st Platoon Sergeant Robert Press and Staff Sergeant Noe Quezada, the 1st Platoon weapon's squad leader. From the beginning I liked Platoon Sergeant Press and Sergeant Q, as we called him; over time I came to respect them as good men and also as soldiers. Sergeant Q assigned me to Private First Class Phillip Henry Clark's gun crew as an assistant gunner;

the other replacements were to be ammo bearers. I liked Clark too; he was quiet and very mature for his age of 19, and was also a drafty. Clark introduced me to the other guys that were originals and came over on the boat, Penny Bunn, David Haskell, Joseph Czarnecki, Jerry R Smith, Sergeant Larry Trowbridge and others.

Clark went on R&R on the 3rd of February 1966 and I took over the gunner responsibilities. When Clark returned, we shared the gunner responsibilities.

On the 4th of March, when elements of Abu Company formed up on line to assault the village of My Phu, I was the gunner and Clark the assistant gunner. We were in the center of the assault formation, and were about 50 yards from the village when the enemy opened up on us. Due to the fact that we were just to the left of the Company Commander (Captain Hal Eaton), his RTOs and his Vietnamese Interpreter, plus there was another M-60 crew on the right side of him, this fact made us all prime targets for the enemy. We took lots of causalities due to being in the open with no cover or concealment, not even tall grass. I was firing the gun from the hip as Clark and I moved to our left trying to get to high ground and cover. The volume of incoming fire was so great that we hit the ground and I began firing from the prone; when we went down, Clark was out of position because I stepped in front of him, which put him on the wrong side to feed the gun. I was firing the gun as fast as it would fire while incoming rounds were kicking up dirt all around us and ricocheting off of the gun. We gained fire superiority over the NVA position that I was firing on, but we were still receiving incoming fire. Clark directed me to fire on a position to our right front; I shifted fire to that position and gained superiority, but as we did, the first position came alive again. I shifted back and as I did, Clark told me to slow up because we were running low on ammo. Clark told me he was going to try and locate some ammo, as our ammo bearers had been close to us when the enemy opened fire. Clark crawled to the rear of me as a great volume of incoming began striking all around us. Clark hollered, "Hornbeck, I'm hit!" As I looked back, Clark had already realized his wound was just a graze and he went on—seconds later I heard Clark call one time for a medic.

I was firing the gun in short bursts of two and three rounds at this time; incoming rounds were going over my head and striking the gun, plus kicking up dirt all around me. Soon after I was out of ammo and the gun was inoperative. I was struck twice by incoming automatic weapons fire—once in the elbow, a through and through wound that didn't strike bone, and once in the upper chest that shattered the upper portion of my sternum. I had rolled over on my back, and called for a medic one time, but then realized there were so many other troopers calling for help.

    I must have been in a small depression in the ground or something; every time I moved, the NVA fired on me, and the rounds were barely going over me with some kicking up dirt all around my head, when I undid my pistol belt and slid out of my web gear. Every time my heart beat, blood would squirt about six to eight inches high, so I took a first aid bandage and held it on the wound. Eventually it dried and sealed it as I never tied it off. I had my sleeves rolled up on my fatigue shirt and it acted as a tourniquet when I raised my arm to stop the bleeding of my wounded elbow…I never did bandage it.

    I laid there under incoming fire, during the hottest part of the day, once even trying to take a drink from my canteen. The enemy must have seen me move because they fired on me and a round hit my canteen, spilling water all over me and knocking the canteen out of my hand. About 2100 hours I heard someone crawling near me. I had my .45 caliber pistol with a round chambered and asked, "Who goes there?" Sergeant Q said, "Shut up Hornbeck, you'll get us all killed!" They told me I was the last one to be located that night. Sergeant Q asked if I thought I could walk, I said I would try, but after being helped up I collapsed to the ground due to the loss of so much blood. A black trooper picked me up and ran with me all the way to where the medevac Chinook chopper was; to this day I'm unaware of his name. I was laid on a litter and informed by Sergeant Larry Trowbridge that Clark was KIA; I was already certain of this. I also was informed I was to be the last one to be medevac that night because the Chinook was completely full.

I was evacuated to the 8th Field Hospital in Nha Trang and by the 6th of March I was up walking, eating solid food, and drinking liquids. General Westmoreland came to see his troopers and awarded purple hearts in our ward, which was full of "Above the Rest" troopers. On the 8th of March I was flown back to the States and hospitalized at Madigan Army Hospital, Fort Lewis, Washington. There I was reunited with my wife, but due to a hospital rule on children, not my daughter. My wife Jo Ann and daughter were staying with her parents in Parkland, Washington while I was overseas.

After my recovery and a 15-day convalescent leave, I received orders to the 82nd Airborne Division at Fort Bragg, North Carolina and was assigned to A Company, $1/325^{th}$ Airborne Infantry. I was reunited there with my old friends David W. Haskell, Jr., Tony Hernandez, and Jim Radley from Vietnam. I completed my enlistment on 3 November 1967.

After leaving the service I worked in construction trades. In 1972 my baby sister and her husband passed on, leaving behind three small children; Guy age six, Dale age five and Charla Dawn age three. My wife Jo

Ann and I agreed to go into court and obtain custody in order to raise our niece and nephews. Jo Ann was pregnant with our youngest daughter Brandi at this same time. The court case was over about the same time as our child Brandi was born. Our family grew from two to six in a very short time.

I went from working in construction trades to owning a few small companies in construction and during the Savings and Loan crisis of the late 1970s and early 1980s we had to downsize as I went broke. We moved to Phoenix, Arizona for the warm weather where I worked as Project Manager/Job superintendent for a general contractor and a Boat Captain before retiring.

What About Me?

By Roger "Chief" Wathogoma

Roger "Chief" Wathogoma.
Courtesy of Chief Wathogoma.

During the morning, around ten o'clock, we were air lifted by helicopters into a valley and dropped off in a rice field. I was with the machine gun squad, 2nd Platoon of Abu Company, 1st Battalion Airborne, 327th Infantry, 1st Brigade (Separate) 101st Airborne Division, as we combed from village to village, I don't remember how many. We made light contact with the enemy during the morning up until noon time.

We incurred a few wounded and they were flown out by choppers and we continued our mission... searching for the enemy.

At the next village we stopped to rest and eat. It must have been around noon when Diego Mercado (machine gunner), Arnell Keys (ammo bearer), and I (assistant gunner) set the M-60 machine gun in position and began talking about what we wanted to do when we got back to the world. Our squad leader, Sergeant Reynolds (Marty) Martinez, came by to ensure that the machine gun was properly placed and ready to function.

After our rest break, our platoon formed up in an assault line formation with troopers well spread out abreast as we began slowly moving forward to search the last village before going back to our battalion CP, walking across a large, flat, dry rice paddy, then we crossed a dike and about half way from the village, which was about a hundred yards wide, all hell broke loose from inside the village with gunfire from the enemy. It sounded as through hundreds of enemy occupied the village. My initial thought traveled back to basic training when I was on the rifle range qualifying with my rifle...hearing the horrendous, large volume of numerous rifles firing simultaneously. I remember spinning around and falling down to the ground, not realizing I was hit in both legs. As I lay there, I couldn't move all I could hear was gunfire and bullets flying inches above my head. It sounded like thousands of angry bumble bees. The enemy had us pinned down; out in an open rice paddy...we had no cover to seek and nowhere to go...we had to just lie there. I tried to move my left leg, but all I felt was a stinging feeling and then numbness.

As I looked at my pants leg, all I saw was bright red blood, and as the battle continued I heard Arnell Keys behind me crying and moaning, I figured he was shot. He cried for a while longer and then he stopped. Arnell must have died right then. Diego Mercado who was to the right of me was not hit. He kept hollering to me, asking if I was alright. I told him I was hit, but I'm ok. We kept hollering to one another, I could hear his machine gun firing; he was firing rapidly, and then stopped. I hollered to him, but he didn't answer me. I knew then that Mercado was gravely hit and dead.

Sergeant Martinez was also hit, but I didn't know that right then. Every time someone rose up to run or moved slightly, they were shot. The enemy was very close to us, about fifty yards, but they were so well hidden that I couldn't see them. We lay out in that open rice paddy as enemy snipers kept picking off anyone who moved, ever so slightly.

A Skyraider airplane was called in and man, did he pound that village. As the plane swooped down to make his runs on the village it zoomed by at about tree-top level. The plane made several runs, right to left then left to right dropping large bombs that when they exploded they shook the hard, dry ground and I saw huge fire-balls, large plumes of dark black and grey smoke rise up. I guess the enemy hid when the bombs came down on them. When the plane pulled up the enemy came out of their holes and continued firing at us. The plane made some runs back and forth, directly over me with 20mm cannon fire, which was the weirdest sound that I've ever heard, a long and loud steady ripping sound. The plane was so close to the ground I could read the writing and see the riveting on the bottom. Then the village began to burn and smoke filled it.

No sooner had the Skyraider departed, the enemy continued firing at us. I laid there in the sweltering heat not able to move, extremely thirsty. I was afraid to move to reach at my canteen for water. I knew that if I moved, I'd be shot.

As I laid there, I couldn't see any movement, until suddenly, our CO, Captain Hal Eaton, with his radio men came running next to me, hollering, "Come on… Let's go get them bastards!" As I saw them running by, the shooting continued, escalating loudly and intensively. I never found out what happened to them. (Author's note: Captain Eaton was WIA while shot in the neck and his Vietnamese interpreter was KIA) The shooting continued off and on for about an hour or two, then it got quiet; it felt weird. My rifle fell about two arm's length in front of me. I thought that maybe they might charge us, so I slowly reached out for my weapon. I heard one shot and saw dirt kick up right in front of my face, so I pulled back my arm quickly. I had to play dead. It sounded to me like every time someone made a sound, a sniper shot him. I guess also that a sniper shot anyone that moved.

While lying out in the hot sun, large black flies kept landing on me crawling over my face and hands, I wanted so badly to swat them away but I was terrified to move. I willed my aching bleeding body into a sort of trance, not moving, except only to breathe slowly and shallow. I knew if I'd moved the sniper would be on me again. I was getting weaker from all the bleeding, then I passed out for a couple hours until dark.

When I woke up I heard faint, undistinguishable voices and movement and I immediately thought it was the enemy searching through us; I was really relieved to learn it was our guys. They walked over to check on me and told me there's a small perimeter a little ways behind, but first I checked on Keys, he was dead, and then Mercado, he also was dead. I stumbled and crawled my way to the perimeter as my legs were aching and I saw about ten or fifteen guys, almost all were wounded.

Later, we moved back further from the village of My Phu to where we had stopped for a rest break. All the wounded, including me, were gathered together and were being treated by the medics. I saw some dead Abu troopers lying on the ground side by side, covered in ponchos, I don't know how many. They put me down next to them. Although I was in pain, all I could do was think of them, their families and mine. I passed out again and don't really know for how long.

When I woke up, I saw all the dead—there were a lot of them. The wounded were all gone; however, three medics were sitting and talking. I asked, "Where is everybody?" They said that they were all choppered out. I asked, "What about me?" They asked, "What's wrong with you?" I said, "I'm shot in both legs" and they quickly started checking me out; and then they were on the radio telling someone that they have another casualty. They carried me further back where the chopper would land to pick me up.

Since that day I still pray that all the KIA are with God. They are my friends, my heroes forever. "Abu!" Finally about two or three o'clock in the morning I was airlifted from the battlefield to Nha Trang Hospital. What an experience it was to wake up in a clean, cool hospital, while moments earlier I was in a hot, filthy battlefield lying with the dead!

I quite often think back about the My Phu battle that afternoon. It's like watching a movie, but it is real, very fierce, intense and scary. God bless all my Abu Brothers that were there to protect me, I pray and thank God for watching and protecting me every day.

~Roger "Chief" Wathogoma
Abu Forever! Above the Rest!

* * *

The Grim Reaper ended up taking 21 "Above the Rest" paratroopers on 4 March 1966; in the battle known as My Phu, as they forever became sky soldiers. They traveled from the silver wings of a paratrooper to be carried aloft on the wings of Angels along with a Vietnamese Interpreter for a total of 22. The following gave all:

FATE UNKNOWN

Abu Company (13)

Harry M. Godwin, 1st Lieutenant, Age 26, El Dorado, Arkansas

Note: (1) Norman J. Buell, Specialist Fourth Class, Age 25, Honolulu, Hawaii

Reuben L. Garnett, Jr., Specialist Fourth Class, Age 23, Steelton, Pennsylvania

Diego Mercado, Specialist Fourth Class, Age 26, New York, New York

James R. Scott, Specialist Fourth Class, Age 19, Fort Lauderdale, Florida

Phillip H. Clark, Private First Class, Age 20, Wisconsin Rapids, Wisconsin

Note: (2) James S. Cocchiara, Private First Class, Age 20, Springfield, Massachusetts

Richard P. Corson, Private First Class, Age 22, Buffalo, New York

Stanley T, Demboski, Private First Class, Age 20, Jersey City, New Jersey

Harvey W. Jones, Private First Class, Age 19, Fort Worth, Texas

Arnell Keyes, Private First class, Age 21, New York, New York

Paul G. Parsons, Private First Class, Age 20, Van Wert, Ohio

Charles D. Wadsworth, Private First class, Age 19, Alvy, West Virginia

> Author's notes: (1) Special Fourth Class Norman J. Buell was a medic attached to Abu Company whose parent unit was D Company, 326th Medical Battalion, 1st Brigade (S), 101st Airborne Division
>
> (2) Private First Class James S. Cocchiara was part of a Forward Observer Team attached to Abu Company whose parent unit was A Battery, 2nd Battalion, 320th Artillery, 1st Brigade (S), 101st Airborne Division

Bravo Company (7)

Woodrow W. Ham, JR, Staff Sergeant, Age 26, Kinston, North Carolina

James E. Bush, Specialist Fourth Class, Age 20, Lebanon, Tennessee

James H. Edge, Specialist Fourth Class, Age 36, Greensboro, North Carolina

John M. Harden, Specialist Fourth Class, Age 21, Island Lake, Illinois

Roscoe L. Vick, Specialist Fourth Class, Age 23, Rocky Mount, North Carolina

Michael R. Young, Specialist Fourth Class, Age 23, Newport Beach, California

Jack W. Lindsey, Private First Class, Age 23, Houston, Texas

Charlie Company (1)

Alberto A. Lucero, Specialist Fourth Class, Age 25, Salida, Colorado

"Only the dead have seen the end of war."

~ Plato

FATE UNKNOWN

Chapter 35

Recovering Our KIA

After completing our tactical withdrawal and establishing a small perimeter, a squad leader meeting took place and Lieutenant New asked for a volunteer to go recover our KIA. Although I would never leave a man out on the battlefield, throughout the battle I had never given any thought about KIAs. This was a different situation, I thought to myself—one duty I would have to be ordered to do, not volunteering for. It's a long standing axiom in the Army to never volunteer for anything. Everyone else present was silent and likely having similar thoughts. Lieutenant New broke the silence when he said, "Get a couple men from each squad and Sergeant Mitchell, you take it."

The most dangerous period of a rocket launch is when it is leaving and re-entering the earth's atmosphere...the angle must be precise or it'll burn up and disintegrate. So too is the departure and re-entry to friendly lines or a perimeter. I coordinated with the adjacent positions before leaving, and used the skyline to identify a tree and other objects to allow us to return to the exact position. We would be properly challenged each time, and there's nothing worse than getting lit up by friendly fire. After a day like this one, the term "trigger happy" could be an understatement; men are totally spent and fully aware that the night could be as tough as the day.

After gathering the men, we moved out in a single file toward the 2nd Platoon area, which had been on the east side of the village of My Phu. The moon had come out and some figures could be observed on the skyline, about 150 meters to our right front. We were halfway there when automatic weapons fire erupted, breaking the silence of the night; we immediately hit the ground. After a short time we continued, but approached cautiously. On our arrival there, I met First Sergeant Press, who seemed to be everywhere this day, and Staff Sergeant Travis F. Martin.

1SG Robert A. Press. He always found a calm center in raging combat to lead Abu's. Courtesy of Press Family.

RECOVERING OUR KIA

I asked them what all the firing was about and they told me they had just killed four NVA that had approached them while at sling arms, apparently thinking it was their men stripping some bodies. My thoughts were that these are some bold bastards, but the battlefield belonged to us assholes. First Sergeant Press and Staff Sergeant Martin had already found a couple of men and had them wrapped in ponchos.

The 1st and 2nd Platoons hadn't fared as well as we did: after leaving the cover and concealment of the last rice paddy wall, they had to cross open rice paddies. They sustained 13 KIA, 21 WIA, plus the company Vietnamese interpreter was also KIA, but not all in the initial assault. The battle raged on for hours and gunfire drowned out any fluttering of angel wings lifting skyward. The wounded lay out there for at least eight hours, and if the NVA detected any movement at all, they shot them in the head. They had begun their assault before we were in a supporting position and we couldn't get there in time.

Staff Sergeant Martin reached down and removed the M-16 from one KIA, who was in a prone position, placed it on safety, and then a couple of my men laid out a poncho to place him on. He was rolled over on his back onto the poncho, while his arms remained up in the air, frozen in position, as if he was still holding and sighting down his rifle—rigor mortis had set in.

These brave men would be forever etched in my mind, leaving an imprint unable to ever be erased.

We made several trips returning the KIAs to the perimeter; while stopping short of the perimeter, I had the men get down and I went forward to be challenged and coordinated with our defensive line. I then returned to guide my men in. We used the same entry and exit point throughout the night—not something I would normally do—but the paddies were open without cover and I couldn't take the chance of getting fired up by our own men, or have a man set off a claymore mine on us. I was first introduced to the claymore mine during the Cuban missile crisis. It was designed after the Korean War for defense against human wave assaults. Both the 101st airborne and the 82nd Airborne were the first in the Army to receive all the newest or latest equipment. After the Cuban missile crisis, claymores were tucked away again until we deployed to Vietnam, and then brought out of hiding for good. We carried as a minimum one for every two men; they were set out every night as a defensive measure and used to cover a kill zone for an ambush. They are packed with steel ball bearings and, although the exact number of bearings in them has always been classified, suffice to say they were enough to stop a human wave assault. The ball bearings are propelled by plastic explosives which are set off by an electrical charge of a small hand device known as a clacker. If one of these were to go off on us, the result would be some bodies resembling Swiss cheese. The NVA were good at night of turning these around and when set off would light up a friendly position. Additionally the VC and NVA caught on quick to these and started making a homemade version of their own for ambush kill zones as we used them.

With one of the KIA, it took six of us to carry him, and even with six it was a struggle. In hindsight, this had to be either Lieutenant Godwin or Specialist Fourth Class Reuben Garnett as they were much bigger than the others. When we arrived, a couple of the KIAs had already been completely wrapped in double ponchos so we couldn't see their identities. I had no curiosity to know who they were; the task at hand was quickly forever etched in my mind and our mission was just starting to get underway. I had just seen enough with the trooper in rigor mortis to know that already far too many had given all. And, hell, we weren't there for a viewing.

We searched the battlefield until all were accounted for; upon completion of this mission, we returned to the company perimeter and to where enemy probing, grenade or a full attack was our main concerns. Believe it or not, these concerns seemed somewhat trivial compared to all the other hardships we encountered during the day. A great burden was finally lifted and I knew my comrades in arms would be there for me if needed. Luckily, and with little sleep, the rest of the night was uneventful. Private First Class Tom Joyce and I manned the M-60 machine gun and pulled 50 percent alert status for the rest of the night. The mosquitoes also retired for the night, so there was dead silence. This gave us time to ponder the deep questions about why it was all happening and what it all meant—somehow these questions remain unanswered.

The KIAs were protected now within our perimeter like a parent holds a child; there were many prayers going—calling all angels to walk them through this one. Throughout this expedition, and particularly on 4 March 1966, some gave all and forever became sky soldiers—men like Lieutenant Harry Godwin, Specialist Reuben L. Garnett and others.

"Harry The Horse"

1st LT. Harry M. "Harry the Horse" Godwin, taken at Ft. Campbell, Kentucky just prior to deployment to South Vietnam. Awarded Distinguished Service Cross for the battle of My Phu. Courtesy of his brother, Thomas H. Godwin.

First Sergeant Robert A. Press described Lieutenant Harry M. Godwin as a good, rock solid officer—one that could be counted on when things got tough. In his words: "I was fortunate to have been assigned to Abu Company for a total of seven years. I served with more of the finest officers, NCOs and troopers with this outfit than with any others during my 23 years of service. Many of us have kept a strong bond of friendship right up to the present time.

Lieutenant Godwin and the strength of his leadership have been on my mind many times over the years. And to describe him as a unique officer would not due him justice. Here is one small example: one day while the Abu's of the 2nd Platoon were on patrol in the Tuy Hoa area, and were moving in a deployed formation, we came under sniper fire. Lieutenant Godwin and I moved up and stood on a rice paddy dike for better observation. Another shot was fired and hit the dike between the two of us. I immediately took cover behind the dike and prepared to return fire, but was surprised to see Lieutenant Godwin still observing the village for any sign of the sniper.

I yelled at him to take cover; he finally did so, but somewhat reluctantly. I didn't agree with his method but I greatly admired his courage. Lieutenant Harry M. Godwin was a respected officer by all that served with him."

* * *

Author note: The nickname of "Harry The Horse" came about because rumor had it that Lieutenant Godwin would run as fast as a racehorse along rice paddy dikes to draw enemy fire in order to locate their positions and then place effective fire on the enemy by his designated snipers.

I recalled in August, as we were clearing Highway 19 and approaching the An Khe pass which was our second objective, when a trooper turned around and said to me, "Have you heard the rumor?" I replied that I hadn't. He told me he had heard that some lieutenant had been killed. Being somewhat naïve at the time, I wondered how in the heck a lieutenant would get killed. I could understand peons getting killed, but not an officer. It didn't take long to realize that a bullet will strike anything in its path—regardless of rank. On 4 March 1966, while we were at My Phu and going up against the NVA that had machine guns and automatic weapons with interlocking fires, all those bullets were destined to strike anything in their path since on that side, most of our Abu's were caught in the open without cover or concealment.

Lieutenant Godwin was only 26 years old and also had completed three years in the Marine Corps. Upon discharge, he attended Henderson State Teacher College in Arkadelphia, Arkansas and enrolled in their ROTC (reserve officers training course) program, rising to Cadet Commander. After graduation he was commissioned to 2nd Lieutenant and entered the U S Army. Lieutenant Godwin was awarded the DSC (Distinguished Service Cross), the second highest medal in the Army, for his heroic actions on 4 March 1966 at the battle of My Phu. Additionally, on 9 November 2012 he was inducted into the Arkansas Military Veterans Hall of Fame. His brother Thomas had this engraved on his headstone: "HEREIN LIES A MAN OF STATURE GOD SELDOM BESTOWS"

Lieutenant Godwin stood six foot 3 inches tall; however, his real stature was that gained by his achievements and his demonstrated performance. Military leaders can demand respect by virtue of their rank and many do, however the leader that gains respect through demonstrated performance will always outperform others, and is the greatest achievement a leader can obtain. Lieutenant Godwin was such a man and leader…he gained the respect of the chain of command, his peers, and subordinates. Such an accomplishment says everything about the man that medals or awards can never say.

1SG Robert A. Press at the entrance to Godwin Hall, Phan Rang Base Camp, June 1966. Courtesy of 1SG Press.

"Sweet Daddy Grace"

SP/4 Reuben L. "Sweet Daddy Grace" Garnett, Jr. Designated 1st Platoon sniper, awarded Bronze Star and Purple Heart for the battle of My Phu.

RECOVERING OUR KIA

Reuben Louis Garnett, Jr., better known as "Sweet Daddy Grace" to most, grew up in Steelton, Pennsylvania; he was the product of a great middle class family whose father also was a military man. Reuben had the ability to walk into a room and turn heads because of his charismatic personality; he was like a magnet—people were drawn to him like bees to honey. He must have possessed this from an early age because he was a natural in his ability to handle it. One of his favorite past times was boxing; his great size, strength, and grace of movement made him a natural where strangers feared him. In reality, however, he was a gentle giant...a complicated individual whose laughter and jokes somewhat masked the real inner man. The pictures contained in this book, taken just prior to My Phu, depict his great size. They were taken on one of those rare times that our platoons had come together for a few hours. All those months of combat did nothing to change Reuben and he continued to gather a crowd. The Vietnamese were enamored with him—they hadn't seen too many black men, particularly of his size. And, that old charisma had a way of breaking the language barrier.

My Phu in Vietnam on 4 March 1966—to some it may seem like an unimaginable place, far in the past. However, to some of us, it's as though it was only yesterday...in a place never to be forgotten. It seems like only yesterday that Specialist Fourth Class Reuben L.

Garnett was taken away from us to become a sky soldier. Sweet Daddy Grace made a massive and everlasting impression on everyone he met. This wasn't influenced by his great size but rather by his character, charisma, presence, and infectious smile that I can still see to this day. I was so captured by that smile, along with his charisma, that it made the situation more tolerable by allowing me to escape from the realities of war. Although we met so long ago, his presence in my life was truly unforgettable. Unforgettable...that's what you are, Reuben! The very thought of you brings a smile to my face as I reflect back on the experiences and remember your smile.

On 4 March 1966, some gave all and went from the wings of eagles to the wings of angels. Reuben L. Garnett was one...never to be forgotten...who always was, and will forever be "Above the Rest!" Reuben was awarded the Bronze Star (fourth highest award in the Army) for his brave actions at the battle of My Phu.

Chapter 36

Walk Through

After stand-to on 5 March 1966, we received orders to again take the village of My Phu and promptly moved out for our objective around 0730 hours, walking right into the village without a shot fired. Later while checking the village, a single shot or two happened as some holes were cleared by fire, but it turned out to be a walk through...a real cakewalk. I observed hastily dug prone shelters, which told me the enemy wasn't prepared for this fight and we had caught them on the move. Perhaps that CS gas did stir them up or they were trying to circle around Bravo Company to avoid contact. Moreover, they were caught with an extra company out there this time. The positions didn't even have brass in or near them from their bullets that had been fired as if they had policed them up also. One body was found under a small sampan type boat, otherwise was fairly pristine. Apparently as night fell when we pulled back, the enemy was doing the same, gathering their wounded and dead to carry off into the night, able to slip through a porous defense that after at least eight hours still wasn't cordoned off.

Captured weapons from Battle of My Phu, 4 March 1966.

Just outside the village to the west, I ran into C Company men who were on line sweeping through the area. I was surprised to see one trooper with a huge machine gun on wheels, a type I had never seen before. I asked where he had found it. He replied that he had accidentally stepped on it in a rice paddy with water—otherwise would never have known it was there. They obviously were hauling ass and dropping the heavy stuff or hiding it for later. I asked if there were any bodies there and he said, "Yeah a lot of them." We continued back to the Battalion Base Camp/FSB—our platoon never did get to search that area north of the road where we had first spotted them in the open ourselves and had lit their asses up. That is the area where C Company had searched and found the machine gun.

Author inspecting a Chi-Com bamboo stick grenade, captured during Battle of My Phu.

Author at Bn. CP/FSB checking out captured AK-47 rifle from My Phu battle.

WALK THROUGH

Captured NVA weapons at 1/327 Bn. CP/FSB, a couple days after Battle of My Phu.

FATE UNKNOWN

We become a product of our learned experiences, and one lesson learned from that battle was the possibility of running out of ammo; even with combat experience to control fire there are times when nothing can get in or out for extended periods of time. I had beefed up to 300 rounds long before My Phu and immediately after, started carrying a shit-load of ammo, 800 to a 1,000 rounds to be exact. My thought process was I may bite the bullet but I was never going to get over run and bite the dust for running out of ammo. Every man carried something extra, whether it be a claymore mine, M-72 LAW or M-60 ammo—now we all carried more M-16 ammo. As a leader, I didn't have to formally tell a man to throw away some ham and lima beans or c-rats, or take a 10 pound crap, as they quickly learn the priorities. For a FNG, combat was an accelerated crash course from the University of South Vietnam where grading on the bell curve wasn't applicable and passing was a go or no go home with that damn Timex still ticking in your heart. Weapons squad 101 would soon begin, with almost a totally new squad enrolled.

Chapter 37

And So It Went!
By Major Eugene R. New (USA Ret.)

2nd Lt. Eugene R. New's CP of 3rd Platoon. Courtesy of Major New (USA Ret.)

Information had been received on 3 March 1966 that an NVA force had moved out of the mountains and were moving toward our Battalion base camp of the 1st Battalion of the 327th Infantry, 1st Brigade (s) 101st Airborne. Based upon the information received, the Battalion Headquarters group developed a plan to catch the NVA between an attacking force and a stationary force. If executed correctly, this maneuver could effectively destroy the force caught in the middle. The plan was to place artillery, naval gunfire and an air barrage along the edge of the mountain range. The purpose of the barrage was to eliminate NVA reserve forces and disrupt the NVA's resupply capabilities. While the barrage was going on, a task force consisting of Abu and Bravo Companies plus some additional support personnel, would maneuver to trap the enemy. Abu Company was to helicopter assault just north of the impact area zone and then sweep back toward the Battalion base camp. The idea being that we would push the NVA into the forces positioned around the Battalion base camp/FSB.

The next morning of 4 March, the barrage began. A lot of fire power, including lots of napalm, was placed on a 500 meter front. Since we did not go into the area where the barrage was placed, no one could determine if there had been anyone in the impact zone and, if so, had there been any casualties. At any rate, it had been an impressive display of firepower. As the barrage began to wind down, we began our helicopter assault at 1030 hours. The landing zone was clear and no enemy resistance was encountered for our platoon. The task force quickly formed up with Abu and Bravo Company on line. With Abu Company on the right and Bravo on the left, the additional support personnel were attached to the companies. We began the sweep north at approximately 1130 hours.

The mission of my platoon, the 3rd Platoon of Abu Company, was to serve as the eyes and ears for the task force. We maintained an interval of between 200 to 400 meters in front and to the right flank of the main body of the task force. We were very familiar with the area we were moving through, having conducted many military operations there prior. The terrain consisted of lots of dry rice paddies, small scrub oaks, banana plants, and underbrush. The entire area was also crisscrossed with small streams and irrigation ditches. There were several little hamlets consisting mostly of thatched huts made from bamboo, grassy brush, and banana leaves. There were not many people to be seen in the hamlets, and those who were seen were the elderly, younger women and children. There were no men between the ages of 12 and 60.

We moved north with Staff Sergeant Ira H. Perkins, the Platoon Sergeant, on point with the lead squad in a diamond formation. This allowed for better all-around security and observation. The other two rifle squads moved behind the lead squad, also in diamond formations. Each of the three rifle squads had two M-79 40mm grenade launchers; the rest of the men were armed with M-16 assault rifles and hand grenades. The weapons squad included: two 7.62 caliber M-60 machine guns, two gunners, two assistant gunners, and four ammunition bearers. My platoon headquarters included 2 RTOs and my weapon squad leader, Sergeant Galen G. Mitchell. We all wore our lightweight packs. Since this was planned to be a one day operation, each soldier carried only a couple of c-ration meals, two canteens of water and lots of ammunition. Some carried their poncho, but most did not. Everyone carried at least one bottle of mosquito repellant. When we began the move I had 37 men, including me, in the platoon; when we arrived back to the Battalion, there were only 18 of us left.

We passed to the right of the hamlet of My Phu and then crossed two small streams. We didn't see any sign of enemy activity, just the buzzing of giant horse flies and occasionally the chirp of a bird. The mosquitoes would be out in the late afternoon. It was like the area was deserted, a walk in the park. I thought we would be back in the Battalion CP by mid-afternoon at the latest. Boy was I wrong! Shortly after crossing the second stream, we heard a sustained burst of rifle fire, machine gun and grenade fire to our left rear. (Southeast) The rifle fire was easily recognizable as coming from AK-47s. Once in a while we would hear the sharp crack of an M-16. It was obvious the majority of the firing was from NVA weapons. An AK-47 sound was chug, chug, chug...a deep sound. The M-16 was crack, crack, crack...it was sharp and very distinctive. I immediately was on the radio to the CO, Captain Hal Eaton, to find out what had happened. He wasn't able to give me any details, but said they had walked into a major ambush in the hamlet of My Phu. He ordered me to get my platoon back to My Phu and attack from the west side—they needed help. So I gave the squad leaders a quick frag–order (only essentials not thorough and complete) on our new mission. Fortunately the squad leaders, along with the men in my platoon, were well trained and experienced. We had been together for a while so I didn't have to spell out every detail; once we all understood what we were to do and how we were to do it, we moved out on the double.

We crossed back over the first stream and approached the second. As we were looking for a place to cross back over, Mitchell yelled to me, "There are a bunch of people across the stream to our left front." We identified them as members of Bravo Company. Moments later Sergeant Perkins yelled, "There's a bunch of fu-king NVA in the open." The NVAs were spotted on the other side of the stream at about 100 meters to our left front. I estimate there were at least 60 to 70 enemy soldiers in the open. Sergeant Mitchell immediately had his machine guns on them and began firing. I yelled to the squad leaders to have their men open up with their M-16s and M-79 grenade launchers.

the largest group of NVA in the open, any of ever seen. We continued to fire on the NVA as we looked for a way back over the stream. They never turned toward us, nor did they return fire. I think with all the firing going on in the ambush area, they didn't realize we were there until the ones we hit began to drop. As they ran, we continued to fire, reload, and fire again. The field they were in was filled with waist-high grass. As the NVA realized they were being attacked from the rear, they started disappearing into the grass field, but they still never returned fire. Since we could no longer see our targets, we swept the area with grazing fire. Mitchell had one of his assistant machine gunners hold the weapon on his shoulder, while the gunner swept the area in front of where the NVA soldiers had started going to the ground. The M-79 grenadiers kept popping their grenades into the same area. The rest of us fired at least one 20-round magazine into the same area.

As we continued to move forward, Captain Eaton called and asked, "What's the hold up?" I told him the situation and he said, "I don't give a shit about those guys, I need you to get here to take the pressure off us. We have dead and wounded scattered all over the rice paddy in front of My Phu. We can't get to them until you put a lot of fire on the west flank of the ambush. That should hold them down, so we can pull the wounded to cover." This was the last time I spoke to Eaton, as he was wounded in the throat shortly after our conversation. It appeared the enemy unit had been moving toward our Battalion CP when the barrage on the LZ occurred, then the helicopter assault went in behind them; they turned to quickly prepare a hasty ambush. We walked right into it.

Disengaging from the NVA soldiers we were chasing was very frustrating for everyone in the platoon. We knew we would probably never again have such a lucrative target, but disengage we did. Note: The next day Charlie Company swept through the field, found over 20 NVA dead, along with lots of AK-47s and even a wheel-mounted 51-caliber Chinese machine gun. No way to tell how many were wounded and carried off by their comrades. I realized later that we had engaged either a reinforced platoon or a company. They were moving in the direction of their mountain hideaway when we saw them. I think they had sprung their ambush and were now withdrawing, while their rear guard kept what was left of our task force occupied. A typical NVA tactic—they were well disciplined, well trained, and completely fearless.

It was afternoon by this time. We had been steadily humping, since we landed on the LZ Abu at 1030 hours. Adrenalin was keeping everyone pumped, but I knew that wouldn't last. We needed a rest break, but I also knew that wasn't possible. We had to get to the ambush site and do what we could. So I gathered the squad leaders for a quick situation report and I issued the frag-order (just essential information for the mission). I told them we had no time for a rest stop, so if the men have anything they can eat on the move, let them do it. We had to move about one kilometer to get to where I expected to begin our assault. Not a long distance, but with the 100 degree heat and high humidity, the conditions made it seem much further.

We moved in our familiar diamond wedge formation toward the sound of the guns. The firing, especially from the NVA, had nearly stopped while we were en-route. There were sporadic bursts of fire from AK-47s followed by short bursts from M-16s. I thought the battle was about over and we would be able to sweep through the area…then take a long rest break before heading back to the Battalion CP. Wrong again! I led my platoon south along a raised cart path that I knew ran about 150 meters to the west of My Phu. The remainder of the platoon guided on the path, but maintained a well dispersed formation. I deployed my platoon along the side of the raised path away from My Phu. I passed the word to the squad leaders to stay down while I found out where we were needed.

When we reached My Phu, I saw a captain with his RTO standing in the middle of the raised cart path, staring across an open rice paddy toward My Phu. I asked,

AND SO IT WENT!!!

"What's going on?" He said, "Everything is screwed up. The enemy is in the tree line; we tried to assault into their position. They just shot the shit out of us." I asked, "Where they at?" He pointed at My Phu, which was only about 150 meters away, where the bad guys were located. I decided I had all the information I needed from this captain. I think he was the Battalion S-2 and had been traveling with Bravo Company. I never found out why he and the RTO were standing on a raised path...in the open...that close to an enemy position.

I called Captain Eaton, but First Sergeant Robert A. Press answered. That's when I discovered that I, a second lieutenant, was the only officer left in both Abu and Bravo Company. The others had been killed or wounded. Press said, "There are several wounded in the open rice paddies on the south side of My Phu and every time we try to pull them in we lose someone else. So you need to move in from the west and clear out that bunch of bastards." I replied, "Roger that, as soon as we are formed up and moving I'll let you know, so don't fire in our direction."

I called the platoon sergeant and the squad leaders to my position. Once we were together I said, "We are going to assault My Phu and clear the NVA, so we can retrieve the wounded lying in the rice paddies on the south side. When I give the signal, move out on the double toward the village. If we have casualties, keep moving until we get to that defilade position west of the tree line, then go back and recover them." No one had any questions, so they went back to their men. When I saw they were in position, I gave the signal to move out and the entire platoon started moving. As we passed over the raised path, I noticed the Captain and his RTO were moving north along the raised cart path, heading to some other location.

As we moved across the rice paddy, I had a machine gunner on my right side and my RTO, with his radio antenna sticking up in the air, on my left. In retrospect, I realized that was not the smartest thing I ever did, because the priority targets for the NVA were always the machine guns, radios, and leaders. They knew if there is a radio, a leader is nearby. We had moved about 50 meters when we began to receive fire from the tree line on the edge of the village. Since we couldn't go back and we couldn't stop in the open field, my sergeants and I began yelling, "Move it, pick up the pace, go, go, go." In a matter of seconds we had reached a raised graveyard, maybe 20 meters from the village and we all hit the prone position behind the cover offered by the small graveyard. Most graveyards and villages were raised above the rice paddies to prevent flooding during the monsoon season. I knew we were too bunched up, but there was no other choice.

AND SO IT WENT!!!

As I began to get my breathing under control, Perkins yelled, "We got wounded!" I looked back across the paddy we had just crossed and realized we had wounded down in the open. Two other troopers, without being told, crawled out and began pulling the wounded up behind the graveyard. Fortunately the graveyard was raised enough so the NVA could not hit those pulling in the wounded. We had suffered several casualties in our dash to the graveyard and still had 20 meters to go to the edge of the tree line. I had looked back to see my platoon and thought, oh my God!

I called First Sergeant Press, "Where's our artillery support?" Press said, "We are too close. They let us walk up to within 25 meters of their position before they sprung their ambush. We have people behind a paddy dike within spitting distance of those bastards. Plus we have wounded in the open and the sons-of-bitches let the wounded scream until we try to recover them and then they zap the one who goes out. Too close for artillery." I shouted, "So what the hell do you expect me to do. We are in the same shape, except we are behind a graveyard and I don't want us to wind up residents." "I understand, but if you get into the village that should take the pressure off over here." "Ok" I said. "We'll give it a shot."

Once again, I got Perkins and the squad leaders together and said, "Ok, we are going to take that position. Get your people ready, and when I signal I want everyone to throw a grenade toward the tree line—if you have white phosphorus, throw those. As soon as the grenades go off, come up firing and run to the tree line." I signaled...grenades were thrown. Once again, we rose as one and started over the graveyard. We were met by the combined interlocking fire of two machine guns and AK-47 rifles. The rounds were cracking by our ears like the popping of a bull whip. CRACK! Men were being hit to the left and right. Fragments were being smashed off grave stones and some of the stones were shattered. I turned to the machine gunner on my left, to direct his fire, as he was smacked by a round in his upper left chest. He went down like he had been hit with a sledge hammer. My RTO was hit in his right leg and his right arm. He was knocked back off the graveyard during the assault. I realized then we were not going to get to the tree line, so I started yelling," Back, get back." The word went down the line and the ones still on their feet dropped back to the cover of the graveyard. We were able to pull the wounded back without being exposed to the deadly accurate fire of the hidden enemy. At most we had made only about two or three steps before we were knocked back.

"Troops on the ground, troops on the ground, this is Sky-Hawk, over." This was the first voice I had

AND SO IT WENT!!!

heard on the company net, except for First Sergeant Press, since the battle began. I responded, "This is Abu, who are you?" He identified himself as an A-1E Skyraider. The A-1E is a propeller driven aircraft that is great for close in support. He said he was on a search mission looking for targets of opportunity and had been monitoring our situation. I said, "You sure found targets of opportunity. What type ordinance do you have?" He replied, "One hundred pound bombs and 20mm guns." I said, "Great, we can use everything you have. I will pop smoke and the enemy is about 20 meters east of that, just inside the tree line on a north south line. Keep the ordinance just inside the tree line because we have friendly's about 75 meters to the east. They are in the open." Sergeant Press came on the net, "I'm monitoring, good luck."

I popped smoke and the pilot said, "I identify green smoke." "Roger that!" I replied. He began his first south to north run. He put three of his bombs in perfect position about 25 meters to my east and barely inside the tree line. Then he circled and made a pass from north to south. Again the bombs were right on target where we had been receiving fire from. He appeared to be flying at tree top level. I thought, damn, I hope he doesn't clip one of the palm trees. He gave a whole new meaning to the term low and slow. It seemed he hung in the sky as he slowly passed by, but he was doing a good job. Right on target!

After making another bomb run he said, "OK now I'm going to make my gun pass." I replied, "Do it, your right on target." He started south to north… riiiiiip…riiiiiip…riiiiiip—the 20mm cannon sounded like a giant was ripping pieces of sheet metal. Along the tree line, it looked like a giant weed eater was clearing a path about 20 meters wide. He made a couple of more gun passes and said, "That's it for me, I'm out of ammo and running low on fuel. Good luck." I responded, "Thanks, you did a super job; take the rest of the day off."

Eight more men had been hit in our next futile attempt to get to the enemy position. The latest wounded included machine gunners, my RTO and the 3rd Squad Leader. I now had 19 wounded behind the graveyard. Several were in critical condition and needed medical help right away—much more medical help than the platoon could provide, as we didn't have a medic. So far I had no KIAs and I was very thankful for that. So now the platoon was down to 17 able-bodied men and me. They were exhausted, but ready and willing to do what they were told. Real troopers! I was proud to be their leader. I now had two NCOs remaining, Sergeants Perkins and Mitchell, as well as a replacement RTO. Both machine guns had been damaged, I thought beyond repair. We were low on ammo, water, grenade launcher ammo, and I was completely out of my favorite Roi Tan Panatela cigars.

I was about to call First Sergeant Press, but he dropped down beside me and said "Lieutenant what do you have?" I have no idea how he arrived there. Suddenly, he was there. I gave him the situation and he said, "We're bringing in a medevac chopper to a covered position about 100 meters to your right rear." He pointed to the planned LZ. "We have the LZ secured and the chopper will take out six to eight each time. You'll have to get your WIAs over there. They'll also bring in some supplies. What do you need the most?" I told him what we needed the most. I said, "Get ready to assault!" Then he said, "Lieutenant I think you should hold what you got." I replied, "I think your right, Top." I knew there was a lot of mumbling, "Thank God," up and down the line when the word passed from man to man, that we were not going over the graveyard again. They would have gone if told but they were sure glad they weren't told. After his short visit, Press went back to what was left of the company command group. I have no idea how he was able to get to my position and back without drawing fire.

Perkins organized a two-man team to carry the wounded to the LZ; they carried one at a time. They also brought supplies back on their return trips. The water was great…hot…but wet, and much appreciated. When one crew was tired out, they were relieved by another two-man crew. Most of the wounded were able to walk, but many required assistance. As that was going on, I had Perkins distribute the supplies as they came in. Both of Mitchell's machine guns had been hit and he was working to cannibalize them to try to get one that would work. He finally had one gun fixed. For the remainder of the battle, Tom Joyce and Mitchell were the platoon machine gun crew. It was now around 1800 hours. In this region it would begin getting dark around 1900 hours. As soon as the sun went down, the temperature would drop from over a hundred during the day, to the 70's at night.

The Battalion Commander called me on our radio frequency. I gave him a full report and he said, "OK, we are going to put a cordon around that village tonight and try to stop the Mothers from getting away. In the morning we'll bring in reinforcements and clean them out." He told me to gather and place the KIAs in Abu Company's CP, in the morning we would evacuate them from the same area we had been evacuating the WIA's. The battle was pretty much over by this time and most of my WIA's had been taken to the rear. I think the NVA was as shot up and as exhausted as we were. Both sides were ready to take a break and lick their wounds.

AND SO IT WENT!!!

I told Perkins and Mitchell what was going on. I had Perkins put the men in two-man positions; one could rest while the other was on alert. We spread out in positions along the south side of My Phu. I asked Mitchell to take four to five men; start bringing the KIAs into my CP area and lay them out in a line. I told him to return to our position and forget the KIAs if he saw any NVA or if he was fired on. Fortunately, he received no fire and he was able to bring in all the KIAs he could find. Usually it took all four men, using a poncho as a carrier, to carry one KIA. When laid out, they were wrapped in ponchos. This was backbreaking and heartbreaking work. The men being brought in were men we had worked with and played with. That morning they were vibrant and alive; now they were bodies in the advance stage of rigor mortis. Mitchell along with his crew, walked all over the open rice paddies where the ambush had taken place and along the village tree line looking for our causalities. No sign of the NVA—I guess they had moved back into the village and were preparing to make their withdrawal under the cover of darkness.

Mitchell brought in 13 friendly KIAs and couldn't find anymore. Included among the 13, was Lieutenant Harry Godwin, Platoon Leader of the 2nd Platoon. I had come to know Harry quite well. Just two days before he and I had shared a poncho hooch at Battalion

Headquarters when we were stuck there for the night. Harry and his sniper, Specialist Fourth Class Garnett, had been shot through the top of their heads. They had been hit while charging forward in a crouch or they had hit the ground when the ambush was sprung. Now they were covered in ponchos, lying in a row in a dry rice paddy. It was close to 2300 hours when Mitchell finished his somber task.

The mosquitoes were out in force that night. They would bite through fatigues and ponchos didn't even slow them down. The rumor was, they would band together and carry away small animals. Also, the temperature was in the 70's by midnight. So all in all, it was a miserable, cold, practically sleepless, hungry night. At least there was no more enemy activity that night. About a half hour before it began to get light, my NCOs and I made sure everyone was up for stand-to. Weapons had to be at the ready and everyone fully alert. The period before first light is a prime time for an attack. We stayed in the stand-to mode until we had enough light to see, then we started moving around and getting ready for whatever the day would bring—eating a c-ration if we had one, drinking water if we had some, and generally performing our morning rituals.

On the morning of 5 March 1966, I was waiting for orders to come down to make a joint sweep though the village with Abu and B Companies combined, when a

AND SO IT WENT!!!

new voice came up on the Abu Company net, " This is Steel 5 on the way in, pop smoke." I popped a smoke grenade and he said, "I identify white smoke." I said, "Roger that." The chopper landed on the same LZ where the WIAs were evacuated and our NDP was. Out hopped the Battalion Executive Officer, Major David H. Hackworth; he was freshly shaven, and wore clean fatigues and new jungle boots. The Battalion Surgeon, Dr. Benjamin, was with him. They were rested, fresh, and eager to make the world free for democracy. We, on the other hand, looked like we had been rode hard and put away wet.

I reported to Hackworth and gave him a quick situation report, to include the fact that there had been no sign of the enemy since around 2000 hours the previous evening. He said, "OK, get your men ready to make a coordinated sweep of the entire battle area. I'll let you know shortly when to start and what your search area will be. By the way, put your radio on the Battalion frequency so I can contact you easier." At approximately 0730 hours Hackworth gave the order to begin the sweep.

Abu, B and C Companies went over the entire battle area with a fine-tooth comb. Evidently the enemy force had found a way through our cordon and eluded us during the night. The NVA were meticulous in policing up their positions. They never left any of their dead, weapons, or even their empty shell casings unless they had no choice. The NVA took everything and everyone they could, but we still found enemy weapons, enemy KIAs, and also some battle gear.

There were no enemy bunkers or reinforced positions—just hastily prepared prone firing positions—just long enough and wide enough for one person to lie in with excellent interlocking fields of fire.

After searching the area for about three hours, we received the order to march back to our Battalion base camp. We reached there about 1500 hours. It was good to be back. A hot c-rat meal, shower, change of clothes, and a cigar—it doesn't get much better than that. That night we were manning our portion of the perimeter; the next night we made a two kilometer march and set up a platoon size ambush. And so it went!

~Lieutenant Eugene R. New (Major USA Ret.)
3rd Platoon Leader

Captain Eugene R. New, 1969. He completed a second tour in Vietnam as a Company Commander and Battalion S-3 (Operation Officer). Courtesy of Major New (USA Ret.).

FATE UNKNOWN

Chapter 38

In My Opinion

The final results were: approximately 118 enemy dead by body count, for which the flies would be grateful, while Abu Company had 13 KIA, 39 WIA, Bravo with 7 KIA and 11 WIA, and C Company 1 KIA. While we won the battle and dominated the battlefield, we also were bloodied after having gone up against their best professionals with many valuable lessons learned from this experience. Major Hackworth, the Battalion XO, had a talk with us a few days later at the Battalion Command Post/Base Camp about 3 miles away; at the time I was unaware who he was as I'd never seen him before. The gist of the talk was that we had made some mistakes by assaulting across the open paddies, and in future engagements we would instead pull back to allow artillery or air power to hammer the enemy, thus preventing unnecessary causalities while softening up the objective. Contrary to statements made by Hackworth in his book *About Face* (Chapter 15, page 521), no speech ever took place on the morning of 5 March 1966 just outside of My Phu. There were also many other blatant fabrications throughout his book.

One of the falsehoods expressed by Hackworth in *About Face* was that he had to kick the survivors in the ass on the morning of 5 March 1966 in order to get them moving to attack the village of My Phu. On page 521 he wrote the following: "Then I tore their collective ass for violating the basics, which had led to all their problems in the first place." As a survivor, I'm compelled to set the record straight…not for selfish reasons, but rather for all the survivors who were unjustly and cruelly attacked by Hackworth…adding insult to injury. His description of the event could not be further from the truth—it never happened that way nor was the village occupied by the enemy when we moved in on the morning of 5 March 1966, without a shot being fired to take it. I never observed any 'fortified positions,' unless you possibly consider a dead enemy NVA under a small thin sampan boat as overhead cover. Personally, I never saw Hackworth there, which is not to say he wasn't, but I can honestly say he wasn't in the thick of it where my ass was. Perhaps his biggest participation in the My Phu attack was putting his ear to a radio. It is my opinion that his award of the Silver Star (third highest award for valor in the Army) for the battle of My Phu—is a total farce—a complete fabrication of events that never happened, much similar to his unauthorized Ranger Tab—easily proven by eye witnesses and actual participants. I would assume that with all the awards he received, some must have been earned, but I know for a fact that

IN MY OPINION

the Silver Star for My Phu was not a deserved or earned award. So much for integrity and honor! Additionally, (page 508) Hackworth has no shame in his game when he attacks Medal of Honor recipient 1st Lieutenant James Alton Gardner, who was KIA on 7 February 1966, while carrying out Hackworth's orders (page 505) at the battle of My Canh (2) by stating, "At fault too, perhaps, were the habits Gardner and Hiser had brought to My Canh." Also on page 506, he gave a backhanded compliment about Medal of Honor recipient 1st Lieutenant Gardner. That kind of 'on the record' statement is indicative perhaps of Hackworth's own jealousy. In summary, I'll riddle you this: who was in charge? In my opinion, to make such statements for personal gain and at the expense of comrades in arms is despicable. It is doubtful anyone there would co-sign such crap and here I thought the shit was flying during the battle only to find the real crap would fly much later. Chapter 15 of *About Face* contained a lot of inaccuracies where Hackworth always came to save the day or to stroke his own ego.

The infantry is taught to find the enemy, fix him, and then finish him—a long-standing axiom. The biggest mistake committed at My Phu was that Major Hackworth, the ground commander, failed to take advantage of the terrain by sending the maneuver element (Abu Company) across open rice paddies for an assault.

FATE UNKNOWN

The exact same mistake took place a month earlier at the battle of My Canh, where he was also in charge—that, again, resulted in heavy friendly KIAs. At My Phu, Bravo Company should have been the maneuver element as they had more cover and concealment on the West side of the village. That is if he had known the enemy was there, and I believe he did, which is why Captain Eaton committed them on line for an assault. I'll give him that one though, as perhaps he wasn't aware of their presence. However, as a leader one must play the hand he is dealt. Throughout this battle, which raged on for at least eight hours, he failed to cordon off a village that was completely surrounded on three sides by rice paddies in order to prevent their escape, and where our full military might could be brought to bear by support elements prior to any attacking or even after we had attacked to completely annihilate them. On our approach to My Phu, B Company was scattered, with gaps and holes in the cordon; this became obvious to me about 1300 hours that day as we passed through them enroute to our attack position. Actually, it was a replication of My Canh (2) that took place on 7 February 1966, where Hackworth was also the ground commander. Nothing outside of the A-1E Skyraider was used for support, and although hugging our belt on the southern end, artillery could have been used on the northern end that was a much broader area, which also would have closed an escape route. No helicopter gunships were used, which would have been excellent even where they were hugging our belt. The enemy was found and caught on the move, whether from the gas or from the element of surprise that another company was in the immediate area. It appears that the enemy then decided to break contact by escaping to My Phu (1) that was surrounded on three sides by rice paddies. To insinuate in his book that platoon leaders on down violated any basics is absurd. They performed admirably with the real failure having taken place at the commander level. Who was in command? The situation was controlled by Hackworth—he screwed it up by not maneuvering and controlling the forces under his command to fix the enemy and destroy them, while taking advantage of their tactical blunder either by a proper cordon off of the village, pounding them with supporting elements, or proper use of the hammer and anvil.

Hackworth remains a controversial figure that isn't without admirers, which I liken to professional wrestling fans. They know it's phony, but in my opinion they just can't help themselves. Given a choice to retire or do an about-face and accept a court-martial, he chose the former, escaping disclosure of the real Hackworth that set an example of 'do as I say not as I do.' The fact of the matter is the commander is responsible. Attempting to pass off or insinuate that others were always the blame was without integrity and totally unprofessional; however, this theme or method of operation flourished throughout his books. As a survivor, I strongly resent such statements. In my opinion, Hackworth failed to conceptualize the situation by not analyzing courses of action and proved to be, in my opinion, worthless in this battle. He was a prima donna who always knew more in his books in the positions he held than all his superiors. He never rose above colonel, and I seriously doubt he missed his calling. However, I digress and shall move on, again without a kick in the ass.

Chapter 39

PFC Clarence E. "Griff" McKinnis

Left PFC Clarence "Griff" McKinnis practices hand-to-hand combat skills with a fellow trooper, October 1965.

After My Phu, Abu Company had the mission for providing perimeter defense or security for the Battalion CP and artillery as we waited for replacements to arrive. After an uneventful night, the morning of 9 March 1966, began with stand-to, much like all the other days. Afterward, around 0715 hours, I went over to check my M-60 position and Gunner Tom Joyce.

On arrival at the gun position, Private First Class Clarence E. "Griff" McKinnis, who everyone just called Griff, was also there. He was born on 4 April 1946 to Gladys McKinnis of Detroit, Michigan. He was raised in a middle-class family, along with his older sister Ermaleta McKinnis of Round Rock, Texas. Griff was a graduate of Northern High School in Detroit. He came over on the boat with Tom Joyce and me. In fact, after the battle of My Phu, we were the only boat members or originals remaining in the platoon, at the time then having been together over eight months. Griff was a good-looking black soldier who appeared somewhat quiet or reserved, but if you knew him, he was just like the rest of us. Clarence was greatly respected and admired by everyone because of his outstanding demonstrated performance as a soldier in combat.

We seemed to never dwell or talk of the bad stuff like My Phu and only discussed the good stuff. Conversation this morning was about normal things, such as getting back to the world, trading for some Kool-

Aid, and the like. I remember noticing that Griff seemed to be awfully quiet, even for him, while he appeared to have a troubled or worried look on his face. He was just listening...not adding to the conversation. I said, "Hey Griff you ok?" His reply was, "Yeah," without looking up or smiling. He seemed content to look at the ground, as if in deep thought. A short time later he said, "Catch you guy's later," and started walking back to his position about 30 meters away. I was thinking perhaps the battle of My Phu had a lasting affect on him and I would go see him later. No more than a minute or so went by when we heard an explosion from an all too familiar sound of a hand grenade. We ran over there and saw Griff lying about 20 yards down in a small stream; the blast had taken him from the bank and nothing could be done to save his life. I won't go into details for his family's sake, but he obviously had tried to get the grenade off his belt after hearing the handle pop. First Sergeant Press was with another trooper on the other side of the stream, heard the handle pop, and then observed Griff trying to get it off his belt. He had attempted to get out of his web gear, but the five-second delay of the grenade fuse wasn't enough time to allow that.

As squad leaders, we were constantly on our men to check the pins on their grenades, at a minimum of every morning and evening during stand-to. Additionally they were also to be checked prior to boarding a chopper and during movement through the jungle. Some men took to squeezing the cotter pin back for nighttime, and then would spread them back in the morning—not a good policy because it wears the pins out and it can easily break off a pin, or a trooper may forget to spread them back.

After all we had been through over the last eight months and then just recently surviving the battle of My Phu—it seemed to just make no sense, but was a sobering reality. I ordered the men who had gathered to provide assistance back to their positions...not for security reasons, but because I knew they couldn't dwell on this tragedy. They all seemed to take one last look...and then slowly complied. Shortly after I did the same, with that image forever locked in my mind. Men don't say much at times like this—they don't have to, as each man retreats to his individual thoughts.

Griff was only 19 on that tragic day that he forever became a sky soldier taken in the prime of life. Although we ponder for a reason and search for meaning without ever getting an answer, we'll forever remember him.

Chapter 40

Premonition

Replacements were arriving while we continued perimeter defense and ambush patrols around the Battalion CP/FSB. One of the replacements caught my eye. His name was Private First Class Dominick "Nick" Fondo, Jr. and I had requested him for the weapons squad through Lieutenant New. I was always on the lookout for good men for my M-60 machine guns, and my weapons squad needed to be rebuilt after My Phu. Nick Fondo would prove to be an excellent choice. He became a hero during the battle of Dak To on 9 June 1966, and received an Army Commendation Medal with "V" device for heroism. Despite being wounded and engaged against a numerically superior NVA force, he continued to place accurate M-60 fire on the enemy while covering Abu Company's tactical withdrawal. After establishing a perimeter defense, Nick's actions prevented their perimeter from being overrun through his fierce determination and accurate fire placed on the enemy positions. He also exposed himself to small arms and mortar fire to provide first aid to wounded comrades.

PFC Dominick "Nick" Fondo, Jr. received a medal for his valorous actions at Battle of Dak To. Courtesy of Nick Fondo.

Then in early April 1966, we loaded on choppers to conduct an airmobile assault 20 to 25 miles north of Tuy Hoa. The mission was to search-destroy around a

Special Forces Camp in the vicinity of Dong Tre where a reported large enemy force was gathering to attack and overrun the camp. Additionally, B and C Companies of our battalion would join in the operation. We began to receive some sniper fire. We had some VC surrenders, found some medical supply caches, and took some prisoners of war. On the 6th of April, C Company found a huge cache of rice. On the 6th of April, as is reflective of combat stress, the Battalion had a man with a self-inflicted wound in the foot; this proved the point that every man has a breakingpoint. The difference between a hero and a coward is measurable in a second or a single thought. Obviously, his self-preservation dominated that battle and choice; however, he'll receive no sympathy from the overwhelming band of combat brothers that claimed victory over their fears or demons in combat. He can find sympathy in the dictionary between shit and syphilis!

The enemy was definitely in the area but seemed to be avoiding us if possible. In addition, we had a CIDG (Civilian Irregular Defense Group) operating with us, which is a militia force trained by U. S. Special Forces. Man did they get the irregular part correct! To me they looked like a bunch of Boy Scouts with adult weapons. I'm sure some VCs were among them—another damn problem we had to deal with. For me, they were like trusting a hard-on in a whorehouse.

Boy Scouts may be an overstatement and perhaps Cub Scouts may be more appropriate. Acknowledgement here is due for the U. S. Special Forces personnel and other advisors for entrusting their lives to these Ruff Puffs, commendable and very admirable. They did get two POWs after we checked out an area that was hit with artillery because of being a suspected enemy location; however, around 1600 hours, our illustrious attached allies refused to go on a hill that was a known VC location. Little candy ass, mother fuc-ers…hard to believe their bloodlines and the NVA are similar. Naturally we checked it out, but no contact occurred as the enemy had fled.

On 7 April 1966, we conducted stand-to and then continued sweeping on into the Special Forces Camp without incident. We were just chilling on the airstrip waiting for the other companies to close in and conduct a lift out by choppers. Our next mission would be to a place called Phan Thiet, which was supposed to be an area not heavily populated with VC and would allow us to hunt the enemy while at the same time train all our new replacements.

Sometime around 1215 hours, we received word that one of our sister companies was in some deep trouble and we would be going in to help them as soon as choppers arrived. We would leave the heavy stuff like sleeping rolls, while taking only the essentials, such as ammo and water. Having accomplished this, we were just waiting for the birds when what seemed like a premonition hit me like a ton of bricks—something told me I was going to get screwed up. In all this time, I never had a feeling like this and always felt invincible with the attitude that there was no bullet with my name on it. I attempted to pass this off, but it persistently kept nagging at me and my mind was racing with all kinds of thoughts. I'm thinking, "Is this what Griff McKinnis was feeling prior to his accident, along with others I had observed prior to My Phu that ended up casualties?" In addition, I'm thinking God is preparing me for something—for sure it had to be death. I became quiet like Griff and wanting to avoid others as I lay back like I was trying to sleep. Meanwhile the real battle is taking place in my mind and this premonition has turned into full fear. For the second time over there I'm really scared, to the point I'm contemplating refusing to get on the chopper. I could hear the sound of the choppers as they fast approached. Decision, decision…what to do?

Picture of fertile rice paddies taken from chopper enroute to an LZ.

I was able to control the fear and forced myself into the chopper around 1315 hours. This unfamiliar enemy still had hold of my ass and my thoughts now are if the damn chopper is going to crash, get blown out of the sky, or that maybe someone's grenade was about to go off inside the chopper. The flight took about 15 minutes; it seemed an eternity to me and at times felt as though it was taking place in slow motion.

PREMONITION

The LZ was small, with only two birds able to fit, and on landing I was surprised the LZ wasn't hot. I quickly set up my machine guns and a crew behind this huge rock that gave all of us cover, with the gun facing uphill in the direction the birds had landed, as the others quickly established security around the LZ. Shortly after placing the M-60 behind that boulder, all that fear just vanished as fast as it had grabbed hold of me. It was gone just as quickly as it had arrived, and I was completely back to normal in a heartbeat.

My thoughts are that I just need a break—some rest and recuperation, perhaps, as I hadn't had a break since Phan Rang back in December. I had been somewhat lucky then to get out of there without getting busted. We had gone from a time of booze, women and song to a time of long months spent in the field; we were wild men living for the present as if there was no tomorrow. They may have been sons of bitches, but their mothers wouldn't have recognized these party animals. At this point in time, Tom Joyce my gunner and I are the only originals that came over on the boat remaining in the platoon. This 47-man platoon must have had 150 men go through it for one reason or another, with most reasons not being of a good nature. In My Phu alone, we lost half of the platoon. Perhaps I could get seven days R&R in Australia; meanwhile, I was damn glad I jumped on that chopper.

FATE UNKNOWN

"If we take the generally accepted definition of bravery as a quality which knows no fear, I have never seen a brave man. All men are frightened..."
~General George S. Patton, Jr.

Within a short time after landing, the second lift was coming in; it began to hover while lowering to the ground, and when it was about ten feet off the ground, all hell broke loose as we started taking fire. Men started un-assing the bird before it could land as they targeted the lead chopper. It began to smoke, sputter, and whine...then suddenly plopped to the ground. The door gunners grabbed their M-60 machine guns and quickly ran out to our perimeter and set up security. The pilots were still sitting in their seats and I observed a 3rd Platoon man from each side run out, open the door to help the pilots out. One of the pilots was WIA in the leg. Funny how war can be, because I can see this just clear as glass today, but I'm still unable to identify the two men. The pilots shut down the aircraft prior to getting out and the smoke from the tail rotor stopped. The platoon took three other WIA as the second lift landed.

Thinking we were on the top of the hill or only a few feet from it on the crest, I couldn't quite figure out the enemy's exact location. Tom Joyce immediately returned fire when they opened up on us, but I had him stop after the second bird took off. We were now down to a one-bird LZ. There was no sense wasting ammo without definitive targets, even though after My Phu I started humping a thousand rounds for my M-16 just for myself and increased machine gun ammo also by getting the Lieutenant to give me some bigger men. I was never going to die from running out of ammo and getting over run. My Phu was a lesson well learned.

Lieutenant New was about 15 feet to my right. "Where they at, I asked?" With all his fingers extended and joined, he pointed with his left hand in the direction up the hill, while moving his hand up and down. His head turned in my direction with this big shit-eating grin on his face that seemed to ask, where the hell do you think they're at? I smiled back at him, but I was really trying to get an exact location while hoping he had a better fix so I could place M-60 fire on them. I took out my binoculars to look around the right side of the boulder up the hill and observed nothing. The left side of the boulder dropped off sharply so I couldn't really look around that end either.

Thoughts of My Phu were in my head, pinned down with the enemy being only 50 to 60 feet from us while unable to actually observe them or pinpoint their exact location. Trying to prevent a repeat of that situation, I was keenly aware that if their positions or line could be pinpointed, a lot of casualties could be prevented by placing effective fire from the machine gun right on them.

Next, I took my binoculars and looked over the top of the boulder. What I observed was that we weren't at the top of the hill as previously thought, with there being a flat area just to our immediate front (saddle) and then it went up again to the top only 30 meters or so away. From the LZ, I could see the skyline giving the illusion that we were on top but really weren't. Now I knew exactly what our situation was and I had a real feel for the problem at hand, so I lowered my binoculars. Just as the binoculars were at my throat level, it felt like someone hit me in the face with a sledgehammer, knocking me backwards down the hill. Things were going black with tiny white spots all over. Then I felt this intense, terrible burning as if someone was holding a torch on my face. I can attest to the fact that the bullet that gets you is the one not heard, as this bullet hit me right in the nose on a left to right downward angle and I never heard it.

The platoon medic, whose name escapes me, came over to begin treatment and immediately administered a morphine shot. The Doc had traveled with our platoon about four months prior, around the time I first made sergeant, so we knew each other very well and had a great relationship. Extremely concerned, I seriously asked, "Doc, how bad is it?" He replied with a shit-eating grin, "Ah, they just shot your nose off and you have a hole I can stick my thumb in!" Then Tom Joyce said, "It's an improvement." With that, we busted out laughing. I'm not sure if it was from the morphine, our sick humor, or the close relationship we developed over time.

I crawled on all fours back to the boulder since no medevac was coming into a hot LZ with one chopper having already been shot down. It would have to be secured, which meant taking the hill. Lieutenant New was attempting to get some naval gunfire, but our position prevented it because a short round would end up in our pockets. Next, he requested some tactical air support and some fast movers came up on his radio. He gave them the necessary information, and they soon swooped down, making a dry run that sounded like they were 20 feet to our front and 10 feet off the ground. Then they made a cannon run that was so fast the cannon sounded like one long burst with no individual spacing or separation. These are some very large rounds similar to putting at least 100 machine gun rounds or more into one round that will penetrate overhead cover and, if accurately on them, will tear their ass up. At the time, we didn't have much incoming fire, and even though they were once again hugging our belt, these fast movers seemed to have them hunkering down. The next one sped by and all I heard was the sound because by that time it was gone and all the air around me started being sucked up the hill. It also felt like the air was being taken right out of my lungs…then this tremendous heat. This was napalm that was grabbing all the oxygen it could muster from wherever; when you first tried to take a breath there was no air—it quickly returned after the heat, as though a switch had flipped off and on. I'm lying there thinking if that had been five feet or so closer, we would all probably be crispy critters ourselves. Damn that was close! We had done this before, but never this close. Even though napalm spreads all over the place rather easily, I believe those pilots could drop it on a dime. In these type situations, you're literally caught between a rock and a hard place. You are greatly dependent on, or at the mercy of, the ability and expertise of the pilot. Man was their shit together! Lieutenant New…this Alabama-born, southern gentleman…was a quick study in the My Phu "lesson-learned department," and he invited these belt-hugging bastards to his flaming pit-barbeque.

Medevac chopper arrives after Hill #264 is taken.

The Doc gave me another morphine shot. The napalm did the trick on the belt huggers, with the survivors fleeing. The platoon took Hill #264 not long after the napalm strike and found 10 crispy critters (KIA), 1 WIA, and estimated 20 KIA as body parts were strewed about. A medevac chopper was able to get in after about five hours and we were on our way. Note: Another huge battle would be fought in this same area by a sister unit after the enemy overran a Special Forces CIDG Company and C Company of $2^{nd}/327$ Airborne Infantry wiped out an NVA company. My next stop was the 101st Brigade field hospital, where the doctor removes my bandage and, takes a look at my wound. He reads my card from the Doc in the field, and tells me they're going to give me another morphine shot and send me to the 85th Hospital, in Quin Nhon. In addition they put an intravenous (IV) in my arm.

    Night is falling as I'm loaded into another chopper. The ride is feeling good and the cool air blowing in through the open door caresses my body. I started becoming queasy sick, throwing up all over the floor of the bird, feeling as if I'm losing control. Things were getting black and I immediately thought my life was slipping away. I attempted to get up and out of the chopper, fighting to keep from letting go of my life. The medic on board was holding me down and closed the door while telling me to stay down. Total blackness overtakes and engulfs me; next thing I hear was a female voice calling my name. Opening my eyes, I see a woman's face looking down on me with a bright light all around her head. My thought was that I had died and she was an angel. She keeps asking my name and I keep telling her, but my voice is all mumbled and agitated, and I'm growing frustrated. I begin to curse until finally she says, "Its ok. Go back to sleep." Now, only a paratrooper would dare curse at an angel. When next awakened I discovered that I hadn't died after all—I was in the hospital with my jaw wired shut because it was also broken. Only then did I realize I would make it back to the world and life with a new beginning. In fact, my time remaining in the Nam was so short I could sit on a dime and dangle my legs. I sure wish that doctor had told me the morphine shot would put me to sleep and everything was going to be all right!

The 95th NVA Regiment proved to be a tough adversarial opponent from mid-January to mid-April; however, we kicked their ass—killing 637 by body count and their disillusioned VC counterparts surrendering in large numbers—losing heart while choosing life. We dominated the battlefield while adapting our tactics to set a standard for our peers to emulate in the future aspects of the war. There wasn't much recognition back then in the form of awards or the likes. Each man fulfilled a vital role and to list any one or two persons would be a disservice to the many others that had served in Abu Company. The greatest reward was to be recognized by your peers as being a part of a great unit and organization, their acceptance saying it all.

FATE UNKNOWN

Chapter 41

McNamara's 100,000

After returning to the world and getting out of the hospital in Valley Forge, Pennsylvania, I was assigned to Fort Dix, New Jersey, teaching target detection and zeroing of the M-16 rifle. One day this unit, that couldn't do anything correctly, came through my range; after exhausting work, however, we finished the necessary tasks. I reported my observations to Sergeant First Class Hightower, my NCOIC, and let him know that they were enroute. He laughed and said, "That's because they're part of Project 100,000!" Of course my reply was, "What is Project 100,000?" He told me it was Secretary of Defense Robert McNamara's plan to lower all test standards to allow 100,000 men entrance into the Army to fulfill the needs for Vietnam. The Project is also referred to as McNamara's 100,000. Moreover, he figured this would relieve pressure on the draft, which also would help quell anti-war demonstrators. Many years later I discovered it was much worse than previously thought—it was more like 120,000 per year for 3 years, for a total of approximately 354,000 men.

These good men went to the bush (Vietnam) and served...some losing arms and legs...while others lost their lives...only to be betrayed later by our politicians, specifically Robert McNamara. When the war was over, the Army returned to its previous high standards and these good men were forced out of the Army through a program called QMP (qualified management program). What this really meant is…you are no longer good enough for us. They were good enough to die for their country during war, but not qualified enough to serve after the Vietnam War. It was another great injustice thrust upon the soldier, quickly buried in the aftermath. As the great radio host Paul Harvey would say…"And now you know the rest of the story."

I despised McNamara, along with all politicians who sanctioned and condoned this to take place. And, yes, that includes you too President Lyndon B. Johnson. When McNamara recently died, my thought was…good riddance to him, as the world is now a better place! It's a shame it couldn't have happened in the 1960s. Men were only numbers to him and the war was about big figures (dollars), as he was a number cruncher or bean counter. The largest thing he failed to recognize was that his own ego caused him to think he knew more than the Joint Chiefs of Staffs.

I seemed to recall about a year or so prior to his death he was making the rounds promoting his new book and finally, after over 40 years or so of no shame in his game, admitted to some of his mistakes. However, he conveniently ignored Project 100,000 and the fact that he was aware of the effects of Agent Orange. It took long enough for his admittance of a smidgen of his deadly mistakes. His conscience must have finally caught up with his ego, most likely because of his age as he drew close to death. It's somewhat like prisoners who come to jail and all of a sudden become religious. Had they had even a speck of it prior, they probably wouldn't be in that situation. After having worked as a Correctional Supervisor in prisons for over 22 years, I can attest to the fact that they're a dime a dozen. Trust me in that I also never met an atheist in a foxhole either. The men that fought in battle were getting those reality checks on a daily basis, if not by the hour or second, and in his case I can't for the life of me see where late is better than never. As a man of numbers, he above all others should have realized that his one "I'm sorry" can't ever undo or equate to the grievous sorrow caused on his behalf to the men and families behind those numbers. We're not good with lessons learned either, as today the same mistakes are perpetrated on a daily basis by our illustrious politicians that handicap our military leaders.

The military keeps a soldier so busy it consumes his whole life, with hardly a chance for anything else at times, including family. Although there is little time to conceptualize the big picture, the picture eventually comes into focus. One lesson I learned after retiring from the Army was that the enemy also existed from within and we were surrounded on multiple fronts. Oh for sure we knew of Jane Fonda, AKA Hanoi Jane, but even today few are aware of McNamara's 100,000 and his knowledge about the effects of Agent Orange. Much later I became aware of a Nobel Peace Prize winner by the name of Henry Kissinger. He was both the National Security Advisor and Secretary of State under President Nixon and then continued on as Secretary of State under President Ford. In 1973 Kissinger was awarded the Nobel Peace Prize for his efforts as the U.S. representative at the Paris Peace Accords, to end the war in Vietnam. He made the following statement:

"Military men are just dumb, stupid animals to be used as pawns in foreign policy."
~Henry Kissinger

McNamara and Kissinger have flown under the radar for far too long, thanks to selective journalism and they deserve this short time in my sight alignment and sight picture. A search of the kill zone reveals the worst enemy perhaps is the one from within. Is it any wonder I have greater respect for the NVA & VC than for Hanoi Jane, Robert McNamara and Henry Kissinger?

Chapter 42

Gut Checks

My life rapidly began changing after my release from Valley Forge Army Hospital in July of 1966. Prior to being released, I saw several of my comrades in arms get assigned to the hospital as a result of a huge battle fought at Dak To against an overwhelming force. Private First Class Robert "Pappy" Papesh of Ohio informed me about the battle and of the deaths of the men I had recently served with.

"T-Bird's" (Blair A. Funderburk) luckiest day came on 6 June 1966 during the battle of Dak To, when the Battalion was surrounded by an overwhelming NVA force of the 24th NVA Regiment and the 88th Regiment, along with supporting elements. The area was infested with NVA and contact was made during which an NVA soldier gut-shot Private First Class Golden Jones and then immediately tried to Chieu Hoi (chew hoy), or surrender. Coming up out of his hole with his hands up, Staff Sergeant Perkins immediately shot and killed the NVA and he slumped back down in his spider hole. Having a NVA surrender wasn't the norm—they would die before giving up—real hardcore die-hards, whereas many of the VC would surrender. Obviously valuable intelligence was lost from this incident. Jones was a very well-liked member of 3rd Platoon. During combat, one's emotions run the gamut at an accelerated speed, to include both hate and respect for the enemy. Was it anger, hate, deliberate, instinctive or love for his comrades in arms? Many others said they would have done the same. Criticism comes cheap for those that haven't traveled in a trooper's jungle boots. Paratroopers were never known for taking a lot of POWs...likewise the NVA. Well, they may have taken you, but you could forget about surviving.

PFC Ernesto Dominguez, participated at the Battle of Dak To. Courtesy of Family and Vietnam Wall.

The 3rd Platoon was in the lead and continued forward on 6 June 1966 with T-Bird on point. His slack man that day was Private First Class Ernesto Dominguez, who had been in Vietnam for 20 days and was assigned to Abu Company on 5 June 1966, the day prior. Private First Class Dominguez was from Bakersfield, California, and was a homeboy of Charlie "Tuna" Lostaunau. Tuna had asked Private First Class Gary Stackhouse to look after Dominguez; he promised to do so. Dominguez had volunteered to walk point, but in this situation Sergeant Perkins wouldn't have it. He did, however, allow Dominguez to be T-Bird's slack man so he could start learning that role. The monsoon season had set in and it rained every day, just as the enemy wanted it to. Because of the rain, supporting aircraft and other support was hindered, including any medevac missions. They were following a slippery trail downhill with a creek at the bottom. T-Bird could see down the trail to the creek which had a ledge with a drop off of about four feet. As T-Bird approached the creek, he slipped and fell onto his back, sliding off the ledge into the creek. Just as he fell, the NVA opened up and killed Dominguez, who dropped and slid down into the creek, landing on top of T-Bird, knocking the wind out of him. T-Bird became incapacitated. When T-Bird could breathe, he found himself covered with blood and wasn't sure if it was his or

Dominguez's. He screamed loudly for help. Later Sergeant Perkins told T-Bird that he didn't know how T-Bird had survived because he observed so many enemy rounds striking the ground all around them. Obviously, Private Ernesto Dominguez had been protecting T-Bird after the wind was knocked out of him. T-Bird said this incident was his most memorable. "On this day I really became aware of my mortality." Walking point takes skill plus luck, and this was without a doubt T-Bird's luckiest day in Vietnam. Funderburk said, "I often think of this incident."

PFC Gary "Stack" Stackhouse, RTO for 3rd Platoon. Courtesy of Stack.

According to Private First Class Gary "Stack" Stackhouse, Perkins' RTO, on 7 June 1966 they again were travelling down the same trail and crossed the creek where Dominguez was KIA the day prior and also where Perkins killed the Chieu Hoi after Golden Jones was shot in the gut. They traveled about a half a mile, crossed another creek, and started up a hill. They heard a large volume of fire to their left flank and then Stack listened to a call for help over the radio as another "Above the Rest" unit was under fire and taking causalities.

Sergeant Perkins was in the lead with Stack and a newly assigned trooper. This was definitely not the place for a platoon sergeant to be...walking point out in front of everyone...it's a private's job. He was over aggressive and should have been further back where he could have exerted his military and combat experience over the situation at hand. Perkins was out of the zone—similar to a football game that's tied late in the fourth quarter and the defense gets a 15-yard penalty to put the offense in field goal range to win the game. Aggression doesn't count. What counts is controlled aggression, and he robbed the 3rd Platoon of his experience which had to cause them additional problems going forward. Hard earned combat experience is irrecoverable once lost. Had I been there, I would have been with the lead M-60 and would have had to say something about this unsound tactic. We had discussed this same tactic before when operating in the mountainous jungles near where Doc Jackson and Perk had made coffee; obviously it was to no avail. However, to Perks credit, he was getting pressure from the platoon leader and the CO Captain Willis to move, move and close with the enemy. They in turn were getting the same pressure from the battalion commander, who at that time was Major Hackworth. Perk should have still slowed down and if they wanted to go any faster they could have taken the lead themselves. Sacrificing good sound tactics for speed is always a recipe for a disaster.

They started up the hill toward the sound of heavy fire from the other company, and about half way up Stack spotted an enemy machine gun position looking down the hill on their left. A machine gun is never alone and they froze in place. Perkins whispered to Stackhouse and asked if he saw it. Stack replied, "Yes." Stack said, "Perkins didn't attempt to back up and I thought he was going to attack the enemy. I told Perkins it was a bad idea to stay there, and thought we should back up and call artillery or air power on them." Without another word, Sergeant Perkins raised his weapon and took aim, getting off maybe two rounds before he was hit in the chest and knocked down." Stackhouse immediately began first aid by putting a bandage on Perkins; he took several rounds and looked like it had blown out his back. As Stack was placing the bandage on, he was struck in the left elbow

by a bullet which also tore up his bic̪
kins looked up at Stack and asked hi̪
Stackhouse said, "Then he died in my a̦
Robert "Pappy" Papesh, a machine gunner ̼   ̠ᴀ-60, was further back but could still see Sergeant Perkins get hit. "His body seemed to turn to jelly, as a red mist engulfed him...Body parts flew from his body and Perkins hit the ground hard. I was sure Perkins was dead," said Pappy.

Private First Class Dominick "Nick" Fondo was providing cover fire and an enemy round went down the barrel of his M-60 machine gun; it hit a chambered round that exploded in the chamber. An inch or so higher and Nick would have drawn his last breath. The NVA had the presence under extreme combat conditions to go after the guns, making them priority number one. Displaying such great poise under fire and other traits, they gained the respect of troopers as real hard core bastards. The strangest things happen in combat. Once I saw a man hit in his steel pot while he was wearing it. Most times it would go through, however this time it ran around the steel pot between the helmet liner and the steel pot. He didn't have as much as a scratch on him but his bell was definitely rung. Another time, a small Bible carried in a trooper's left breast pocket stopped a round to save his life. Other men looking for luck or divine intervention started carrying one there as well. Most of us contributed it to pure luck, the perfect shot or angle.

Major Hackworth ordered Abu Commander Captain Willis to leave Perkins' body to go assist another unit in trouble, and he remained out there among the enemy for days before being recovered. This was the first time a trooper was ever left on the battlefield, and needless to say, the Abu's weren't one bit happy about the situation. They could visualize their own fate ending the same way. Also the fact that on the day prior to 6 June, when artillery was called for by Captain Willis, it landed in the middle of 2nd Platoon, which wasn't a morale builder. The collateral damage of this friendly fire incident was: three Abu's KIA, six WIA and one missing, according to the official record taken from the battalion Staff- Duty Journal, form 1594. The Vietnam Veterans Memorial Wall confirms three KIAs. However, on page 536 of Hackworth's *About Face* he states it was five. In an after action report written by CO Willis on 6 February 1967 for the U. S. Army Infantry School, he states on page 8: "Fulford and four other men were killed."

One of those killed was the 2nd Platoon Sergeant, a Sergeant First Class with 14 years of service named Varl E. Fulford from Bowling Green, Florida. His MOS (military occupational specialty) was 11-C, which is an indirect fire specialist or mortar man; ironically, he died by friendly indirect fire. Also killed were Sergeant Franklin W. Smith from Columbus, Ohio, and Private First Class William D. Hopson of Hampton, Virginia.

On page 8 of CO Willis's after action report he writes: "The time was 1730 hours. Platoon Sergeant Fulford was told to withdraw and bring in more artillery and air. The enemy followed Fulford and took up positions fifty meters from the 2nd Platoon perimeter. The enemy assaulted by fire. As the artillery and air began to get on target, the enemy crept closer to Fulford's platoon. The enemy maneuvered around to Fulford's rear. He was receiving heavy fire from both north and south of his perimeter. At this time the 105 howitzer battery in direct support was asked to split the battery and have three howitzers adjusted on the enemy to Fulford's south."

The artillery battery did not want to do it and for good reason as it has proven to be a problem with only one FDC (fire direction center), and it goes against doctrine developed over many years in both peacetime and war. "A 155 howitzer battery was in general support. The 105 battery's FDC wanted the 155 battery to fire the mission." According to Captain Willis's report dated 6 February 1967 he states; "This was rejected because experience had proven that the time required to get the 155 fires on target would be excessive. Also, it would not have been possible to adjust the 155 fires in close enough to do any good." This is one bogus ass defense because it wouldn't take the 155 howitzers any longer to get on target as splitting the 105s would take. Also saying they couldn't be adjusted close enough for support is like saying they could never be used for close support. They were used throughout the war in close support roles and the greater burst of a larger round is taken into account when walking it in or adjusting it in. Willis states, "The 105 Battery agreed to split the battery. An azimuth was given to the new target. The first target was designated AE 101. The new target was designated AE 102. As Platoon Sergeant Fulford began to adjust AE 102, a volley of artillery fire fell on Fulford's platoon. The artillery had used the azimuth to AE 101 to adjust AE 102. The result was that the rounds dropped on top of the 2nd Platoon." While he states the 105 battery agreed to split the battery, he conveniently leaves out why they changed their mind or who convinced them to change their mind. In my opinion a commander of an artillery battery isn't going to listen to anyone that's not at least equal to or of a higher rank. Was it CO Willis? Was it perhaps Major Hackworth, the battalion commander? You make the call and fire for effect.

On 9 June Abu Company was moving through mountainous jungle terrain as nightfall was approaching. They were enroute to assist C Company of 2nd/502, who was taking heavy casualties and were facing the threat of being over-run. The 3rd Platoon led Abu company forward and the NVA were conducting area ambushes to catch all relief forces while they continued their attack on C 2nd/502, who were OPCON (operational control) to our battalion, the 1st/327th. The NVA allowed 3rd Platoon to get almost on top of them when they sprang up out of their well-prepared positions with a heavy volume of fire.

PFC Robert R. "Pappy" Papesh, M-60 Machine Gunner of 3rd Platoon, participated at the Battle of Dak To. Courtesy of Pappy.

The 3rd Platoon was climbing a mountain at the time and the NVA held the high ground; the terrain was wet and slippery. Private First Class Robert "Pappy" Papesh moved his M-60 forward with his gun crew to support the lead element. On arrival with the point man, the NVA started lobbing hand grenades down on their position going after the machine gun. An enemy hand grenade hit Pappy's left shoulder, bounced off, then exploded with a very loud KABOOM. Then two more grenades exploded...KABOOOOOOOM. Pappy was seriously wounded with shrapnel wounds on his left side, to include his hand, arm, forearm, shoulder, foot, shin and left knee.

The 3rd Platoon withdrew, broke contact, and Pappy was unintentionally left for dead. It quickly became dark and Pappy was trapped between the NVA and his platoon. The 3rd Platoon pulled back down the hill about 150 meters to set up for the night and were scattered in small groups with gaps between their lines. Aerial flares from artillery kept the area lit throughout the night, perhaps giving the enemy second thoughts about attacking and exposing themselves. Members of 3rd Platoon could see the enemy on the ridge lines while the flares were swaying back and forth above. The NVA is known to search the battle area for the dead to capture weapons, ammo, grenades, and equipment. Pappy tried to remain quiet, and must have passed out from lack of blood and pain as the NVA missed him in the dark of night or took him for being dead.

The following day the 3rd Platoon returned to retrieve the KIAs and Pappy. This is a classic example why no one should ever be left behind if at all possible because they may still be alive. On the battlefield, one can't know for sure if a casualty is truly KIA unless verified by an accounting and recovery. Was Staff Sergeant Perkins dead or had he just passed out when left on the battlefield by Hackworth and Willis? How about the others who left on 7 June 1966 as ordered by Hackworth and Willis? In the meantime, they can bite the dust from lack of first aid or medevac if possible. Just knowing that you won't be left is priceless peace of mind on the field of battle.

Hackworth ordered that they be left so Abu Company could go help Tiger Force who was surrounded and in danger of being overrun. A tough call, but probably a correct decision, however, it was a situation that was created when Hackworth deceived the brigade commander of the intelligence reports he had on the enemy in the area and the other battalions were withdrawn from the area. This placed our battalion up against a force the whole brigade (three battalions, plus support) should be opposing. The units continued to operate to a large extent by platoon size forces which would get them surrounded, and the relief forces ambushed enroute to help. For the most part, economy of forces wasn't used or units massed to counter the larger forces. Hackworth was being outmaneuvered by the NVA at every turn. What really saved his ass was that these troopers were so good they were able to hold on where other units would have folded or had their asses totally annihilated, similar to how the 101st held on at Bastogne. Now don't get the idea I'm some great tactician, because I'm not, but in 20 years of military service I learned a thing or two. One thing I learned is that regardless of rank, to include that of a general, we all expect those above us to know more than we do and to lead.

Abu Company evacuated casualties of Tiger Force and policed the battle field where they were assaulted, until about 1100 hours of 9 June 1966; they were then ordered to return to the area where Sergeant Perkins was KIA on 7 June 1966. Later that day of 9 June, Abu Company was ordered to relieve C Company, 2nd/502, who were in danger of being overrun and were surrounded by an NVA battalion. Captain William "Bill" S. Carpenter, Jr., AKA "Lonesome End" and an All-American football player at West Point, was the CO of C Company 2nd/502 which the Abu's were attempting to reach. He called napalm in on his own position and troops, to prevent the NVA from overrunning his unit, which broke the NVA attack and for which he received the DSC for his actions. Enroute to assist, Abu Company was heavily engaged by an NVA force which lay in waiting for a relief force.

On 6 June 1966 Abu company and the rest of our battalion (1st/327) was surrounded by an overwhelming NVA (North Vietnamese Army) force consisting of the 24th NVA Regiment and the 88th Regiment, in one of the bloodiest battles of that first year at Dak To. Peter S. Griffin (from the 2nd/502nd) was one of just four who were able to get in to render assistance by repelling from a CH-47 chopper. My men Nick Fondo, Robert "Pappy" Papesh and Blair A. "T-Bird" Funderburk speak highly of his great contribution and participation to provide a much needed airborne assistance from fellow troopers and brother in arms. By their accounts, Griff missed his calling and instead of a "Widowmaker" should have been an "Above the Rest" trooper as he truly is, as well as an Abu. Peter S. Griffin was the author of the poem "That Rusting Crate."

Sergeant George A. Morningstar of Ocala, Florida, was also one of the four to repel in, and was KIA on 9 June 1966 enroute to provide help to C Company of 2nd/502; he received a Silver Star for charging an enemy machine gun emplacement. Sergeant Morningstar was a member of A Company 2nd/502 (Widowmakers) but was fighting as an attachment to Abu Company. Sergeant Morningstar, Private First Class Peter S. Griffin, and only two others were able to make it in on 6 June 1966 when Abu was surrounded by an overwhelming force. The four men were able to rappel by rope from a Chinook helicopter through the thick jungle and make it in before the NVA drove the chopper away by heavy accurate fire. They remained with and fought with Abu Company throughout the battle of Dak To.

Abu Company ended up surrounded throughout the rainy night on 9 June 1966. By daylight, the company was consolidated and a perimeter was formed for defense. Artillery fire and air support probably prevented an all-out attack as the enemy was kept at bay. Patrols were sent out all day to look for a gap in the NVA's positions on 10 June, and about 1800 hours the enemy was found to have withdrawn from the west side.

Abu Company was ordered to link up with Tiger Force on the night of 10 June. Abu sent a small recon unit down a creek bed because the jungle was too slow for movement, while the creek bed was a major highway through the area. Travel was still slow and a new moon helped conceal their movement. The point and recon unit discovered that the creek ran right through an enemy base camp and they notified Willis. Captain Willis ordered his men not to shoot, despite receiving sporadic fire, so as not to give away their location. At the same time, artillery was called and walked down the banks. T-Byrd and Fondo don't remember if the artillery was used, however if so it was a good call to cover their retrograde movement (withdrawal) and force the enemy to hunker down as they moved through the area. This tactic is also great for snipers, U-shaped ambushes, and to prevent reinforcement or resupply by the enemy. This forced the NVA to hunker down and also served as cover for any noise they may be making. Abu Company was also carrying their wounded. This was the night Nick Fondo, despite being wounded himself, carried Bobby Papesh and helped his assistant gunner Private First Class Lawrence "Pineapple" Kalawe from Hawaii, for several hours through darkness, to an LZ for medevac extraction. After traveling all night, they reached their objective and linked up with Tiger Force at a LZ they had prepared, early on 11 June. The wounded were evacuated and Pappy spent 13 months at Valley Forge Army Hospital in Pennsylvania. Nick Fondo had multiple wounds, spent several months in a Japan hospital, and lost the middle finger of his left hand.

The 101st was one of the few units to conduct night operations in the past at various times, whereas hunkering down was the norm. The NVA were hugging their belts and staying close during daylight hours, but at night they were breaking contact and pulling back into their base camps. Despite having the advantage of knowing the terrain, they weren't comfortable in the thick jungle at night.

From the period 3 June 1966 through 11 June 1966, Abu Company suffered fifty casualties including four platoon leaders and two platoon sergeants. They received forty replacements. Twenty-two of them were men who were gathered up from Headquarters Company and eighteen were new men. They included two new lieutenants while two staff sergeants continued to run the other two platoons. The KIAs and WIAs would continue through 17 June 1966 in the battle for Dak To and dominance of the terrain and AO.

Then we have Major Hackworth, who by this battle should have been shit-canned, but was still in charge as the brigade commander had to make do with what he had, just like the line companies. The NVA was tactically kicking his ass as he continued to screw up; seeing the situation at brigade level, General Willard Pearson ordered a tactical withdrawal to place a B-52 Arc-Light bombing on the NVA. Before a B-52 strike could be conducted, all the $1^{st}/327^{th}$ units and attachments had to get out of the immediate AO. Tactical withdrawals were conducted to obtain a safe distance.

The B-52's carpet bombing can easily cover an area a half mile wide and two miles long, while each aircraft can carry a pay load of 84,500 pounds of bombs consisting of both 750 and 500 pounders. Carpet bombing is designed to inflict damage in every part of a selected area of land. An Ark-Light strike approaches the potency of a nuclear weapon. The NVA trenches, tunnel systems, and fortifications were pretty much not penetrable by artillery and fast movers, while some could be as deep as fifty feet. The B-52 Bombers solved that problem with the craters easily being thirty feet deep and more.

The planned B-52 strike came at 0830 hours on 13 June, obviously their unlucky day. If they had breakfast by then, it was their last meal for many. The strike targeted the areas where all the major contacts took place, plus the base camps that had been discovered. They were either out looking for our disappearing units or were waiting in their base camps for our next attack. Either way, they were out maneuvered by General Willard Pearson. They made a huge mistake by not maintaining contact and constantly hugging our belts at all times once the battle commenced to include the night. There were 24 waves of B-52s on this day. As the mist was rising, it was raining bombs as their payloads were dropped, creating a maze of craters throughout the AO. The Ark-Light carpet bombing tore their asses up and broke the backs of the 24th and 88th NVA Regiments while tearing up their well-prepared positions and turning the tide of this battle of Dak To even more so in favor of the 101st.

All the units plus an additional battalion were moved back into the AO; they found numerous weapons and 1,200 NVA bodies by body count. Only a few small groups of diehards were encountered in the mopping up operation. The 24th NVA Regiment and other supporting units were rendered ineffective as a fighting unit; their fate was really sealed when the Screaming Eagles descended down on them, seizing them with their talons. The Eagles released their prey by a classical military retrograde movement (tactical withdrawal), hunkered down for the storm and thunder of the B-52 Bombers, and then the Eagles soared back into the AO looking for prey to reclaim and sink their talons into.

On 17 June 1966, CO Willis also called in helicopter gunships that resulted in further collateral damage and the wounding of 26 troopers, to include every single medic assigned, most of the NCOs, the rest of the officers to include Willis himself, and the killing of 1st Lieutenant George E. Perry. Lieutenant Perry was the grandson of the famous Admiral Perry; at the time his tour was complete and he had orders to return to the States, as he was past his return date. On page 542 of *About Face*, Hackworth's states, "Willis played it safe and called for fire support." Hackworth also stated on the same page that the helicopter gunships were at fault. "Gunships that came to his aid made a terrible error."

In CO Willis's after action report (Personal Experience of a Company Commander) dated 8 February 1967 he states: "A flight of aerial rocket artillery helicopters was in the area. The Air Force forward air controller was asked to control the strike, as he had controlled the previous air strikes. He knew the Company location. The forward air controller marked the target for the ARA (aerial rocket artillery) ships. The flight leader was told that the Company location was one hundred meters east of the smoke and not to fire east of the smoke. The first pass was good. The first two ships were relieved by two additional ships. These ships were not certain of the company location as they had not seen the first two ships expend. The forward air controller asked the Company to throw smoke. The Company had used the last of their smoke to control the air strikes. The forward air controller went through the process of marking the target and orienting the flight leader on the Company location. The flight leader rogered. The first pass was initially on target, but toward the end of the run, the ships turned up the ridge and walked rockets into the Company position. One was killed and twenty-six were wounded." (Author's notes: Could he observe this through the jungle? Hackworth's book states it was 21 wounded from the incident and Willis's report states it was 26.) I believe the Company Commander (Willis) would have better firsthand knowledge and 26 wounded is probably the correct number.

FATE UNKNOWN

**Captain George E. Perry,
West Point Class of 1963.
From Vietnam Wall, courtesy of classmate BG ONG.**

Killed by friendly fire was 1st Lieutenant George E. Perry the XO (executive officer) of Abu Company who Hackworth said volunteered to go from Phan Rang to Dak To. Lieutenant New and Staff Sergeant Robbins, however, said he was ordered by Hackworth because Willis needed help and most of Abu leadership were casualties. That we know to be true because by this time Captain Willis was stepping on his crank with both his left and right foot and seemed to never miss a step. Lieutenant Perry was married, a father and already had plans to meet his wife in Hawaii. His tour was up and he had orders to return to the States. A new 2nd lieutenant at Phan Rang was assigned to gather his personal effects and ship them home to his family. A Congressional inquiry occurred, as shit rolls downhill, when his family discovered that his famous grandfather, Admiral Perry's corn cob pipe, a family heirloom, was missing from his personal effects. An investigation ensued with the 2nd Lieutenant admitting to thinking it was insignificant and had thus thrown it away. To a family member, the smallest thing is the most important thing in the world if it belonged to their loved one. Getting started off on the wrong foot and lacking common sense, I doubt this lieutenant's career flourished.

Captain Willis called for ARA fire; he also directed and controlled it…therefore he was the MMFIC and the one responsible. He can delegate his authority but not his responsibility; this is a long standing Army axiom and many leaders have been relieved for far less. Another problem they encountered was not having enough smoke grenades. Page 5 of CO Willis' report states: "The specified equipment included six claymore mines per platoon, twelve smoke grenades per platoon, four hundred rounds of 5.56 ball ammunition per man armed with the M-16 rifle, two grenades per man etc." In *About Face,* Major Hackworth states on page 535, in reference to equipment, "So the single order was a simple one; lighten up!" Normally a platoon carried a claymore mine for every two men or at least 17 to 21, at least four grenades per man and two smoke grenades per leader or roughly 24, depending on strength. In two tours in Vietnam and after My Phu, I never carried less than four grenades, two smoke grenades and 800 rounds of M-16 ammo. Traveling light to keep up with the enemy or to catch him is fine, but what are you going to fight him with once he's been caught? It's no wonder they ran out of smoke grenades and were lucky not to have a problem with the other items.

If the air strikes, 105 howitzers, and 155 howitzers were ineffective it's doubtful at best that the gunships with 2.74 inch rockets, totaling 48 per gunship, were going to be more effective. Also, the gunships could have been controlled by radio until they were over the Company's location and then given further instruction. Remember, the units are in triple canopy jungle and from the air they can't see through the canopy top…plus smoke from artillery could have been used to mark their location. Perhaps with that much confusion and doubt, cancelling would have been the best scenario. An immediate investigation should have been ordered by Hackworth or the brigade commander if for no other reason than to prevent any reoccurrence in the near future. If one was ordered and conducted, we're not privy to the results.

GUT CHECKS

Four (or six) dead and thirty-two wounded from friendly fire or collateral damage in a thirteen day period is more than coincidental. Also, there were more friendly fire dead and wounded that occurred during Willis' tenure than all the Abu Commanders for the conduct of the whole war, of almost seven years, as there was only one other in 1967, and after at least a minimum of 18 commanders. You make the call—was Willis at fault? Was Hackworth at fault? Perhaps both were at fault. You make the call!

Hackworth never relieved Willis of command—was it because Willis had protected and assisted Hackworth in the past and now he owned him? Specifically, when he shacked up with a Vietnamese women (Miss Vinh), who was an "uncleared" national, thus exposing classified information such as unit maps, unit locations, call signs, and radio traffic while AWOL (absence without leave) in Tuy Hoa, as he pretended to be on duty and operational as if being in the TOC (tactical operations center). Captain Willis was aware of his status and covered for him while assisting in his necessary needs for this charade. On page 514 of *About Face*, Hackworth said, "While Willis and the girl organized the accommodation end of things." Additionally he stated he would stay in contact with Willis at the battalion CP who would aid and abet this cover-up while the battalion was in the field. Hackworth also on page 514 said, "It was not a bad way to fight a war." I suppose all this disclosure served to feed his ego and prove him a macho man or stud. Meanwhile real macho men were out in the field ducking bullets from AK-47s in the paddies and jungles. Miss Vinh didn't make him another KIA but then again he probably was more valuable alive than dead. A "prima donna" that wasn't reined in by superiors, until much later in his career, he was allowed to flourish to the detriment of the unit and many KIAs.

There is a huge difference between a mortar platoon sergeant and a rifle platoon sergeant and incorrect assignments by proper MOS was a hindrance to the unit's efficiency. Truck drivers were being assigned to infantry units and needless to say, many bit the dust before they could get their feet wet…but we are forced to play the hand dealt. Having officers rotating every six months for career progression was another hindrance to the unit's efficiency—by the time they were trained they were replaced with the likes of Captain Willis. Meanwhile the poor enlisted man or NCO had to endure a whole year of combat. The way the Army handled the replacements with over 30,000 airborne qualified airborne troopers in the U.S. was downright atrocious and one of the NVA's best weapons, just like another enemy unit fighting us. Of course the units had to accept and make use with what they were given. Under these adverse conditions, the 101st still set standards for other units and the enemy never saw any deterioration in their fighting capability.

    I can't help but wonder if I had been there, what differences I may have been able to effect for a different outcome of my good friend Sergeant Perkins, the 3rd Platoon, or had I not been wounded in April would it also have resulted in my death in this great battle known as Dak To. In the first year that Abu Company was in Vietnam, 32 Abu men were KIA, while the 101st Brigade(S) killed 1,814 that first year and another 327 by air. (Figures were taken from Vietnam Odyssey, the story of the Brigade) Who knows how many were carried off or buried by B-52 strikes that were never counted—I would surmise it to be many.

    All or part of the 101st Airborne Division served in Vietnam for almost seven years and was the last division to leave Vietnam. During those years 4,022 troopers were KIA, twice as many as in WWII, and 18,259 (more than a whole division) were WIA. (National Archives & Wikipedia) I haven't been able to find the enemy KIA or WIA from the whole 101st Airborne Division although the numbers exist somewhere. However, based on the above figures of our Brigade my best SWAG would be 30,866 enemies KIA and 138,897 WIA. I used a WIA ratio of 4.5, the same ratio as ours while normally 6.0 is the accepted norm. Now these figures may appear or seem high, but they're not high when one considers that in 1995 the North Vietnamese government acknowledged 1,100,000 NVA and VC were KIA during the war to include their MIAs. Did they admit the real figures? You make the call; regardless, the admitted number can be accepted as true and it's a significant number disclosed by their government. The 101st Airborne Division made a significant contribution toward that 1,100,000. The ratio of KIA of the U.S. (58,282) to their admitted number of 1,100,000 is 19 to 1 or 19 NVA and VC killed to 1 U.S. soldier. Based on that ratio and 4,022 101st KIA, they would have killed 76,418 of the enemy. This number would include all supporting elements under control of the 101st, such as artillery, gunships, B-52s, etc. We'll never know the exact number, whether its 30,866 or 76,418. One thing that is evident is they became the prey of the Eagles, while the 101st Airborne Division set an example for other units to emulate. We had our "Rendezvous With Destiny."

I was on medical leave from the hospital and had orders to report to Fort Dix, New Jersey for my next assignment and realized the girl I had been seeing, named Irene, wouldn't be going with me. It was at that point I asked her to marry me and she accepted, although my family wasn't thrilled with the idea and were somewhat shocked by my choice. She had been previously married and had a young daughter, Linda, whom I later adopted. We were married on 11 June 1966, honeymooned in Atlantic City, and remain married to this day. So much for everyone thinking they know what's best for me.

We moved to the Fort Dix area, settled in and remained there for about a year and a half. During that time we purchased our first TV and car on credit, and on 17 May of 1967 my son Galen Randall was born at the Fort Dix hospital. I was also promoted to Staff Sergeant E-6 and my base pay was increased to $305.40 plus $110 per month for housing and about $40 for rations. Then in November of 1967 my enlistment was up and I had to make a decision whether to re-enlist or get out. I felt as though I had a calling with the Army; in working with trainees to teach target detection and marksmanship, I strongly believed I could make a difference in their making it out of Vietnam, where most would eventually wind up. However, when you witness such things as McNamara's 100,000, I also came to realize I'm just another number in the big scheme of things. So eventually I made the decision to get out (second time) and to make another go of civilian life. I went to work as a pipefitter's helper at Sun Ship in Chester, Pennsylvania. Used to a routine that changed on a daily basis in the Army, I found this job to be extremely boring. I would wait in the bowels of the ship as my pipefitter would go to the shop to bend or fit one piece of pipe while I waited for hours for his return. At this rate, I could learn this craft in about 40 years or just before retirement. I made the decision to return to the military and thought it best to raise a family. It proved to be a good decision since for unknown reasons, the shipyard eventually closed; lack of efficiently employing a workforce surely must had been a huge contributing factor. Later I would return to Fort Dix to attend Drill Sergeant School and as the Honor Graduate become a Drill Instructor.

Author's promotion picture while in Germany, 1970.

The author in 1974 as a Drill Sergeant at Fort Dix, New Jersey.

I was assigned to the 82nd Airborne at Fort Bragg, North Carolina and while there, attended Jungle Warfare School, Jumpmaster School, and Air Movement Operations Course which would enhance my military career. Ideally one would go to Jungle School then to Vietnam, not the reverse, however I still learned a great deal. Actually, about 12 years later I would return to Panama with an assignment to the Jungle School or JOTC (Jungle Operations Training Center) as a committee chief of platoon combat techniques, teaching the ambush and search and destroy operations, somewhat coming full circle. Each unit was allocated just a few school slots and the men wanting to attend were always numerous with final selection coming from the chain of command. In fact if selected and failed to graduate you could forget about ever getting another chance at redemption or other schools for that matter.

Things were going great for about a year, and then I received orders for Germany in 1969. Irene and I were greatly looking forward to this new assignment. Irene loved to travel and the prospect of going overseas to Germany was for her very exciting. It presented an opportunity not many of our background ever have in a lifetime. I was also ecstatic because having a family now meant my responsibilities had dramatically changed and getting orders to return to Vietnam was always looming in the back of my thoughts. Germany was a three-year assignment and I figured the war would be over by that time. I preceded my family over and lived in the barracks until housing was available. In the meantime, the Army spent thousands of dollars shipping our household goods and privately owned vehicle over for us.

Irene and the kids assimilated quickly to their new surroundings and she loved the country, people, and food. We were able to bring her father over for a visit and also my parents. My mother was born in the U.S. but was of German decent from her grandparents and the trip was one of the great highlights of her life. As for me, Germany was a tough tour because during the winter we went away hundreds of miles to the field for 30 to 45 days at a time, returned for about two weeks and moved out again to the field. In the summer they were sending me hundreds of miles away to schools, such as Land Mine Warfare (three weeks), Seventh Army NCO Academy (four weeks) and Field Sanitation Course (three weeks) where I learned all about everything from mosquitoes to the Musca Domestic (common house fly). While not the same type flies as in Vietnam, I considered myself an expert with this pain in the ass little guys from my tour in Vietnam. My daughter Tara was born the day of my graduation from the Seventh Army NCO Academy on 12 June 1970 in the Wiesbaden Hospital. I would forgo graduation and the chance for honor graduate to get my diploma, and began the trek home to my wife and family.

After about a year in Germany I received orders to return to Vietnam, with a reporting date of 13 December 1970 to Oakland, California. Thinking Germany would be a three-year tour, we were somewhat in disbelief at first. Irene and the kids would remain near my family where they could help look after her, even though by now she had very much adapted to life as an Army wife with a family. She learned to drive and became completely independent. One of the first things I did on arrival at home was to contact the Department of the Army at the Pentagon to get an extension of leave through the holidays to spend time with my family. I was told they would consider it however if I didn't hear from them I was to report on 13 December as my orders indicated.

While at home, my old friend Bob Richmond came to visit me, and since last seeing him, his life had changed as rapidly as had mine. He married a girl who already had two children and had become unbelievably religious and very antiwar. He gave me a sermon on how the war was all wrong, that I wouldn't return alive, and how I should go to Canada to choose life instead. Psychologically this just blew my mind and I was totally unprepared for it. It's one thing to go to war unaware of its realities and quite another to return knowing you're most likely not going to survive. Additionally, life was more complicated this time around as I was no longer a single, 20-year-old cocky kid. I had a wife and three kids. It played with my mind for days and it took a gut check, but I would return and follow my calling. Even then it played with my mind, causing additional hardships that I damn sure didn't need in a combat environment. Some years later I found out my father had put Bob Richmond up to talking to me about not returning to the Nam because he didn't want to lose me. I never heard from the Department of the Army and reported to Oakland as ordered on 23 December. I called home to let them know of my safe arrival and learned the Pentagon had called, giving me an extension of leave through the holidays. In the meantime I had already reported in and was 3,000 miles away, so I decided to just go with it and hopefully would be home for the next Christmas.

On arrival in Vietnam, I was assigned to the 173rd Airborne Brigade, and after several months my enlistment was up. I was then faced with a choice: reenlist and stay in Vietnam…where I would be getting shot at…and continue a career, or get out of the Army and return to civilian life and survive this ordeal. This weighed heavily on my mind for weeks before I could decide on the best choice. Many a career NCO's in the same predicament chose to get out and live. After a lot of aggravating and gut-wrenching weighing of pros and cons I decided to reenlist and gut-check it out. It was another gut-check that in the long run would prove to be the right one, at least for me.

FATE UNKNOWN

Chapter 43

Gathering Eagles

Left Carlos Torres, center David W. Haskell, Jr., and right Ricardo C. Velez. Taken in 2004 at the Phoenix, AZ reunion.

Carlos Torres lost a leg in an old French minefield; David W. Haskell, Jr. suffered greatly from PTSD; and Ricardo G. Velez was one of many WIA in the Tuy Hoa area as the intensity of combat greatly increased. We hooked up for a final blast at the Phoenix reunion in 2004, and a few years later they passed away. They were original Boat Troopers and had originally gone over on the USNS Eltinge.

Eagles always return to their perch…may they forever be at peace on a perch in heaven. It was a peace that escaped them while here on earth, as a result of being an Abu soldier, humping the jungles and rice paddies of Vietnam.

The manifest of gathering eagles continues to grow and take flight. Our final muster shall be the greatest reunion of all. On behalf of all your Abu brothers and comrades in arms, both living and deceased, we wish you peace.

Chapter 44

In Retrospect

My Army career began in August of 1961, and upon completion of jump school in February 1962, I went to B Company, 1st Airborne Battle Group, and 506th Infantry at Fort Campbell, Kentucky. I always had a fondness in my heart for the Bravo Bulls of the 506th, as it gave me the foundation for the successful military career that eventually followed. We become the product of our learned experiences and those early lessons carried me far. I am sure that many have heard the old adage that in the Army, your best assignment is always your last. There's much truth to this, perhaps because of the unknown of a future assignment and because in human nature we tend to focus on the now. However, the present doesn't last long and the past lasts forever. In reflecting on my assignments as Drill Instructor, Jungle Warfare School Instructor, First Sergeant, as well as a gut-check to return to Vietnam for a second tour with the 173rd Airborne Infantry Brigade, I can truly say that through my career, the best unit I ever served with was A Company (Abu), 1st Battalion Airborne, 327 Infantry, 1st Brigade (S) 101st Airborne Infantry Division.

 I deployed with them to South Vietnam on the USNS General LeRoy Eltinge in July of 1965. Initially

FATE UNKNOWN

I went over as an M-79 Gunner of the 3rd Platoon and in December 1965 was promoted to Sergeant. Upon my promotion I was given the M-60 machine gun squad. Despite a high turnover rate and too many hardships to mention, this unit was "Above the Rest" and the best unit of my career. Our darkest day was 4 March 1966, at the battle of My Phu which saw 13 KIA and 39 WIA. I made it to 7 April 1966, before being wounded in action from a gunshot to the head.

In my career, I saw the typical Army commendation medals, Good Conduct awards, Master Parachutists Badge, etc. However, the awards I'm most proud of came from my time with Abu Company: the Combat Infantryman Badge, Purple Heart, and Bronze Star Medal with V device—and prior to ending my career, the combat patch of the Screaming Eagles on my right shoulder.

I was aimlessly soaring around in my youth, as most of us do, unsure of the correct path to take—in fact I was discharged twice before deciding on a military career. In retrospect, there were two profound influences in my life. The first was the Army, who took a 17-year-old, street-smart kid that quit school in the eighth grade, allowed him to obtain a high school diploma and some college, and gave him the opportunity to have an impact on so many men throughout my career through my leadership positions and assignments.

IN RETROSPECT

The second influence was a wonderful woman named Irene whom I married in June 1966, and who gave me three wonderful children. She has always been there providing the strength I needed to overcome life's daily challenges. Irene is truly "Above the Rest."

After completion of my military career, I worked for over 22 years as a Correctional Supervisor in prisons for the New Jersey Department of Corrections. If I had known some of the significant advantages of employment in this field, perhaps I wouldn't have stayed in the Army for a military career. But, in retrospect, it all worked out for the best. All of our experiences, such as mine in the Army, are required for us to become who we are…and no one endures without mistakes in their journey. One can never appreciate another person's journey without actually traveling in their shoes—but hopefully through this book and the stories it relates, I have been able to place you in my combat boots for a tour of combat in the rice paddies and jungles of Vietnam. Presently, I am enjoying retirement and my favorite sport of horse racing, in the Sunshine State of Florida.

"Some must be warriors that others may live in peace."
~Mercedes Lackey, Exile's Honor

FATE UNKNOWN

Glossary

AIT   advanced individual training, Training that takes place after Basic Training that pertain to an individual's specialty

aka   also known as

AK-47   a Soviet or Chinese made automatic rifle of 7.62mm (.30 caliber), the standard weapon for the North Vietnamese Army

AO   area of operation

APC   all-purpose capsule or can also mean armored personnel carrier

ARA   aerial rocket artillery, of a helicopter gunship that carries forty eight 2.75 inch rockets

Arc Light   USAF B-52 bomber air strike

ARVN (arvin)   Army of the Republic of Vietnam (South Vietnam)

asap   as soon as possible

AWOL   absence without leave

battalion   an Army unit composed of four to five companies with a total of 700 to 1000 men and commanded by a Lieutenant Colonel

BMNT   before morning nautical twilight

Bronze Star   awarded for heroic or meritorious service during combat. Heroism is indicated by a small "V" device which is attached to the ribbon. The medal ranks below the Silver Star or 4th highest award in the military.

C-4 a plastic explosive used to destroy enemy equipment, mines, and booby traps; commonly used by infantry troops to heat up c-rations or water

Charlie slang for Viet Cong or guerrillas

chopper slang for a helicopter

CIDG Civilian Irregular Defense Group, usually under the control of U. S. Special Forces

cloverleaf a patrol pattern

commo slang for communications

company an Army unit composed of three rifle platoons and a weapons platoon plus a Headquarters section, consists of 175 to 185 men and is commanded by a captain. Normally four to five companies make up a battalion.

CO Commanding Officer

CP command post

CQ charge of quarters

C-rations or c-rats military canned food

CS a gas that is the defining component of tear gas

DSC Distinguish Service Cross, the U S Army's second – highest award for valor

DZ drop zone

dust-off slang for medical evacuation by helicopter

EENT ending evening nautical twilight

fast movers jet aircraft

FEBA forward edge battle area

FDC fire direction center

GLOSSARY

FNG fu-king new guy, a term used by grunts to replacements of all ranks

FO forward observer—normally an artillery 2nd lieutenant accompanies an infantry unit on field operations—for mortars normally a sergeant

FPL when every man in a unit fires his assigned fields of fire or assigned sector—used as a final measure to stop an enemy assault

Frag order just enough essential information given to accomplish a mission, not a complete 5 paragraph field operations order

FSB fire support base

FTA fu-k the Army, a common Army expression

GED general education development

GI member of the U S Army

GM Group Motor

GP general purpose

HEAT high explosive anti-tank

H & I artillery or mortar harassment and interdictory fire

KIA killed in action by a hostile force

HE high explosives

JOTC jungle operation training center

KP kitchen police or kitchen duty

LBE load bearing equipment

Leg any non-airborne soldier

LP/OP listening post & observation post; normally deployed away from the main element to provide early warning, deceive the enemy of main units true location and force enemy to prematurely deploy for their attack

LZ landing zone

medevac medical evacuation by helicopter also known as a dust-off

M-16 standard service rifle for U S armed forces since Vietnam War, also used by many allied nations and over 8 million have been produced, uses a 5.56mm caliber cartridge. In 2010 after almost 50 years of use the Army began phasing it out for the M-4 carbine which itself is a shortened derivative of the M-16A2

M-17 a nomenclature for an Army protective mask against chemicals

M-60 a 7.62 caliber U S light machine gun

M-72 LAW shoulder fired light anti-tank weapon

M-79 a grenade launcher that fires a single shot 40mm shells with an effective range of 375 meters, breech-loaded shoulder fired weapon

MIA missing in action

MMFIC main mother fu-ker in charge

mortars both 4.2 mm & 81mm are indirect fire weapons that fire explosive projectiles known as (mortar) bombs at low velocities short ranges and high trajectory

MOS military occupational specialty

MP military police

NCO noncommissioned officer

NCOIC noncommissioned officer in charge

NDP night defensive position

GLOSSARY

NVA North Vietnamese Army, aka People's Army of Vietnam or PAVN

PAVN People's Army of Vietnam, aka NVA

platoon an Army unit that has 43 to 48 men and is made up of 3 rifle squads and a weapons squad plus a Headquarter section, led by a 2nd Lieutenant Four platoons generally make up a company.

PLF parachute landing fall

PTSD post traumatic stress disorder

opcon operational control

QMP qualified management program

RCT regimental combat team

REMF rear echelon motherfu-ker, anyone and everyone in the rear areas that is not in direct combat with the enemy on a regular basis

ROK (rock) Republic of Korea

ROTC Reserve Officers Training Course

R&R rest and recreation

RTO a radiotelephone operator

SF Special Forces

Silver Star the third highest award for valor in the US Army

sit-rep situation report

SOP standing operating procedure

stand-to all personnel are 100% awake and ready to fight from their positions

starlight scope a night vision device that relies on ambient light, introduced in Vietnam and crude by today's devices and standards

SWAG scientific wild ass guess

squad a small Army unit made up of two fire teams with each being led by a sergeant. May consist of 10 or 11 men and is led by a Staff Sergeant for the squad leader. Four squads make up a platoon.

TAC Air tactical air support

TOC tactical operation center

TOT time on target

USNS United States Navy Ship

VA Veterans Administration

VC Vietcong or guerrillas; generally not a fulltime regular Army force, similar to U.S. reserves however a Vietnamese Communist soldier, unit or party member

Viet Minh (VM) fought the Japanese during WWII and the French in the 1950s. Its popularity and reputation was in ruins in the late 1950s and in 1960 became the NLF (National Liberation Front) more commonly known as the Viet Cong, a communist movement to overtake South Vietnam

VIP very important person

WIA wounded in action

Annex A

Movement Order

Headquarters
101st Airborne Division and Fort Campbell
Ft. Campbell, Kentucky 42223
AJCGC-O   27 May 1965
LETTER ORDERS
NUMBER 5-116

Co. A 1st Bn. (Abn.) 327th Inf. to be deployed in accordance with LO 5-116 this Hq, 27 May 65

HILBERT DONALD C .... CPT
HOWARD JOHN D .... 2ND LT
LITTNAN CHARLES L .... 2ND LT
REYNOLDS GEORGE W .... 2ND LT
ADAMS EARNEST H .... PVT
ALBRITTON CLIFFORD .... SSG
ALLUM DANIEL K .... PFC
ANDERSON DALE E .... PFC
AROYO CARMITO SP/4
BARCZEWSKI DANIEL .... SGT
BELANGER ADRIEN O .... SGT
BLALOCK JOHN W .... SGT
BOALS TERRY L .... PFC
BORDEN OTTO .... SSG
BRELAND ODDUAR .... PFC
BROWN JOHNNY M .... PFC

FATE UNKNOWN

BROWN ROBERT J .... SGT
BUNN PENNY A .... PVT
CAMPBELL TOMMY G SP/4
CAMPBELL MICHAEL .... PFC
CAMPLIN BAXTER SP/4
CLARK PHILLP H .... PVT
COGGINS HAYDEN P J .... PFC
COLEMAN JAMES .... PFC
COLEMAN BILLIE L .... SGT
CRAWFORD CHARLEY J .... PFC
CUNNINGHAM JAMES H .... PFC
CURRIE PETER G .... SGT
CZARNECKI JOSEPH .... PFC
DENNIS L M .... PVT
DOLAN JOHN D .... SGT
DOUGLAS GERALD A .... SGT
DUBIELAK STANLEY E .... PVT
DUFFINA JAMES M .... PFC
DUNBAR EARNEST S SP/4
EADES RODNEY C SP/4
EMEL DONALD E .... SFC
EPES FORCE   JR .... PFC
FARETTA ANTHONY P .... PFC
FELTS PHILLIP L .... PFC
FERNANDEZ MANUAL F .... PFC
FINLEY DUANE E 1SG
FIPPS EUGENE .... SGT
FLORES GARAY RAMON .... PVT

MOVEMENT ORDER

FLUKER CLINTON E ....PVT
FRANKLIN GILBERT ....PFC
FREEMAN LAWERENCE SP/4
FRYE LEONDUS G ....PFC
FUZZELL CURT S ....PFC
GARNETT REUBEN L ....PFC
GONZALEZ SALVADOR ....PFC
GOOSEY ARVEL D ....PFC
GORDON JEFFERSON ....PFC
GOREY STEPHEN J ....PFC
GORE HOWARD C ....PFC
GRACE MAJOR ....PFC
GRAF LARRY J ....PFC
GRAVES JERRY E SP/4
GRIFFIN CHARLES E SP/4
GRIFFIN CLARENCE E ....PFC
GRIMES HOMER L JR ....PFC
GRISSOM STUART W ....PFC
GUERRERO FRANCISCO.........PSG
GUEST RONALD V ....PVT
HARLEY HARDRICK SP/4
HARRIS EDWARD T SP/4
HASKELL DAVID W JR ....PFC
HAYES SAMUEL J ....SGT
HENDRICKS SAMUEL ....SSG
HICKMAN LINZY ....PFC
HOLLOMON THEOLOGY.........PFC
HOLSTER EDWIN C..................SP/4

HUGHES JAMES JR ....PFC
HUMPHRIES JOHN T ....PSG
JAIME PEDRO..........................PFC
JOHNSON JAMES W ....PFC
JOHNSTON CLIO......................SGT
JONES ROBERT W ....PFC
JONES CHARLES ....PFC
JONES HARVEY W ....PVT
JONES EARL ....SGT
JOYCE THOMAS R...................PFC
KING JOHN K ....SSG
KOVARY JOSEPH B..................SGT
LAFLER HAROLD L ....PFC
LARGE RONALD......................PVT
LEWIS JOHN H SP/4
LIBBERT HAROLD W SP/4
LIES GARY W ....PVT
LONG WILLIAM H...................PFC
LOSTAUNAU CHARLES L SP/4
LUCAS MICHAEL A ....PFC
MAHON EVERARD E ....PFC
MALAKAS STEVE G SP/4
MARTINEZ GILBERT ....PFC
MARTINEZ REYNOLD.............SGT
MARTIN TRAVIS F ....SSG
MCQUEENEY MILTON............SSG
MEDINA ANDERSON A...........SP/4
MEEK MAURICE L JR............SSG

MOVEMENT ORDER

MERCADO DIEGO ....PFC
MITCHELL GALEN G SP/4
MONICAL LARRY D ....PFC
MORAN PATRICK W ....PFC
MORRIS CALVIN D JR SP/4
MORRIS WILLIAM D ....PFC
MULLNS JAMES D ....SGT
NEAL JERROLD E ....PVT
NELSON JOSEPH JR SP/4
NELSON GEORGE T JR ....PVT
NEWTON WARREN R SP/4
NIXON CLAYVON ....PSG
NORTON RONALD S SP/4
NOWLEN JAMES J ....PVT
OWENS CLAUDE R JR ....PFC
PEREZ AMOS G JR ....SGT
PETTY JOHN E SP/4
PILGREEN DONALD R ....PVT
PORTER EMMITT ....SGT
PORT JOHN E ....PVT
PRESS ROBERT A ....PSG
QUEZADA NOE ....SSG
RAY BENJAMIN D SP/4
RAY KENDALL H ....SSG
REYES RENE ....PFC
RHEA FORREST E ....PVT
RICHARD EARL ....PFC
RIVERA JORGE A ....PFC

RIVERA MILTON C SP/4
ROBBINS BILLY R .... SSG
ROGERS DAVID T .... PFC
ROGERS HUBERT .... PFC
ROGERS JOHNNIE K .... SGT
ROMERO FLORES RAUL .... PFC
ROWLEY DONALD B SP/4
RUTLEDGE MORRIS L .... PFC
RYAN RAYMOND T .... PFC
SALINAS JOE G .... PFC
SANTIAGO PEDRO M .... PFC
SCHJOLL MICHAEL .... PVT
SCOTT JAMES R SP/4
SCOTT JOSEPH   JR SP/4
SHAMP PAUL D JR .... SGT
SIMMONS GARY N .... PVT
SIMON FELIX .... PFC
SMALL DOUGLAS B .... SGT
SMITH FRANKLIN .... SGT
SMITH JERRY R .... PFC
SNYDER DAVID E .... SSG
SPEER WILLIAM D .... PFC
STACEY JIMMIE LEE .... PFC
STALLWORTH REGINAL .... PFC
STETSON ASHLEY JR .... PVT
STEWART ANTHONY .... PVT
SULLIVAN LEO F .... PFC
TAFT RICHARD R .... PFC

MOVEMENT ORDER

THOMPSON MITCHELL SP/4
THOMAS ROY JR ....PFC
TONEY JOHN L SP/4
TORRES CARLOS ....SGT
TROWBRIDGE LARRY ....SGT
TRUDEAUX HERBERT B.........PVT
TRZEBUCKOWSKI FRANK.....SGT
TURNER ROBERT C ....SGT
VANDIVER CHARLES ....PVT
VELEZ RICARDO G.................SP/4
VIGIL JOE G...............................SGT
WAGONER JAMES V.................SSG
WALKER KENNETH L ....PFC
WEAVER HAROLD D...............SP/4
WENZEL CHARLES L ....PVT
WHITE GEORGE G....................PFC
WHITEHEAD HOWARD L........PVT
WILLIAMS JOSEPH ....PFC
WILSON PABLO M SP/4
WOLFE PAUL F ....SGT
ZAJAC THADDEUS...................SP/4

Notes: Other original Abu's that went over on the boat and were assigned to Abu Company after the original order was cut on 27 May 1965 were:
GODWIN HARRY M..............2ND LT
  SKLAR RICHARD R. ....1ST LT

~Abu deployment roster to South Vietnam 1965, courtesy of Abu John H. Lewis.

FATE UNKNOWN